the diary of a BAD BITCH

PALMETTO
PUBLISHING
Charleston, SC
www.PalmettoPublishing.com

© 2025 by Selene Ashé

Harcover ISBN: 9798998631405
Paperback ISBN: 9798998631481
eBook ISBN: 9798998631412

the diary of a
BAD BITCH

TRUE STORIES OF SENSUALITY, SELF-DISCOVERY, AND SPIRITUAL ALCHEMY

Selene Ashé

PREFACE

What Makes a Bad Bitch?

Bold **A**uthentic **D**ivine.
Beautiful **I**ntelligent **T**alented **C**ompassionate **H**onest.

There is no specific formula. She could be the CEO of a big corporation, an escort, or a housewife. There are many flavors of bad bitchery, but there are some fundamental ingredients that we all possess, or are in the process of obtaining. A bad bitch has an immense sense of self-awareness. She knows herself, loves herself, and respects herself more than anyone else could. A bad bitch has boundaries and is comfortable establishing them. She experiences fear and doubt, but that doesn't stop her from taking the next step.

A bad bitch knows that she is part of universal consciousness, divine in her existence, and powerful in her purpose. She is patient with her journey and doesn't skip the mundane human processes because she knows that even the small moments shape her greatness. A bad bitch allows herself to feel the full range of emotions that run through her body. She knows how to love, and she knows how to grieve. A bad bitch prioritizes herself unapologetically. She takes care of her physical, mental, emotional, and energetic health, knowing that self-care is a crucial part of her existence.

A bad bitch can recognize when she has pushed herself too far, and if she chooses to continue, she doesn't love herself any less. Because she does it with the awareness that sometimes a bad bitch has to do what a bad bitch has to do. A moment of weakness, failure, or imperfection does not define her—her resilience, growth, and the ability to rise above it do. A bad bitch leads with grace but stands firm in her power. She knows that life is an ever-evolving process, and through it all, she remains unstoppable, knowing that her worth is innate, unshaken by external circumstances.

A bad bitch isn't unbreakable, she's resilient. Strength doesn't mean she never falls apart; it means she embraces the moments that shatter her. In the midst of chaos, she remains calm, knowing that when the time comes to gather her pieces, she won't just rebuild—she'll evolve. Each break refines her, shaping her into someone wiser, bolder, and more unstoppable than before.

INTRODUCTION

I thought this book was going to be about sex, but it turned out to be so much more than that. I always dreamed of being an author but never felt intelligent or worthy enough to be called one. I have kept a diary my entire life, but my journaling practice became a lot more consistent when I met a lover that filled my world with amazing stories to tell.

One day, I was recounting one of my encounters with this lover to my dear friend Vero, and she gave me the idea of putting it all in writing and sharing it with friends. I followed her advice, and I realized how much I loved storytelling and oversharing. And that I didn't need a master's degree in literature to write about my own experience with sexual reclamation and personal growth. At first, I focused a lot of my writing on the sexy and romantic experiences I was living. But as I became desensitized to the newness of it all, my focus shifted toward personal development and the life lessons that I learned through my journey.

It's important to note that my perception of the world was shaped by the way life unfolded in front of me. I share very raw, explicit, and vulnerable stories. I don't skip over any of it. I love and accept all aspects of the human experience, including the not-so-godly ones like rage, jealousy, and shame because they are some of the greatest teachers. In the pages that follow, you'll read my experiences through my lenses. I engage in relationships, friendships, and situations that bring both joy and conflict. Here you will read my point of view of these, and not those of the other people involved. My stories are not complete because they are one-sided. I ask that as you read, you use discernment and remember that I am a simple human. While I always strive to do the best I can, I am often wrong, make assumptions, and project my own fears and insecurities. This is not a book about the good person that I am. This is my process of becoming the best version of myself.

I was born and raised in La Havana, Cuba. I have two sisters from my father's side, but I was raised as an only child. For a large portion of my childhood, I lived at my father's house with my mom, my aunt, and my male cousins. I was a kid with lots of energy to spare, always dancing, running around with the boys, climbing just about anything climbable, monkeying around my father's outdoor gym, and always plotting the next fun adventure. I dreaded going to school and sitting still in front of a TV. I hated when they made me wear dresses, get my hair brushed, and have pictures taken.

But I always had an insatiable appetite for the foods and things I liked. All year long, I looked forward to summer break because school was finally over and I could play all day, every day. Every summer, we would go on beach vacations, where we would fill up an entire house with about twenty-plus members of the extended family and friends and have a great time connecting with each other in nature.

I loved the weekly scheduled power outages and hurricane season because all we could do was get together with neighbors to hang out and play dominoes, card games, and bingo. I loved when they allowed me to play at the adults' table and make bets on the games. At one point, I had won so much money playing that I thought I was rich; I would count my money every day and plan how to invest it. Perhaps that's when the entrepreneur in me was born.

Like most girls, I was my father's little princess, and he was my everything. He was always the fun one, and my mom was the strict one. He taught me how to ride a bike, skate, and, later in life, drive. I always anticipated my dad getting home and the whistle call he would do as he approached the house. My father, to this day, practices a religion called Yoruba, in which he's a priest. The religion involves sacrifices of all kinds of animals, and this was a totally normal thing for me to witness around the house. I didn't like the part with the sacrifices, but the culture has many beautiful practices, and one of my favorites was the drum circle. I loved dancing to the African beats and watching others. It wasn't unusual to see people dance and embody the spirits of ancestors. When this happened, they were always treated with respect as they would walk around the place, sharing wisdom and prophecies. Sometimes they would totally lose control over their bodies and move in very intense and interesting ways. We call it *se montó*.

When was a baby, I was initiated into the religion, but when I was nine years old, I went through a more in-depth initiation alongside my mother. I can't share much of what happened there, and I also don't remember much, but it was a yearlong initiation of a spiritual rebirth. It started with a week of rituals, where they first took us to bathe in a river where we collected rocks, then took us to a property where we stayed for the entire week. A lot happened there, but what I remember the most were the animal sacrifices, the shaving of our heads, and the beautiful white temple in which we stayed. The temple was a representation of the womb, and offerings of fruits and flowers were made to our altar daily.

After the first week, we went home with a lot of rules to follow for the next year to come. For the first three months, all mirrors had to be covered, no technology was allowed, our heads and entire bodies had to be covered in layers of white clothes, we couldn't be outside at noon or midnight, we couldn't be photographed, and we were not allowed to dance until we were presented in front of our first drum ceremony, among many other rules that I don't remember. I hated that I couldn't see what my bald head looked like, just the reflection on the bathroom tile.

After the three months were over, we could finally stop wearing all the layers, and I could see myself in the mirror. I did look cute with my grown-out pixie hair, but we still had to be dressed in white all the time for the rest of the year. The rule I hated the most was no swimming at all for the year, so no beaches, rivers, ponds, pools, etc. The rest of the restrictions were hard, but this was the worst.

Shortly after the religious initiation, my father left the country. I still remember that painful day. He was wearing a light blue agbada, and I watched from afar as he disappeared into the distance of the crowded airport. Reliving this memory as I write has brought up a lot of sorrow and helped me realize that this was the first time I felt abandoned. It's such an interesting paradox. My inner child was so deeply hurt, and she detested him for it, but my higher self knew that he was paving the path to my future. He would call often and visited a couple of times in the four years that he was gone. But I was so resentful that I hardly ever got on the phone. He supported us from afar, and I never lacked anything materially, just his presence.

At the age of fourteen, after many failed attempts, my mom and I were finally able to join my father and make Miami our home. The relationship with my father didn't fully restored upon our arrival, but I knew I was finally where I belonged, and even though things were a little rocky at the beginning, I knew the potential for growth in this country was massive compared to the island.

High school, though, was a bit traumatic. I went to Miami High School, which is one of the largest high schools in the city. It certainly felt humongous compared to my little school in Cuba. I struggled a lot at first getting around the place, but thankfully I wasn't the only one who didn't know English. The school was packed with kids just like me, and it was not long before I belonged to a small group of friends. Most of my classes were in Spanish the first two years of high school, so I didn't learn much English in school. Most of what I learned was from watching TV and learning the lyrics of the songs I liked. I remember watching my little cousin sing Lady Gaga's "Poker Face" and wondering if I could ever sing it fluently like she did.

This was right around the time I realized I needed to start taking risks in life, get used to discomfort, and build my independence from my parents. I had already survived my first year of high school in a new country, so anything was possible. I was really scared of getting on a plane without an adult, so I asked my parents if I could visit Cuba by myself. I didn't think they would let me, but they did. I was so nervous waiting for my flight that after boarding, I realized I left my carry-on at the gate. It was absolute chaos, but I got it back, and I survived. I didn't know it at the moment, but I was a young kid with a big desire for personal development, and overcoming this challenge was a big win.

Although my parents were never on top of my grades and were completely hands-off when it came to school, I always strived for the best. I performed all right in most classes, but it always felt like a struggle. I was riddled with anxiety my entire senior year because I didn't know what I wanted to do with my life, and it seemed like all my friends had a clear vision. I always loved nature, so I started college with environmental science in mind and then changed majors to nutrition.

At this age, I was old enough to recognize my parents' toxic relationship patterns. My mom and I only had each other to vent to about my father's temper. At times, I would try to talk my mother into leaving him after listening to her complaints, and one day we did. After he left for a religious workday, we packed all our stuff and left. We had no idea where to go, but we found a tiny efficiency studio in Little Havana where my grandma, mom, and I all slept in the same bed. This was an intensely difficult time in our lives. My mother was working two jobs, I was starting college and had my minimum-wage job at the airport, and we had three mouths to feed. I experienced real hunger for the first time in my life. I would hope my friends would invite me to their homes for dinner, and I counted pennies at the store to be able to buy food. A month later, we had no choice but to go back home when we found out my mother was pregnant. Then about another month after going back, she had a miscarriage. It was almost like a move from the universe to get us back.

A few months later, late in the night, I was at Denny's with my friends. I got a call from my mom telling me that something happened and to head back home. When I got home, everything was a total mess, and my room was a disaster. My father got arrested for drug possession. But all they found was some cash and a gun that used to belong to my grandfather, who had recently lost his mind to dementia. Since they couldn't find drugs, they told my father that if he didn't turn it in, they would pin it on me, his daughter, and that I would be the one paying the price. That's when he finally told them where it was. A few grams of methamphetamine weren't enough to incriminate him as a dealer, and my father tried to prove that it was for personal use by snorting it in front of them, but that wasn't enough. He went through a short trial in which he was convinced that pleading guilty and doing three years was better than losing a trial and going away for ten.

I hate to say this, but although I was deeply heartbroken about my father's fate, I felt relieved that it was just my mother and me again. I was completely oblivious to the full story of the arrest; they sheltered me from the truth. It wasn't until years after his release, when my father and I had a meaningful and beautiful conversation about our relationship, that I learned the full story, and I told him that if I had known this then, I would have supported him to fight.

At the time my father's sentence started, I was working as a lash-extension technician for the family business of my boyfriend at the time, and I was making good money for the first time in my life. But I was anxious and depressed, trying to keep up with school and work. I paid close attention to my misery, and I followed my inner guidance. One day, I sat down with my mom and told her that I was dropping out of school, that I couldn't take it anymore. I had just recently started learning how to tattoo eyebrows, and I thought, *You never know; this might actually lead to something good.* I was so right about that because my career in cosmetic tattooing has been a blessing to my life.

From ages nineteen to twenty-seven, I was in a committed relationship with a man that I have so much gratitude for. When I met him, his family was looking to expand their business with more lash technicians, so they plucked me from my minimum-wage job and taught me to do lashes. This was the start of my current career path. I worked with them for a couple of years, then at the age of twenty-two, I decided to be my own boss and signed a commercial lease where I started my business. The first three years were extremely rough because I had no idea what I was doing and I was learning as I went. I got into huge debt, trying to grow my reputation as an artist. I even considered giving up multiple times, but eventually my investments started paying off, and I reached a level of success that allowed me to make my crazy ideas come to life. My entrepreneurial journey has been such a beautiful process, and I have learned so much about myself.

This long-term relationship was a huge learning experience where my personal development started. Like most nineteen-year-olds, I didn't know myself or what I wanted in life. I shaped myself to fit into his lifestyle, and I was happy in those shapes for most of the relationship. He was a surfer / sailor / beach bum—a simple guy—and I loved that about him. But I didn't realize how dim my light was next to him because he wasn't into shiny things. In the year 2020, we decided to get married because we had been living together for so long, and it felt like a smart move to be able to save on taxes and to buy our home. I made the proposal myself. Not like a big-deal proposal; it came up in conversation. We knew we didn't want an actual wedding, so we just went to the courthouse and got it done. On the way to the courthouse, we argued for multiple reasons. There was one red flag after the other, and I had a gut feeling that this was the start of the end. Looking back at it, I see how I emasculated him by being the one with the initiative. Clearly, we were not getting married for the right reasons.

In January 2021, I started my pole-dancing journey, which inspired my embodiment process. Although I always loved dancing, I carried a lot of shame around the desire for attention that sometimes accompanies it. Before falling in love with pole dancing, I used to judge pole dancers who would post their videos on social media, wearing almost nothing. Clearly, this trigger was meant to bring attention to the part of me that resonates with it that I didn't accept fully.

Since I have always been very athletic, it didn't take long to learn. I installed a pole in my living room and practiced almost every day. I started sharing my videos on social media, and I could tell that my partner wasn't happy about that. Many people in my life weren't happy about it. Through pole dancing, I learned to love the process of acquiring a new skill and learned to love my body in new ways I didn't know were possible. I started to embody the woman I always envied and the attention whore in me in a way that was healthy and enriching. I started feeling more comfortable wearing extravagant things and being the center of attention. I started getting gigs performing and realized how much I loved being on stage. Pole dancing was truly a portal into my reclamation journey, and in the process, my life changed drastically.

Around this same time, I also started learning about the female hormonal cycle and the moon cycles. Ever since my reproductive years started, I have experienced extremely painful periods, and I learned that all these symptoms that have been normalized in society are actually signs of imbalance. So I adopted a lifestyle that supports my body. Throughout my journal, you will read comments about where I am on my cycle; that's because I am always aware of the current phase and how it's affecting my mood, energy levels, hunger, and creativity. I have some book recommendations in the acknowledgment section if this is something you're wanting to learn more about.

Scattered throughout this book, you will find my blood art—paintings created using my own menstrual blood. This is a controversial topic, as period blood is often seen as something unclean or taboo. I understand that perspective since I wasn't always in tune with my own cycle. But as I deepened my connection with my body, I grew more comfortable with it and began using it intentionally as a medium for expression and healing.

In 2020, I began my Reiki practitioner training. While I don't practice Reiki often, I'm grateful for the wisdom it gave me—especially my understanding of the chakra system and how to balance our energy centers. Each chakra painting in this book carries a piece of that knowledge. It is my hope that you see the magic in them and turn to them whenever you need guidance or alignment.

Midyear of 2021 was one of the hardest moments of my adult life till this day. The relationship I invested seven years in was feeling like a dead end, and I struggled to make the final decision. I would cry in the shower almost every day and felt so ashamed to be in that situation that my face broke out in painful cystic acne that would not go away, even with all the expensive facials and life adjustments that I made. I would pick at my face every night, followed by the haunting feeling that my acne would go away when I finally listened to my intuition. That was not the only way my body would speak to me. I had recurring yeast infections every month that would make sex very uncomfortable, and my jaw would lock any time I tried to perform oral sex. I would wake up crying in the middle of the night from having psychic dreams telling me it was time to end it. In every dream, he either broke up with me or did something that gave me the perfect excuse to break up with him, and I would feel so much relief in the dream, only to wake up to a different reality. The last dream was very clear: there was no reason other than my sovereign decision that it was over.

I came home from work one day, knowing that was the day. I was so nervous and fighting the need to say it. I panicked so badly that my hands cramped up and bent inward. He saw me from the room inside and came out to help me calm down. When my hands started to feel normal again and the tears calmed, I said, "I can't do this anymore." He was confused; I had to elaborate, but I don't remember how I did it. From there, we tried to work it out for a couple of months, but it never felt right moving forward until it finally ended. We were on good terms for a while after that and were in each other's lives often, but that slowly came to an end when we both started dating other people and moving on with our lives. This is when I started creating the life I wanted.

Fast-forward to the present moment. I see how all those dreams and intuitive hits were my future self helping me make the right decisions. It felt like an eternity, but I don't regret how long it took me. Because of that, I'm now so much more aware of my energy leaks and can easily change my course when I need to.

I wasn't always a sexually liberated person. I do have memories of me grinding on the corner of the bed as a child and feeling ashamed; then during my high school years, I would touch myself and video chat with strangers on Omegle. But I didn't masturbate to the point of orgasm until I was in my early twenties. I had just discovered a podcast called *Sex with Emily*, and I learned so much about exploring my sexuality and the importance of self-pleasure. I asked a friend if she masturbated, and she said, "Of course I do. I just watch porn and use my hands." This was another wake-up call: everyone out there is doing it but me!

So one night before bed, I found a video that I liked, and I started touching myself until I climaxed. It was pure ecstasy; tears rolled down my face from the intense energy rushing through my body for the first time. That's when it occurred to me that all this time, I was having sex with but not actually reaching this point, and it was all due to lack of knowledge of my own pleasure. I became obsessed with self-love and would find moments throughout the day to give myself quick orgasms here and there. I was basically a horny teenager in my twenties, and that was a fun time!

Interestingly enough, I would often have full-body orgasms with my partner during sex, and those were always so epic. These days, I have more awareness on the topic to know that those were energy-based orgasms since they did not stem from any part of my body but rather the entirety of my body. I also would have orgasms in my sleep all the time, and they weren't even linked to sexual dreams. I would simply wake up with the urge to press on my vulva as it throbbed with pleasure. I wasn't sure what that was or why it happened; it was just a surprise sprinkle of pleasure. There are times in my life when they happen often, and other times they don't happen at all.

When my partner and I were still together, I would go to bed early every night while my partner stayed downstairs watching TV, and I would give myself a nice little good-night loving, making sure I had at least two orgasms—and sometimes I would even lose track. I felt ashamed because I wasn't having sex with him instead, but I saw my self-pleasure as something separate from our sex life. He didn't like it when I used my vibrator during intercourse, so that was just my private thing. We were still having sex regularly, and it was pretty good, but it was feeling a little monotonous and performative. It would start with oral, then switch to the other person, then we would fuck for a few minutes until he came, and that was the end. My communication skills weren't there, and I didn't feel comfortable telling him when something didn't feel good, so I just let him do whatever.

When we were trying to repair our relationship, I started speaking up more about those things, but he would get offended. One day while making out, he was fingering me, and there was a piece of cuticle scratching me; I suggested that on top of trimming his nails, he should also file those little corners. He got upset and left the room. It's easy to say that he just didn't care, and that's exactly how I felt at that moment. But if I step into his shoes, I can easily see his frustration that after all the years, I was just now bringing awareness to this issue. We were both equally at fault for our failed sex life, but I'm the only one responsible for learning and communicating about my pleasure.

After this break up, I felt free to finally live a fantasy that I'd had since I started pole dancing. For some reason, I really wanted to know what it would be like to be stripper, and I figured since I was pretty good at pole dancing, I should be able to make a lot of money. After hours of research on YouTube University, I drove up north to one of the most popular clubs in Miami, Scarlett's Cabaret. It was a long drive of over an hour, and the entire time I was mentally preparing myself. Pretending I wasn't about to shit my pants, I approached the not-so-friendly-looking hostess and told her what I was there for. When the manager finally showed up after what felt like an eternity, he looked at my ID and, without much explanation, told me that there was an error on my ID that supposedly I needed to fix.

I've grown from and I've healed many wounds, but back then, rejection still hit a soft spot. However, I wasn't about to let this put me down after the long drive and internal work I had put into getting there. I knew there is another strip club just a few miles down the highway. The worst possible scenario just happened and stripped me of all the fear and insecurities. Convinced that the manager just gave me a BS excuse to not take me in, I drove my ass to Tutsies.

At the other club, the manager presented himself. He was much nicer, and I had a better feeling overall. He briefly looked at my application and asked how long I'd been dancing for.

"Well, I've been dancing my whole life, but I've never danced at a strip club."

Confused, he asked, "Are you sure you can be fully naked on stage?"

"I guess we'll find out."

He took me to the locker rooms and asked me to change into my outfit and let him know when I was ready. Walking up to the stage, I was feeling the pressure slowly build up. I don't remember the kind of music that was playing, but I made sure to feel good about it. Coming up with the flow as I moved around the pole, my little black dress came off first, revealing most of my body, leaving just my thong and my top. Next was my bra; I smoothly unclipped it from my back using only my fingers and slid it down my shoulders.

I tried to make eye contact for as long as possible with the audience, but it was the hardest part of the dance. I was so vulnerable and alone and small and innocent. My confidence was the result of a shot of adrenaline, but deep inside, I was scared and intimidated. Eye contact felt much more personal than exposing my naked body. I'd struggled with the size of my breasts in my self-love journey, and I could hear the critical voices in my head. No matter how much I'd learned to love them, the voices were still there, and I put myself in this situation to listen.

The moment came when I had to drop the panties. I slid both my thumbs through the straps on my hips and, facing the back of the stage, pushed my thong down my legs. Slowly to avoid tripping on my seven-inch heels, I bent over and peeled the straps off my skin, revealing my ass and flashing my pussy to the audience. In my mind, it glistened, and everyone stopped what they were doing to admire the source of life. But I couldn't see anything, just my heeled boots and my underwear on the stage. I continued to dance on the stage completely nude except for my shoes, surprised that it didn't feel strange at all. It was like an ancient and wise part of me came alive and took over my body.

I was about to start working there for the night when I confirmed that my ID card indeed had an error and the other manager wasn't lying. Although I couldn't work that night, I felt amazing about the experience and was looking forward to coming back. But when I was actually able to go back and work, I had a very unpleasant experience. I confirmed that this was not a place where my artistry could thrive. It's not a place for artists; it's for hustlers, and I was way too innocent to survive there. I was depressed for days after and realized that if I were to continue to go back, the way I see men would change for the worse. I wasn't interested in creating that kind of reality.

This stirred up some drama on my mom's side of the family. They didn't understand why I wanted to do that kind of work when I had a well-established business. These days, they understand me better, but they had a hard time accepting my reality.

This stripper fantasy was something I wanted to try as part of my human experience research, and it didn't work out as I expected. In this book, you will read about experiences that I put myself through. Some of these stories are embarrassing to share, and I can't believe I am being this open publicly. My purpose in sharing is to push myself out of my comfort zone and show readers that we are not as unique as we think we are. Everyone goes through difficult, embarrassing, sad, happy, loving experiences, but we tend to only share the good stuff. As embarrassed as I may feel to share some of my private moments and thoughts, I am as proud of my failures as I am of my achievements because they played an important role in my development.

I couldn't tell you if this book is about sex, love, entrepreneurship, or self-help. I can't say this book was made to inspire or empower anyone, although that would be great. What I can say for sure is that this is the real story of someone who is doing her best to navigate through Earth School while staying true to herself and the reality she wants to create.

THIS IS HOW IT STARTED

Sex was fun, but there was something missing. Even with my regular occurrence of full-body orgasms, I knew that there was more to explore. Excitement and newness with my new boyfriend started to wither as time passed. Physical attraction lasted, but intimacy wasn't the same anymore. The only new experiences that were happening were coming from my endless cravings for exploration. For the first time ever, I dove deeply into being the pleasure provider; to say I loved it is an understatement, and he was the happy receiver of my newfound passion. I touched him in places and ways that neither of us had ever tried before. He would beg for my touch, and I was always enthusiastic to deliver. Watching him get off was the best part; we were so connected energetically that I could feel everything he was feeling. The buildup, the teasing, and the powerful release were mutually felt every time.

But eventually, I wanted the same special treatment back, and that's where it didn't work out. I communicated about my need to have the same energy reciprocated, and while he tried his best, and we did have plenty of exciting nights, often I was left wanting more. It was never just about me like I would happily make it just about him. It would always somehow end with him inside me. Resentment built up. I couldn't have it my way; I felt so wrong and depleted.

I wanted more. I wanted someone that would put as much enthusiasm into my pleasure as I did for theirs. Someone that would go much deeper than the physical body. So I created this person in my head, and I daydreamed about him all the time. He would do anything to watch me in my powerful, divine orgasmic energy. He knew my body like a map, and he knew exactly what to do to make me want him. That's when I met J.

It started with a comment to an Instagram post where I was promoting my Pole Infused Goddess Circle, offering to help with cross-promotion since most of his clients were also women. I briefly checked his page.

Hmm, interesting. He probably wants to get into my pants, I thought.

And before you label me as a shallow bitch for thinking that, know that I share very provocative videos (also known as thirst traps to those that diminish my art), and my comment section and direct messages and are constantly being flooded with thirsty men. So yes, I assumed based on my limited view of the world. But it also felt different. The energy in this message was nothing like the fire and peach emojis I was used to receiving.

I knew my partner would most likely have a problem with me taking on such an opportunity. Subconsciously, I also knew that this man had a lot more to offer than a collaboration. So I stopped myself from even responding to avoid conflict in my relationship. I did respond three weeks later. It was also around this time that things started to feel complicated with my boyfriend, so that helped.

I followed him back, and every now and then, his content would pop on my feed.

He's hot but definitely not my type. He's too beefy and old. I can tell he is so into himself. Look at him talking so highly about his work and how his bodywork is way better than average. He's probably a pervert, I reasoned with myself.

Ever heard that we judge what we have not healed? Yeah, my inner judge was going at it! But I also knew that I had many of those same characteristics. I speak proudly about my talents like he does, triggering a part of me that I wasn't completely at peace with.

The love for his work was omnipresent on his page. My restrictions slowly faded as I witnessed his promotional content and client testimonials. And even if a little bit of judgment was still there, it wasn't enough to stop me from seeing that this man was truly living his purpose.

Curiosity built slowly with every testimonial he shared. Many of these came from very attractive women, which added to the list of reasons why I didn't like him. Why? Deeply ingrained insecurities.

My relationship with my boyfriend turned slightly toxic. The only way we were able to bond was if I was as stoned as him. Pot was our bond; things may not have been as good as I wanted them, but when I was high, it didn't matter. So I surrendered to it. I settled, knowing that sinking into this shadowy side of the relationship as opposed to fighting it would be the easiest way out. I knew that eventually the light would shine and help me through this painful loss. For two or three months, I had tried my best to push us forward, with the fear of losing my romantic love. I saw us married, with a family and thriving business, but my attachment to that wasn't enough to keep me.

I initiated the end of our relationship just about two weeks before my birthday. Surprisingly, it was much easier than I thought. Nothing compared to my last breakup. I had prepared myself this time, so I spoke with certainty and courage. I knew the kind of behavior he would display and fought the urge to overexplain myself. The decision was final—no going back this time.

Now I felt completely open to finally book with J. I knew what I wanted, a tantra session, but since I had my reservations about the guy, I booked a regular massage to get a taste of him. After all, according to his reviews, even just a regular massage from him was already an upgrade from the regular spa therapies I'd had before.

JANUARY 19, 2023

I arrived early—unusual for me. I checked in at the front desk.

"I'm here to see J in 818."

In my head, I was wondering how many women came here asking for him. They were probably thinking, *Here comes another one!* The lady phoned him, and I could hear the friendly tone in her voice

The guy in the back was analyzing me while overhearing the phone call; at least it felt that way. Who knows what was going through his mind. It felt like a long wait, but in just a moment, they let me up the elevator. Passing by each door, I checked the apartment numbers; to my right was the expansive view of the bay and downtown architecture. I found his apartment and knocked.

He opened the door and welcomed me in with a big smile. He looked just like his Instagram pictures. All I could see were muscles on top of muscles. Very distracting even for me, the girl who "doesn't like beefy guys." Deep smile lines on his face and grays making up most of his beard revealed his mature age.

Immediately, I could feel his secure masculine energy making me shrink in size. Where was all that confidence I'm used to carrying with me?

I removed my sandals and placed them by the door next to his altar. We sat down on his couch, and he explained how his process worked. I had already done enough research to know exactly what he was about, so my ADHD mind was doing her thing. I liked how articulate he was.

I would have appreciated that when I was still learning English in high school; every letter of each word pronounced to perfection, especially the last ones, gesturing with his hands and making eye contact.

I'm a huge fan of massages. I've been getting them regularly since I could afford them, but I only had female therapists in the past. This was the first time with a straight male, and on top of that, it was at his home. No manager to run to for safety—it was just him and me. I was feeling vulnerable, another feeling I'd grown fond of.

He gave me some privacy to undress. For a second, I contemplated if I should keep my panties on, but then I lay completely naked on his table with a towel over my butt as I waited for his return.

Every massage I had received in the past would get straight to the point, but not this one. It started with the dynamic music and vibrating bed, then the first soft stroke of what felt like feathers, followed by warm fur, then the gentle glide of his fingers. After the teasing foreplay, he proceeded to give me the best massage I'd received in my life. He completely ruined regular massages for me, and I confirmed that he is not your average body worker. Every single detail of this experience was meticulously planned, and I could tell.

"You have a very quiet soul," he said, referring to how quiet I was during the session.

I am not *a quiet soul*, I thought. Oversharing is my not-so-hidden talent.

"Do people usually speak during their sessions?"

"Most people moan, cry, or even laugh, but you were completely silent the entire time. You have a very quiet soul."

This made me think a lot, because I am one to moan even at the sight of delicious food or good music. I wondered why I never did during massages. I would just quietly receive and feel. Maybe it's time to explore that.

His shower was ready for me with everything I needed to remove the oil from my body. When I came out of the shower, he was sitting on the couch, and I sat next to him. Still feeling speechless from the session, I didn't know how to tell him that was the best massage of my life. I didn't want to feed his ego by adding to the endless list of compliments he receives on his work. But it happened for a reason, and I had no choice.

He told me about other modalities he worked with, and he offered me a tantric experience for the same price of his regular sessions. This was a price gap of over $500. I was already willing to pay his full price for this experience, but the generous discount was a good reason to come back sooner than planned. I made it clear that I was interested in taking his offer, so he sent me some videos and information for me to look over. I watched all the videos, I read his reviews, and I was convinced this was going to happen.

I reached out to book my next appointment, and it just so happened that the only day we could both make it work was on my birthday. The previous year, I had taken my first solo trip to Costa Rica for a plant-medicine ceremony, which also landed on my birthday. I was planning on doing some sort of plant medicine this year as well, but perhaps the universe has something else in store.

JANUARY 26, 2023

It's my birthday. I dedicated my entire day to myself, starting with a delicious morning practice that set the tone for a powerful healing pole dancing session. Dancing is one of my favorite forms of therapy—a meditative practice where my focus turns inward and I connect deeply with my body and emotions.

For those who don't dance, it may be hard to understand what it feels like when music enters my consciousness and transforms my body into water. Slow and fluid, I wave my spine and my legs along the floor like a mermaid swimming through the depths of the ocean. Then, in contrast, rough and choppy like the crashing waves when I twerk—my ass catching the rhythm of the bass as my body moves with unapologetic freedom.

When I'm on the pole, I'm very intentional about feeling everything: the calluses forming on my knuckles as I grip the pole with all my strength, the delicious ache of a deep stretch, the pull of my skin against the pole, the steady rhythm of my breath, and the intentional flex or point of my feet. The burn in my muscles even becomes a pleasant sensation when my intention is to express what I'm feeling through movement.

Today, my routine reflected the grief of my recent breakup, but what I love most about pole is the freedom to embody any emotion for the sake of experiencing it, even if it's not related to my current state of mind. It activates a beautiful flow—a fully authentic, unfiltered expression of feelings in motion. It's hard to describe with words the feeling that takes over my body when music speaks to a part of me that was quietly wanting to emerge. I am a writer, and yet I can't find the words to describe it. I am grateful to also be a dancer; otherwise I may never be able to express it.

Often, we get so caught up in perfecting a skill that we forget why we started. For me, it's about allowing the sensations to guide me, holding poses until they feel complete. This practice remains one of my favorite spiritual rituals—a way to honor my emotions and my being.

From there, I picked up food and went to the beach. I bathed in the freezing water and lay topless on the sand. The night before, I was feeling a little nervous about the appointment, so I asked the universe for a sign of green light; the sign was a white bird. I had almost forgotten about the sign when, while I was lying on the sand, a flock of white seagulls clouded me and my neighbors. It was clear and in abundance; that was my sign.

After witnessing the beautiful sunset by the bay, I headed to his place with plenty of time to pass by the store and get myself a small brownie or something to celebrate. When I walked into the store, I saw him standing in line, holding a cake. I couldn't help but laugh as I made my way in; he saw me and looked away. I could tell that, for a second, he contemplated pretending he wasn't there, but it was too late. I approached him in a playful way and said hi. I completely ruined his surprise, but this was perfect. I wouldn't have had it any other way.

His offer of the tantra session at a ridiculously low price was already a sign that he was interested in seeing more of me, but a whole cake for my birthday was a sign that he wanted me to stay around. I mean, he's very professional and goes out of his way to help clients, but a cake felt kind of personal. I could get used to this.

After arriving at his apartment I took a shower to remove the salt and sand from my body, then we sat down at the couch. The room was lit with candles; the temperature was warm, with soft, healing music playing in the background, the same music I listen to at home while relaxing. I told him about my intentions for being there and my recent breakup. Then he went over the details of the tantric massage and how many of his clients used this modality to heal after heartbreak.

Removing all expectations was crucial to allow this experience to flow where it needed to go. This was a much more sensual and intimate modality. He said, "I will read the energy in our space and allow it to guide me toward what your body needs tonight. All you need to do is follow my touch and focus on the sensations. Just like a meditation, when you find yourself distracted, go back to your breath and find my touch again; let it ground you into the moment. I will utilize this healing energy to cleanse and remove any residual energy left from your relationship. Then I will introduce my own safe, masculine energy to fill in the void. The difference is that you will not be carrying it with you; everything that happens tonight stays in this safe container."

He brought me over to face his altar where oracle cards were spread out for me to pick one. He was standing beside me, his hands softly running through my shoulders as he gently moved my hair out of the way and whispered into my ears. My body anticipated his touch, and chills invaded my skin.

"Close your eyes and slowly run your fingers through each of the cards. Feel the velvety texture, the sharpness of the edges, and allow your intuition to choose one. This card is what you will go back to in case you are not able to connect with my touch."

I followed his guidance, my attention focused on the aroma in the room, his touch, his voice, and the cards. I chose the card, and holding a small light next to the booklet, he read the meaning for me (it was nothing memorable).

From there, he directed me to remove all clothing and wait for him on the massage table while he cleaned his hands. My eyes were closed when he came back and applied some sort of ointment on my forehead. Then I felt him do some sort of signs with his fingers before he asked me to flip over to lie on my stomach. Then the massage started.

Like the last time, he began with the gentle caress of feathers, sweeping through my body in a combination of slow and swift movements, the unpredictability of his touch completely sending me to a different dimension. He went from my feet to my neck and often worked on two separate areas at the same time. I couldn't tell where he's standing or what hand was where; at times, it felt like there was more than one person in the room working on my body. I surrendered to his touch with ease, my mind for once in complete stillness, bathing in the bliss of his touch.

He was massaging my neck with intensity, his fingers and knuckles digging into my skin in such pleasurable ways, tapping and moving the energy buildup. My mind started to wander for a moment, remembering some of his reviews talking about a neck orgasm.

Is that what he's trying to do? Am I about to have neck orgasm? If I'm expecting it to happen, it's not going to happen; forget about it and just surrender to the pleasure.

He continued to massage the rest of my body and then returned to my neck. Without thinking about it, when I least expected it, it happened.

The left side of my neck and part of my shoulder sent a current down my spine and quickly filled up every part of me. At the same time, it felt like I was falling into a dark, endless void. I could hear him breathing heavily as I spasmed in and out of consciousness. My head lifted and tilted, my body convulsed, and I moaned intensely. I bathed in this pleasure as it turned into a deep cry. I bawled my soul out in the most beautiful way. I allowed the full range of emotions to take over. Slowly, I felt myself come down from this powerful orgasmic release, my crying turned into sobbing, and my tears dried out as a new wave of emotions took over me. I laughed uncontrollably at what just happened; everything about it was hilarious.

I just came from the fucking neck! And not just that, but it was one of the most intense orgasms I'd ever had, and this man had not even touched my genitals!

It was in this moment I knew I would let him do anything with my body. If that was what he could do with just my neck, I could only imagine what he was capable of if I just allowed him the rest of me. He had my trust.

I lifted my head from the pillow to ask for some tissues, and he had them ready for me. I dried my face from all the tears, mucus, and saliva I released just moments ago, and I lay back down for more.

He continued to massage my body while I was still laughing at myself and the massive neck orgasm I received. But I finally calmed down and brought my focus back to his touch, now even more sensual than before. He would go from my back to my bum to my legs, brushing my pussy very slightly, almost as if by mistake, when massaging my inner thighs. The sexual energy had already filled up all of me; even the most delicate touch was enough to make me arch in pure pleasure.

He teased me in that way for what felt like forever, each stroke applying more pressure on my skin. The anticipation made me spread my legs open just enough to give him more access to me. He could tell I was inviting him to touch more. Now he was completely focused on it. His smooth and slippery palms gently massaged my entire vulva, going over my pubic mound, clitoris, outer and inner lips, gradually adding more and more pressure. His fingers stimulated my clitoris, as if he were playing an instrument he'd known forever.

To be completely honest, I couldn't tell you what he was doing exactly; I think his other hand was massaging another body part, directing the energy to my pussy, intensifying the pleasure. This slow buildup of energy suddenly erupted. I moaned and perked my ass up, and just when I thought he had all of me, his thumb slid inside me, applying pulsing pressure on my G-spot and clitoris simultaneously, making me come even harder than I already was. With his other hand, he was brushing my stomach toward my pussy; I don't know why, but this was building up the intensity even more. Another full-body orgasm, with all my favorite components: euphoria, tears, laughter, release.

For close to two hours, I was climaxing every few minutes, each growing in intensity and then tapering down as my body grew tired. I wasn't counting, but there were multiple, very intense orgasms.

At some point during the massage, while my body was moving with the orgasmic energy, I felt his face between my legs. I was not welcoming of this kind of touch and my body went completely still. He noticed immediately and stopped. I feel conflicted about this, but it didn't ruin the experience either.

From the cake to the candles, the temperature, and the music. Every little detail that went into this experience was carefully thought of and put together to impress me, and he did. He also didn't want to charge me the already greatly discounted session. When I pulled out my wallet and asked again how much I owed him, he shrugged and hesitantly told me to just pay him whatever I wanted.

Trying to sleep that night was nearly impossible. Orgasmic pleasure was still flowing through my body every time I remembered our time together. Just the memory of his touch would send me to moaning land. In the morning, I texted him about it:

> J: Very happy to hear ;) Strong feminine energy flowing through you in abundance tonight. It was hot, it was magical, it and you were delicious.
>
> Me: I'm definitely interested in receiving more of these sessions and learning more. I've been interested for a while.
>
> J: Music to my ears...well, eyes in this case. Going to be some beautiful energy in this exchange. Relax and recharge and tell me when you're ready...this new year of yours is starting off great. Btw, still smiling about your burst of laughter.
>
> Me: I felt cared for like never before. You're going to ruin not just massages but also other men for me lol. You've also ruined my vibrator.
>
> J: I prefer the word replaced ;) Btw, leave your wallet at home next time...from now on, all our sessions will be a trade, a fair exchange of divine energy. We grow together, you and I :)

That was one of the hottest things I've read. This text lives rent-free in my head now.

FEBRUARY 6, 2023

This was our third encounter, I had already been served with multiple orgasms, each more explosive than the last. All resistance I carried into this encounter dissipated as I fully surrendered to the experience. I was completely melted on the massage table facing down. My back arched, and my hips swayed involuntarily as the waves of orgasmic pleasure filled every cell of my being.

Keeping my body from sliding off the table was impossible. I had no strength or desire to hold myself up and lie back, but whichever way I ended up, he would make it work. As I lay facedown, my left leg hung off the side of the table and found a place in between his legs. I could feel his erection through his pants as he gently rested on my thigh. My upper body was still supported by the table as my right leg followed my left, and then I was bent over in front of him. My hips, pressed against him, continued to sway up and down in a fluid, circular motion. I could feel my juices wipe off on him. I was open and inviting when he leaned over to my left ear, his chest briefly resting on me while the warm oil rubbed between our skin.

Then he said something. I couldn't hear what exactly, but I knew what it was: a request for consent. He wanted to feel inside me, and I him. Words couldn't roll out of my mouth, so my body spoke for me. His pants came off with ease, and I knew in just a moment, our energies would collide. All my awareness was calmly focused on the sensations. As he entered me, reaching areas his fingers couldn't, rapture took over in a ripple effect from deep inside me. I savored each stroke as I felt the energy move throughout my entire body. The intoxicating aroma of masculinity invaded my nostrils; it was faint and powerful. It would come and go, but I was connected to my breath in constant search for it.

I would never have his cock inside me for the first time again, and it's a memory worthy of worship.

At this point, all my friends and family knew about J. They knew about him since our first encounter, and I kept them updated in the newsletter. There was no escaping the oversharing of our experiences since many of them would go out of their way to find out more. "When do you see him again? Are you going to date him? Tell me more, tell me more!"

All the questions were so overwhelming, I couldn't even wrap my head around what was happening. My ex was still living in my space, and I was already slowly developing intimacy with another man; it was too much all at once. I told my friends that I didn't know: "I don't know when I'll see him again, I don't know what this is going to be, I don't know what I want, and I don't want to think about it. I just want to enjoy our time together, and whatever comes out of it, we'll find out."

But to be fair, all the questions scared me, specifically the ones regarding his job and how I would feel about it if we were to start a relationship. He is a massage therapist who also offers tantric experiences in which a yoni massage is available and performed upon request. Curiously enough, this is one of my biggest turn-ons, but would it be forever? Or do I feel this way only because we are not in a committed relationship?

My lifelong curiosity about polyamory and nonmonogamy tells me that I am perfectly equipped with the mindset to sustain a relationship in which my man is out there, fingering other women as a career. But that didn't mean the journey would be a trigger-free one, so just like everything in life, time would tell. And that's my answer.

Digging deeper into my mind and creating scenarios in my head like women are known to be good for, I thought of the possibility of J meeting and creating a connection with someone who is the opposite of me. Let's say an older woman around his age with way more life experience who embodies the mature feminine energy that I could not give to him. No matter how much I try to ignore it, I would always be fifteen years younger than him, and I would not be able to provide him the kind of experiences that she could because we are so different.

I could dwell on that and just feel bad about myself, or I could pay attention to the beautiful contrast that is. I, too, have something that she would not be able to replicate: my playful curiosity, my daddy/baby dynamic, and so on. Every romantic/sexual partner brings their own spices to the mix, and it doesn't make anyone better or less than.

FEBRUARY 2023
SHROOM TRIP

If I remember correctly, I walked into this encounter knowing that we would be taking psilocybin mushrooms. This was not my first time using plant medicine. I had participated in a couple of ayahuasca ceremonies in the past, as well as a few experiences with small doses of magic mushrooms. But this was my first time taking them in this kind of tantric ceremony.

J explained the nature of plant medicine, how it intensifies our sensations and enhances remembrance. The importance of having no expectations and just going with what the trip offered. He let me know that I was safe, and no matter what happened during our journey, he would take care of me. He even said, "If you end up throwing up all over the apartment, it's fine." He really emphasized that I could let my worries go and just surrender to the experience. This really put me at ease.

I ate a much smaller dose than he offered, about less than half of what he ate. Then we went off with the usual start of our experience. After our oracle card pull and eye-gazing exercise, I lay on the table, waiting for the medicine to kick in while receiving his magical touch.

My memory is blurry from there on; it was a slow but intense incline to the weirdest, hottest, longest sexual experience of my life. A few unforgettable moments that I could put together included us snuggled up on the massage table after making love intensely. I was completely immobile, melted in his arms, my legs wrapped around his, the heat from his body keeping me warm and comfortable. A sudden burst of tears arose from within me, deep and loud bawling as if I had just lost a loved one. The reason for my crying was unknown, but the release felt so good that I didn't want to stop. He encouraged my sorrow, allowing me to sink even deeper, each tear bringing me closer to pleasure than pain.

A strange memory of my childhood came up. It was an image of the stairs from my childhood home. There was nothing else but that image, yet everything about it meant so much in that moment. My cries became deeper as he caressed my hair, face, and shoulders. Then he started pulling the pain away from me. I made my way back into my body, and unsurprisingly, I started laughing uncontrollably; I think he followed.

I stayed in his arms for a few more moments, but then I got a sudden urge to pee. It came out of nowhere, and I knew I didn't have the strength to get up and use the toilet. Then I remembered what he said earlier that night. I relaxed my pelvic floor muscles, and I peed. Giggling as I did, wondering if he could also feel the warm liquid running down his thighs like I did.

I looked at him and said, "I peed." He nodded, affirming that he was happily aware. I didn't feel any shame or embarrassment; it was the complete opposite, although at this point, he was still more of a stranger to me. I had never felt safe enough with anyone to be this vulnerable, dark, and raw. All my colors showed, and I left nothing behind.

After lying in my urine for a few minutes, he went to get me some water to drink, but I was unable to get up—well, more than unable. I didn't want to—so he found a straw for me to drink from. I was licking and sucking on the straw, but for some reason, I couldn't get water to come out of it. It was such a playful moment where I was just being a complete silly-willy.

I believe from there I followed him to the couch where he was sitting. I lay on the floor by his legs, looking up at him. He looked so beautiful from this angle, and his feet! I couldn't stop staring at them. After staring long enough, I finally grabbed his toes and pulled them toward my chest, where his feet rested for the next few minutes. He was pushing down on my body; the weight felt heavy on me, but it felt so good. This was an interesting power play. I was fully in my submissive state, zero resistance. It was hard to explain, but I felt like his little property, and it felt good.

After taking his feet off me, he started playing me with his fingers like an instrument. Going to the beat of the music, his fingers found their way into my mouth. I stuck my tongue out and invited his fingers to play. They danced together the entire song. He massaged my tongue, the inside of my cheeks, the roof of my mouth, deeper inside my throat. I honestly don't understand why or how this happened, but we let it be, and the experience was so fun and weird and sexy. The sounds I made and the sensation of his fingers in my mouth kept the turn-on very high.

The rest of the night, we kept trying to go to bed and sleep, but we failed as every step we took into that direction turned into the hottest new sex position. He fucked me from every angle. His hands, his mouth, his dick made me reach for heaven every few minutes. Without failing, every single time we got into it again, it was another different type of orgasm. We went for hours and hours on end.

I'm doing my best here to put this into words, failing miserably because the memory is so faint. Maybe that night was only meant to stay there, in his space and our subconscious memory.

> Me: J, I feel so small in your arms. I had never experienced such a secure masculine energy. It's so easy to follow when you lead. I expand in your presence. I'm grateful for our energy exchange and your generosity. I'm excited to continue to learn and grow with your guidance.
> J: You manifested me, all things you desired in your world seem to match up with exactly who I am. I'm just myself around you and that's beautiful. Thank you for being as appreciative of me as I am of you. You have my attention and appreciation, those are powerful things. Our adventure together has already begun, I'm beyond happy for this path, it'll lead us to something wonderful.

I experienced his magic while going through my breakup; him effortlessly cutting all spiritual and emotional ties I had with my ex showed me the power of his work. He is a sexual healer, and I am fascinated by the work he does, so much so that I asked him to teach me. I wanted to learn the ins and outs of this practice. Helping women embody their feminine essence is a calling of mine, and this was a tool that I would love to incorporate into my practice.

I wasn't sure he'd had someone that admired his career as much as I did; he was so happy that I asked him to teach me. He left it up to me to find a model and a date, and he would share all his secrets. It took me a while to find someone that would be open to this kind of experience; after all, it does include some sensual energy and touch, but I finally found the perfect model. My friend Aby shared that she had also been curious about tantra and she's thrilled to be my practice partner.

MARCH 12, 2023

J, Vero and I went to an event called Turn On Miami. This is a tantra and BDSM experience night tailored to people who are starting to tip-toe their way into conscious sexuality practices. With multiple sensory stations like Shibari (Japanese art bondage), electrical play, erotic eating, sensory domination, orgasmic sound bath, and more, this is a night to awaken your senses and learn cool tricks to play with your partner later.

Being a guest for the first time at this event, I had an amazing time exploring and playing. We had reservations later in the night at one of the most popular nightclubs in Miami, and we knew that our time at Turn On Miami was going to be cut short. But I left feeling like I would somehow end up coming back as more than just a guest.

Arriving at E11even felt a little intimidating; the line for entry almost went around the corner, and here we were, just like in the movies, skipping the line and going straight in after a quick name drop that J facilitated. First time in, and it was a success! As we pushed our way into the crowded space, I noticed the beautiful dancers on the side and the ones in the center stage of the club. I was mesmerized by their outfits and confidence, and I remembered a flashback of my stripper night last year. Ha-ha-ha, what a mess. At least I now know how to be a good guest and tip generously. I had taken some cash that quickly flew out of my hands, and then J went and got me some more change. I ran out of singles so quickly; the next thing I knew, J was handing me another stack of cash to give out. I felt like a kid in a candy store, being generous and respectful to the dancers, something I knew they appreciated.

MARCH 17, 2023

Today was my first massage class. J and I were sitting on his couch, waiting for my friend to arrive. He was mentally preparing me for our experience. I was excited and anticipating my friend's arrival. When she did arrive, J explained the entire process to us. I was familiar with everything he was saying, but I was paying close attention to his words, expressions, and hand movements. I could tell he thrives being in this position—the guide, the leader. This role looks good on him. He was not shy to show his expertise or use fancy words, he was confident, and he owned the room.

While my friend undressed and lay on the table, J and I went over a quick meditation and eye-gazing exercise in the bathroom. When we came back into the room, my friend was lying facedown and ready. We started with the gentle caress of feathers while he explained how to confuse the mind with unpredictable patterns. I was now feeling some level of nervousness. I could tell that my touch didn't feel confident for the receiver, and this was the first rule: whatever you do, you must do it confidently.

I watched him flow, not just with his hands but also his entire body. I could now see what I was only being able to feel before. His feet slid on the floor as his arms reached opposite ends of her body, his eyes closed, only opening to check on me. I was just kind of frozen. I couldn't do what he was doing without feeling awkward, so while he was massaging, I used my long nails to create patterns on her back, arms, hands, and legs. I figured that having both—the firm and masculine touch and the soft and gentle feminine caress—would also add to the hypnotic effect of the session, and this was a territory I was a lot more comfortable walking on. So I let go of the expectation of doing what he was doing and instead focused on what felt good to me.

After getting out of my head and into my body, I slowly started feeling more and more confident, more rhythmic, more feminine. I started using my elbows to press down on her hips, and then I started using my entire arms and shoulders. My top was getting in the way, and the temperature was hot in the room, so I took it off, and as I did, my confidence multiplied. I was now on top of the table, using my shoulders to massage her glutes and thighs. My entire body weight was on her back, gliding with the help of generous amounts of oil. I was in the energy bubble and feeling good. I was flowing, and I was impressing him.

The last part of the massage ended with the receiver sitting up straight on the table. With both of us standing behind her, J explained how to bring the client down from the cloud they've been floating on. But this was when the energy felt the most intense. I was following his directions, wrapping my right arm around her chest and neck, pressing my chest into her back, her head leaning back against my left shoulder. My arms unwrapped from her neck and embraced her from under her arms. I used my nails to gently stroke her skin, gliding from her upper belly to her breasts to her neck. Her hands softly held mine. This was a moment hard to describe. It was a beautifully sensual experience, yet it felt so pure, so wholesome and healing. After this experience, I felt so much more connected to my friend.

As we unwrapped from each other, I burst into tears. This experience exceeded my expectations—wow. So much healing happened for me, and the best thing about it was that when the experience ended, our energies stayed within the vortex that we created. There was nothing to carry out with us. We let go of all inhibitions—no shame or weird vibes, only love and appreciation for each other and the experience we shared.

J had a busy day with clients after our lesson, so my friend and I relaxed by the pool while he worked. We shared our desire for more of these lessons to come and how we wanted to switch roles for me to be the receiver while she learned. A few hours passed by, and I said goodbye to my friend and went back upstairs with J. He had mentioned that I would never have to beg him for a massage since, for him, it was always a pleasure. So...I asked for another one, and he happily provided. During the massage, we talked about the amazing time we had earlier and how beautiful, intimate, and healing it was.

And then, just like that, unsurprisingly, the massage turned into another hot, sensual experience. His hands found a way inside me and created more of those amazing orgasms. But to be completely honest, we had spent a few days in a row together, and my genitals were very sensitive from all the sex we had. Without me even saying anything, he could tell that I wasn't enjoying his touch as much as usual due to the discomfort. I needed a break, so we stopped.

I was sitting at the top of the massage table. He was standing in front of me, his still-semi-erect penis tempting me to grab it, and I did, but I used my feet. My right foot pushed it up against his stomach, gliding my soles smoothly with the help of some leftover lubrication from just minutes ago, feeling all his textures underneath and between my toes, so warm and slippery. Then, using both my feet, squeezing and sliding them back and forth, I spread my toes and tried to fit his head between them. I felt how it grew with every pulse of his heartbeat. I was amazed at how my feet could maneuver their way around almost as well as my hands do. This was just a tease; I should have been heading back home by then, so just the way I started, I let go, leaving both of us wanting more.

MARCH 20, 2023

Well, that was a stressful day. I went to court to place a restraining order on my ex because he wouldn't leave. We broke up in January, but he still hasn't found a place to go. I have been floating around houses avoiding my home because I can't stand to see him.

I have been staying at J's apartment on the beach, then at my mom's house, and then house sitting for my friend Kelly. I love house sitting for Kelly because it's such a beautiful home with a luscious garden and a tall pole with plenty of space to dance around it, but there is nothing like the comfort of home. Luckily he has his own separate room, but still, he's always leaving a mess around. He gets upset when I'm dancing because he thinks that I do it to piss him off. *What the fuck is wrong with him? I've been dancing way before I met him.*

I can't even be on the phone because he thinks that I am talking to other guys, which is hilarious because he brought a girl home a few days ago. She was actually nice and friendly and complimented my outfit while I was on my way out. He can't stand seeing me happy after the break up. The other day, he started yelling at me because I was dancing, and he slammed the door so hard that he broke the handle. I left for the park for some fresh air and realized I had left my phone. When I got back, he had gone through it and saw that I was talking to someone new, and that made it even worse.

On top of that, last week he got into a nasty argument with my other roommate, and she called the cops on him because of how he was reacting to a simple request to keep the kitchen sink clean.

Since he was added to the lease when he moved in (because everyone living here needed to be on the contract), I couldn't just kick him out. The only way would be with a restraining order. So I went to the court to initiate that, but they didn't approve it. There wasn't enough evidence that I was at risk, which is true. The guy wouldn't dare to lift a finger at me. However, they did give us a court date for two weeks from then. I told him that if he left by then, I wouldn't show to court and the case would be dismissed. Hopefully we won't have to go to that extent.

I really don't think he's a bad guy. He's just so emotional right now because things didn't work out. Funny how hard I tried to make it work while in the relationship and he never saw it until it was too late.

APRIL 1, 2023

Things with J have progressed quickly but smoothly. We spend time together at least once a week and sometimes more. We are both very busy in our own lives, which creates a healthy distance between us. He is so loving, caring, and affectionate. He finds ways to make my life easy every day. Anything I need, he's happy to provide, often without me even bringing it up. My favorite is a beautiful sign that he created from scratch with my information so that when I take my pole dancing to events and gatherings, people know how to find me and even tip me through the QR code. When I stay over at his apartment, he happily pays for my parking and Uber rides to move around the beach town to avoid the endless search for parking on busy weekends.

He wants me around and eliminates any obstacles that might get in the way. He emptied out a couple of drawers so I can keep some clothes there and not travel with my stuff every time I go. He bought me a toothbrush and hairbrush just after the first night I stayed over. He sends food delivery my way if I mention a craving or lack of motivation to cook. His natural desire to support and see me grow is so refreshing. In past relationships, I always felt like I was the overachiever, and my success would outshine my partner. But with him, I don't need to dim my light to help him shine because he is part of it.

I also make it very easy for him to love me. I respect his space and support his career, two things he's lacked in past relationships. From what he's told me, the tantric experiences he facilitates were always a subject that brought discomfort with ex-partners, forcing him to tip-toe around this topic, leaving him feeling unlike himself. But I do more than support his career; actually, what he does is part of why I'm attract-ed to him. And it reminds me of my own struggles in past relationships where my dancing career was not accepted fully and I would go as far as declining gigs to avoid conflict.

I understand how relaxed he must feel in my presence because it goes both ways. We accept each other fully.

APRIL 7, 2023

I just got back home from a cosmetic tattooing conference and I'm so happy to finally live in a home without my ex. He moved out while I was gone for the week. Phew, these last four months were so draining and exhausting. I want to turn the empty room into a tantra temple but I'm not sure it's going to make sense financially. Most likely I will need to find another roommate.

APRIL 15, 2023

I just finished hosting one of the most amazing Goddess circles ever! It was a small group of four and the vibe was immaculate. We danced, we cried and shared stories we had never shared before. I love when in the middle of sharing someone says " I've never told this to anyone but..." I feel like I'm doing a good job at creating a safe space for vulnerability when I hear this.

I read one of my journal entries to them in which I described a sexual encounter with J and they were all fascinated by what they heard.

Also, one of the girls shared that she recently moved to Miami and she is looking for a room to rent. We both were amazed by the synchronicity since I just happen to be looking for a roommate. She is a burlesque performer that I met recently at an event where we both performed. I think she is a great addition to the witchy house!

JUNE 19, 2023
FATHER'S DAY

I went to see my dad today, as I do about three or four times a year. We met at the beach, where he was spending the weekend with his girlfriend. My dad is a ball of high energy. He's extravagant, loud, and somehow always the center of attention.

He's super happy to see me, and he can't shut up. I can barely talk because he is constantly interrupting me. He's been telling me about how happy he is at his new job. He regrets deeply not having found this job before he made all the mistakes that landed him in prison for three years. But honestly, I think he needed that to be able to feel this gratitude. My dad and I are in a good place now. I accept him for the human that he is and don't try to change him. We have had a couple of deep conversations about our issues that helped rebuild our bond, and while it is not the same as when I was his little girl, I am grateful for the person I grew up to be, and I am grateful for the role he plays in my life.

I was telling my dad how proud I am for all the work he's done and the drastic change that he's made in his life. My dad is the biggest pot-head I know, and he even stopped smoking because his job can do random drug tests. I was proud of him for that, and I was making it known. Then things went south when he felt comfortable enough to share something he really shouldn't have. In Cuban slang, he said, "Baby, I'm gonna be honest with you. I love weed, and that is my favorite thing. I don't care for all these other drugs, but weed stays in the system for three months, while cocaine only stays for a few days."

I was confused but not surprised at all.

"Right now, I'm so happy to be here with you, and I feel comfortable telling you this, but I don't feel comfortable with you watching, so just stay where you are and don't look. I'm gonna go behind you and do a quick line."

We were sitting inside a little beach tent, and he leaned behind me to do his thing. I fawned; I didn't know what to do. My father did it again. I didn't know how to act, so I took a page from my childhood trauma book and acted like everything was fine and just went with it.

My father knows who he is, and he knows he has not been the best father to my sisters because he's never been there for them to the extent that he's been there for me. I know my sisters hold resentment toward me for getting all his attention, but they don't know that I dealt with my own daddy issues that they will never understand. I'm not sure what's better or worse, or if it's even worth comparing. What's important for me to remember is that I can love my father and, at the same time, not take his lifestyle personally.

JULY 17, 2023

J and I hosted an event today, and we had a misunderstanding that turned into a slight conflict. Nothing crazy, just the stress of creating an event and handling all the things. But this is a very new thing to me; I still don't know how to navigate it. J's energy is *so* intense when he's not in his usual loving state. He doesn't do or say anything that would make me feel so small and afraid, but being highly empathetic, I can feel the energy, and it's so intense that I can barely speak my point. I just cry and try to speak up, but I feel like a child.

It had been a long time since I felt this way, and it reminded me a lot of my relationship with my dad. I was so afraid of him erupting and lashing out that I would make myself small. I know that we tend to relive childhood experiences with our partners to bring awareness of unresolved trauma and patterns. It was only a matter of time before I met someone that would bring this out of me, and I'm so happy it's J. I feel comfortable letting him know about this, and he puts in the work to not trigger me. Either way, it still happens, and it's an interesting place to be. Yay to me for breaking family curses and elevating my bloodline by doing the hard work!

Anyway, we had a small conflict that turned out to be funny:

After our argument regarding the event, I grabbed my things to head back home (I had stayed at his apartment the night before). He seemed confused and told me that he thought we were going back to his place together after the event. But I had other plans, and we had not really discussed that part.

On our way to the event, we addressed our previous disagreement. I made sure to tell him where I went wrong and apologize for my part. Then he goes, "Well, I'm just sad because I thought we had plans after the event, and you going home felt like a punishment for the disagreement."

I said, "We had plans? What plans?"

He pressed his lips and tilted his head.

I said again, "What plans? I don't remember any plans."

He hesitated and then said, "I thought we were going to have anal tonight after we were done."

I was genuinely thrown back. Like what?

He said, "You said we can have anal after the event."

And I immediately start cracking up because I realized where he was coming from and where the silly misunderstanding happened.

Since I had been dealing with a dry skin rash near my butthole, we had been abstaining from anal sex for some time, but noticing that the issue had been resolved, I told him that after we were done with the event, we could have anal sex again. What I meant by that was that after finishing up with all the commotion of launching an event, we could start to reintroduce it into our intimacy again. But what he understood was that literally after the event is done, we would be celebrating with anal.

Aw, poor baby was so excited that he really thought this was going to happen like this. I couldn't help but feel so bad and, at the same time, so relieved.

I made it known that what I meant was different from what he understood, and just a moment later, we were cracking jokes about the argument and back to our usual energy like nothing happened. I must admit, it's nice not dragging arguments out for days.

Multiple private experiences with my lover showed me what complete surrender looks and feels like for myself. It's beautiful, truly a work of art that deserves to be witnessed. We challenged ourselves to demonstrate our creation, fully aware that it may be easy to surrender in the privacy of our space, but having an audience poses special obstacles to overcome.

During the surrender workshop tantric massage demonstration, the massage table is right next to the wall mirror; the audience can see both sides of the performance. The VIP area was just about five feet away from us, and behind them were the rest of the guests.

After a brief introduction and a beautiful intention setting speech from Vero, J removed his shirt, and I removed my kimono. I climbed on the table and lie facedown, completely naked. J continued his instructions on the hypnosis process for a few minutes before sliding his eye mask down and diving into our demo.

To be honest, not much consideration about my discomfort went into the creation of this event due to the short notice for planning. I was aware that it was going to be an interesting place to be in, but I trusted the process and my ability to thrive in the unknown. It wasn't easy being in charge of the night and then completely letting go. It wasn't until the moment to surrender came that my mind realized what was really happening

I was in my head for sure. The audience was composed of complete strangers that found the event online or through the other facilitators. There were people here I have met before briefly at the acro park days. Some of them were very close friends, including my dear friend Vero who I love like a mom. I started to wonder how I ended up here, divulging my most private and vulnerable moment for all to witness. I knew I had a little bit of an exhibitionist in me, but this? How much of an attention whore can one be? My mom would die if she knew what I was up to. I mean, more than likely, she does know since I shared details of the event on social media, but she doesn't seem to pay much attention and may have missed it. This might be a difficult conversation with her later. It doesn't matter how much I logically understand that my life is mine and I live it how I wish; intrusive thoughts still find their way in somehow.

The music could be a little louder, in my opinion, and I hoped the videographer was getting the right angles I'd asked for. At least the temperature was right. My feet were a little cold, but I knew once we start, they'd be just right. The oil felt cold when it first glided on my back and slowly melted between my skin and his hands.

Noticing that I am still in my head after a few minutes, I started to build my own energy with my breath. Although I hadn't yet reached that heavy breathing that naturally happens with arousal, I made it happen, knowing that it would send the right signals to my brain. I took deep breaths and sighed out continuously until I found myself in my body again. This was right around when J started to massage my inner thighs and brush against my vulva almost as if by mistake. This continued for a few minutes, and it became more and more obvious that he was intentionally teasing my genitals and building up the orgasmic energy.

A current was weaving down my body from the left side of my neck where J always gets me from. I wanted more of that, but he kept teasing and leaving the area, making me want it even more, so I spread my legs apart just enough to give him more room between my thighs. He used the tops of his knuckles and fingers to brush on my vulva from top to bottom, crossing over my clitoris every time. The pressure was tight and very slippery. I could feel my pussy opening and asking to be penetrated. When the angle was right, I could feel his middle knuckles attempting to go in but stopping right before reaching my G-spot, spreading my natural lubrication.

Right when I thought he was about to make me orgasm, he stopped. I was feeling the urge to press my thighs together against my clit as tight as possible to continue the delicious pressure. He went back to my neck and returned to the yoni massage. He repeated the same teasing steps, and I couldn't tell if he was going for it this time or just building on the explosion.

He was going for it, his right thumb found its way inside me. The second it happened, I started to feel the orgasm build up and erupt. He was pressing against my G-spot on and off while his hand went up and down as if he were shaking water off. My spine curled back, and my ass perked up, giving him easier access to all of me. I moaned and projected my voice across the room. My head was tucked into the headrest, and I couldn't see, but I could feel all eyes on us.

Slowly, the orgasm started to diminish, leaving a residue of the energy still flowing up and down my spine. J continued to massage the energy, and I wondered if the demo was done now that I had fully surrendered. Now that the pressure was off, I wish he would continue.

He started to address the audience and answer some questions. He was still massaging my back, and I can tell he's waiting for me to get up to stop. He approached my right ear to check on me.

"I want more."

"What's that?"

"I want more."

"Oh, she wants more."

He didn't go straight for it; he slowly found his way into my yoni, and with ease, we did it again.

Another beautiful, explosive, and full-body orgasm. This one left my body curling and sliding all over the table.

"Where you going?" he said in a playful tone.

I was laughing. My body was so open and free, all restrictions completely liberated.

He knew that, at this point, he could make me orgasm multiple times. All barriers had been broken, and we felt as comfortable as at home.

So he went for it, even more explosive than the last one, reaching full body waves and shivers.

As the orgasm started to fade, I noticed a very familiar feeling, a strong urge to release emotions. My sobbing turned into crying and then intense bawling. This was way more than I could have planned to surrender. This was deep, and I knew exactly where it was coming from. The pressure of the day, the small argument with J, the expectations and everything I had carried with me that didn't serve me were being transmuted with my tears.

Shame surged from my shadowy depths, transmuting into love. I felt so much love and acceptance. Love for myself, my lover, the audience, the universe.

There is still a mysterious part in all of it that I've never been able to recollect. I know the crying feels amazing, and I know that I'm profoundly healing a part of me that lived something, but I don't know what. It's like I collect bits and pieces of it, but I don't have a full image of what it is that erupts in this way. It's a very familiar place, yet so unknown, and it feels like I'm holding back from remembering while, at the same time, chasing the memory.

I call this an overwhelming feeling of feelings being released with my cries.

〜 ᘒ 〜

I received the videos from the videographer, and I was not too happy with them, but all day I've been smelling the sweet aroma of my juices from this morning's self-pleasure practice while watching the videos. Every whiff is a beautiful reminder of where my writing about the workshop took me. I rewatched the video of our demo and couldn't resist the urge to feel myself.

JULY 29, 2023
GODDESS CIRCLE

I hosted a goddess circle that ended up being a close circle of friends since I had no sign-ups. At first, I was bummed about not having attendees, but I ended up having such a meaningful gathering with close friends and a special guest. Jaqui is someone I met through Instagram, and I've always admired her aesthetics and the way she works with rope. When she asked if she could bring rope to the circle, I immediately said *absolutely*. After connecting for a few minutes and ingesting a small dose of psilocybin mushrooms, we started a sensual bondage scene in which I fully surrendered to her experience.

We were both on the floor. She was sitting behind me with her legs holding my hips, my weight supported on her and my head rested on her left shoulder. I could feel her breathing near my ears and the hair on the back of my neck standing up. She was running the rope through my chest; I was feeling every fiber of the rope slowly but firmly brushing my skin as she built a tight bondage around me. I couldn't move my arms; all I could do was let go of control and let her take charge. She was grabbing me from the rope, and as she leaned back and pulled me into her body, rocking the weight of mine on her pubic bones. She pushed me back up and into other shapes, and as I continued to let go of control, I realized how busy I'd been all day, how even when I was taking a nap, my brain would not stop thinking. This was the first time in the day and perhaps in a long time that I was not doing anything. I started sobbing, feeling supported and guided, then giggling, then crying again.

The scene ended with my head resting on a pillow, my arms tied together, rose petals on my body, and my friends feeding me fruits and caressing me. When the tight ropes came off, a newfound sense of freedom took over my body. I felt like I just came back from another planet and saw this one so differently. I was feeling the effects of the mushrooms, and they felt so much more intense than I anticipated. I only had a tiny dose, but this experience totally magnified the intensity, and my body was feeling light and wavy.

The rest of the night we conversed, we cried, we laughed hysterically. I called J and just said, "Daddy, I'm hungry. I'm so high I can't do anything right now." About thirty minutes later, food arrived for all of us to share, and I got to show off the amazing man I have.

This was the night I learned how much I loved rope, and it wouldn't have been that night if I would have had sign-ups to my circle. Yet another clear reminder that not everything is always going our way, but it often ends up being better than we even imagined.

AUGUST 15, 2023

It's been so hard to sit down and write about the wonderful things that have been happening lately. I can barely take a break from it all. Great things and opportunities are happening all the time, yet I don't have much energy or time to sit down and write eloquently about it, so here is a summary of these last few weeks or so.

• I was part of Turn On Miami on June 3, and that was a blast. I knew from the first time we went that I was going to be a performer there. So I reached out, and they offered me a paid gig for the night. My job was to perform at one point of the night, but I was an entertainer the entire time. I was dancing on the pole and on the floor throughout the night, and the guests would gather around to watch. I was also inviting anyone that was interested in playing with the pole to interact with it in a beautiful and intentional way. I also walked around and tried some of the other sensory stations just for fun.

At the end of the night, I chatted with the organizers, and they expressed their gratitude toward the work that I put in. They were very happy with my performances and the way I was part of the night. They wanted to hire me for future events, and I'm so happy about that because I felt right at home with them. I can see us potentially going into future ventures together, but also without setting too much expectation.

• J and I went to the nude beach. It was my first time, and I guess he thought I would be intimidated or shy. I proved him wrong so quickly because it was so hot and my clothes were bothering me so much that before even finding a place to settle, I took my shorts off like it was nothing, ha-ha-ha. We had been relaxing for less than five minutes before being approached by this couple (we believe there is a chance that they weren't a couple and that they might have just met there or not long before then) trying to socialize. It's very common for swingers to meet people at this section of the nude beach, and this was what they were up to. They were OK, but it still feels a little weird to have total strangers butt naked causally talking to you. We were nice to them, but it also was clear from our energy that we weren't interested.

While in the water, I asked J about his experience as a veteran. He shared intense stories from his time in war and appreciated my willingness to listen, noting that few people can hold space for such memories. I'm fascinated by the resilience it takes to endure such life-altering events and deeply respect that he not only survived but is now thriving.

After hanging out at the beach for a while, we headed back to the car because it was raining. We placed a food delivery order, and while waiting in the car, we had some of the most amazing sex of our relationship.

I don't remember exactly how it started, but I think I was licking and sucking his dick from time to time, and then he would finger me. All just playing around without the intention of having sex, then next thing you know, I climbed on top facing him, and I rode him. The space inside his Tesla was actually very comfortable and convenient. I was so wet; I guess the excitement of the nude beach and being in a public place added to the steam. A car drove by slowly, and we immediately stopped and dropped. It was our food delivery driver looking for us, but we couldn't tell. After he drove away, I sat on J again, this time facing the front of the car, leaning forward with my legs closed together and grabbing the steering wheel for support. I slipped his brick-hard cock inside and swayed my hips back and forth and up and down. Oh my Goddess, it felt so fucking good. My pussy was dripping all over him and squeezing with every entry and exit; feeling his erection so deep inside me in this specific position was to die for. After we finished our quickie, we realized that the delivery guy had been calling and looking for us. He casually went out of the car to get the food, and then we ate while bragging about the amazing sex we just had.

J and I have been making the nude beach a place we visit frequently and have realized that there are some regulars, as some of the faces have become familiar.

• I have been dealing with some health issues lately, the reason why I lack the energy to write how I like it. It's not a major health crisis but rather a few little things here and there that get in the way of me living worry-free. The rash on my butthole I mentioned earlier was one of them, but thankfully, after I took care of it for a few weeks, it went away. It was just a dry and flaky patch but it was itchy sometimes.

• My vaginal pH being off is something very new to me. I had dealt with yeast infections for a long time in the past, and now I recognize the symptoms and know how to address the issue from the root. My yeast infections have reached a point where they don't even finish manifesting fully. The second I would start feeling the symptom, which is mild itching, I would follow my protocol, and it's gone.

However, I'm now dealing with a whole new vaginal condition that I never had before; she smells. It's a very strong smell that is sometimes fishy or rotten. It's so embarrassing, and it really gets to my head. J says he doesn't smell anything, and I believe him because he has a bad nose due to some injuries. But even if sweet J makes me feel good about it, it still bothers me so much, and I'm extra self-conscious about it, especially when I'm working close to my clients or when I'm doing Acro at the park or taking pole classes. I have some days when it's not so bad and I think it's gone, and then it comes back around.

I have done so much research about it, and there is basically no real answer to how to get rid of it. Antibiotics don't work long term. Probiotics aren't proven to really work either, and I already eat a very balanced, healthy diet. It makes me wonder if my body is telling me something about J. We have extremely different diets. I'm mostly plant based and alkaline, and he is a literal carnivore; our pH is probably so different. I hope it's just my body adjusting to a new partner and that eventually it balances out again. The fact that he ejaculates inside me (since he had a vasectomy) probably doesn't help because semen is alkaline and it disrupts the naturally acidic pH of the vagina.

The pH thing is hard to deal with, for sure, but the biggest issue I've been dealing with that started right before my breakup with my ex is a hard lump on my right nipple that sometimes gets so big that it hurts pretty bad. I noticed it gets bigger and harder during the luteal phase of my cycle, which tells me it fluctuates with my hormones.

My gynecologist first recommended a prolactin test to check if for some reason my brain was creating milk, but that came back negative. The next step was an ultrasound and a mammogram. Going into the clinic for the ultrasound was rough. Even though there was a deep, intuitive knowing that I did not have cancer, entering that room was so difficult that I broke down and almost walked away. J came with me and was so supportive and loving; he gave me the strength to go through with it. Though I'll be honest, if I would have gone by myself, I would have been a big girl and handled it like a champ, but since he was there, I gave myself permission to be a big baby about it, and I don't regret it.

After seeing the ultrasound, the doctor told me that the mass was not on the breast tissue, and it was on the skin itself, so a visit to a dermatologist was recommended since it was most likely just a cyst.

I went to the dermatologist, and they were confused by what I was presenting to them. They insisted on a biopsy, and I accepted it, again knowing that I didn't have freaking cancer, but I understood that there was a protocol that needed to be followed. They made an opening and took about three millimeters of skin, and when they took it out, a smelly pus came out, which they drained but not completely. They told me in the case that it was a cyst, I would have to go to a breast surgeon to have it extracted.

The results came back with a staph infection, and they prescribed antibiotics. I immediately said, "*Hell no.* I'm not taking antibiotics. There must be a better way." A round of antibiotics would make all the years healing my gut go to waste.

I tried some other remedies like light therapy, but the nipple kept getting worse. Not knowing what to do, I finally budged and decided to take the antibiotics. I thought maybe this would help with the pH thing and the rash (I still had it at the time); maybe my body needed to take the damn antibiotics and start off fresh again.

I made the conscious decision to go through with the treatment, hoping that it would bring the suffering to an end, but the antibiotics only helped with the infection itself, and the seed of the cyst stayed. At this point, I had already spent so much money and time worrying that a visit to a breast surgeon did not sound appealing.

So I made a visit to the Akashic record masters and asked for a solution. They recommended a treatment to apply every night for a week, which brings me to exactly where I'm at. Last night was the last night, and I have noticed significant decrease in size and hardness, which brings me a lot of hope. It is still not gone, but the improvement is noticeable.

My friend Kelly—who is a rogue MD, only practices holistically, and believes firmly in German New Medicine (a controversial alternative medicine that suggests a connection between emotional trauma and the development of diseases)—told me that this is something likely related to mother conflict, that the issue is already being resolved and all I can do is support my body in the resolution. I was a little skeptical at first, not because it was too out there but because I couldn't think of a mother conflict at the moment. It wasn't until the goddess circle that I realized how deeply connected this really was to the mother wound.

Since my spiritual awakening, my relationship with my mom has not been the same. I'm in constant search for personal growth and healing, but my family is not, which has led to some distance between us. Realizing that they have their lives to live and that all I can really do is accept them as they are has been a big turning point and what I believe to have been a catalyst for the healing of my nipple. I'm still processing all of it, but I'm making progress.

• Note from June 2, 2024, after reading back on old chapters: My nipple is fully healed! I applied castor oil packs every night for a few weeks, and that helped significantly. The tiny lump that was left after that slowly disappeared. This was an interesting process of learning about and trusting my body. It's so easy to feel scared and overwhelmed after visiting conventional doctors and the endless tests they do. But returning to our inner wisdom and allowing our bodies to process disease at their own pace is the ultimate form of freedom and personal reclamation.

SEPTEMBER 20, 2023

In much need for introspection and alone time, I'm taking a break from J. My health, both physical and mental, needed this. I'm not the same as I was a few months back. I don't receive as much joy in the simple things in life. It's hard to feel inspired to dance and flow as usual. I know this is not going to last forever, and I'm perceiving it as a great reset in my life.

Summer was extremely slow for business; it was fun because I had the extra free time to be at the beach and take a little staycation. But part of this break in the relationship is also to focus my energy back into my business. I have big moves to make next year, and I know I haven't been focusing enough energy into Sacred Ink. I'm going through a treatment for my vaginal infections now, and I still have another month to go. My symptoms are now gone, and I can finally relax about the smell, but I must continue the treatment to ensure that my vaginal microbiome is replenished fully; that means no sex without protection. No toys inside my vagina, no fingers, no tongues, nothing inside me without a protective barrier.

This was a difficult conversation with J and one that really annoyed me. He would much rather not have sex at all than use a condom because in his eyes, it is limiting intimacy by having a barrier in between us. What he fails to realize is that at least with a condom, I can still receive pleasure that my vibrator alone cannot provide me.

I know he's just being hardheaded right now and is probably regretting having to wait so long to be inside me again.

Aside from everything, I am unsure whether this comes from my lack of enjoyment in the good things in life, or the natural course that relationships take as time goes by, but things have just not been the same anymore.

I get annoyed easily with him and annoyed at myself because he's such a caring and supportive boyfriend. I get annoyed in the same way kids get annoyed with their parents. I'm such a brat, and he always gives me what I want. Part of me resents him for being so supportive and giving, the masochist in me. Maybe the part of me that needs to feel like I must work to earn things? I don't know, but the point is that I get annoyed when he's constantly asking me if I need help. "Is there anything I can do to get you more clients? How can I help you do this? How can I help you with that?" Ahh, I know I sound like an ungrateful bitch, and maybe I am, but it feels like people pleasing times a hundred, and I really dislike it.

I don't like that he kisses me so much. I like kissing when the moment is right, when I feel it. I love peck kisses on the lips throughout the day, when we say hi, and on other simple occasions when a gentle act of love is desired. But he loves big, tongue-twisting, slobbery French kisses at any point in the day. Now, of course, I like those too, but I don't feel the need to do it randomly. When I'm turned on, yes! We are out dancing and feeling good and the atmosphere is right? Hell yes. We are having a meaningful conversation and it naturally happens? Absolutely. But not while waiting for the elevator, and then inside the elevator, and then outside while the dogs poop, and then while waiting for the elevator again and inside again and outside again. I hate the feeling of saliva surrounding my mouth when I'm not ready for it. In private, I don't mind it, but I hate wiping it off in front of people.

Venting about this dilemma makes me wonder if this is an issue with kissing in general that I never encountered with my ex-partners because they weren't very affectionate and I'm just now learning this about myself, or if this means something else for J and me. I don't recall being so in my head about kisses in the past, but seeing how my body reacts to it brings a lot of discomfort.

Remember how, before meeting J, I had my first impressions and opinions about him? Cocky, into himself, and he talks highly about his work and skills? Yeah, I'm not sure that ever changed. For some time, I saw it as part of this grand man on the pedestal I had him on, but as I started to know the flawed human that he is, I confirmed a realization I had years ago: no one belongs on a pedestal.

J did something that I still haven't fully forgiven him for. Two weeks ago, he created a collaborative post on Instagram with a beautiful caption. I complimented him on the writing and accepted the collaboration for the post to show on my feed as well. A couple of days later, before going to sleep, I see a comment on it. "This writing sounds eerily familiar..."

I went to her profile, and it didn't take me long to find the original writing she created. My gut wrenched. The constipation from two days was suddenly ready to come out lol. I couldn't believe it—the pedestal he was slowly walking down from crumbled in front of my eyes.

I immediately wrote her an apology about the whole situation:

It felt important to reach out regarding the writing on a post I collaborated on. I have not yet talked to J about this, though I see he removed the post. I cannot speak for him, but I personally don't support plagiarism, and I was not involved in the creation of this caption. I just came across your page today when I saw your comment and was shocked to see it. Again, though I was not the creator of this post, it does affect me, and I send my sincere apologies.

To which she responded:
I appreciate that. Yep, I did tell him it's ironic the post was about not taking from a woman and attuning to her, and he literally enacted that very pattern on me by stealing from me.

I respect that he at least owned up to it. But I also expressed to him that's a very dark aspect of the masculine psyche and, in fact, the place where rape comes from: "I see it. I want it. I will take it." And that it's important he does some deep work to address that if he wants to be an authentically safe space holder.

Really concerns me that people who are holding space for the most delicate aspects and often most trauma filled aspects (like tantra) could operate with such low integrity. Very, very concerning!

Wishing you both deep healing and fantastic teachers who can guide your path and hold you to account.

Just because it comes from the same place as rape doesn't mean he would do such thing, and it's very far-fetched. However, I do agree this was a very low-integrity moment for him, and he should know better. If you like what someone wrote so much, you don't just copy and change some things around. You either give credit to the writer or write it in your own words.

My inner judge was tearing him apart, I admit that. But even after internalizing that he is a human and humans make mistakes, I still have a very strong feeling about this.

He removed the post and didn't tell me anything about it. If I would not have seen the comment minutes before he deleted the post, I would have been completely unaware of it. I waited an entire day, and he didn't say a word about it, so I brought it up. I knew it would be an uncomfortable conversation because there was a lot of shame, and I hate putting others in uncomfortable situations, but he did this to himself.

He took credit for something he didn't write, then told me that the current circumstances in our relationship inspired him to write about it. Then he went on and buried evidence when he got caught and pretended that nothing happened. When I confronted him about it, he played it off as, "Yeah, I used some of her words." He admitted that it was wrong, but he still didn't own up to how big of a fuck-up this was.

In my eyes, this is what I saw: He read a nice caption about something he could relate to because of our current situation, and he took it, edited some things, and added some of his words. Maybe he wanted to impress me? Regardless, it's plagiarism. Deleting the post and not mentioning anything about it was the worst part.

Has he fabricated a false image of himself? What else has he hidden from me? I don't know what's real and what's manufactured anymore, and it's got me in a state of alert that I can't get past.

This may not be a big enough reason for a breakup, but it made me realize that, at the moment, I just do not have the capacity to deal with these relationship predicaments. I couldn't sleep for two days after this issue, just going over this scenario in my head, and that got in the way of my healing and well-being. Time spent worrying about drama is time and energy not invested in my growth, my career, and my health, all things that I value more than a relationship at this time in my life.

It is my hope that after this break, I have gathered enough energy to work on our relationship. These are built and not found; it's all about the effort on both ends. I know J is an amazing person with flaws like everyone else. He treats me like a queen, he fucks me like a king, and as long as the communication is there, he is willing to listen and grow from his mistakes. That alone is something hard to find, and it would be a shame to let him go at a time in my life when a lot of things don't feel right. What feels right now is distance from him to reassess my values, boundaries, and desires.

SEPTEMBER 30, 2023

It was a full moon last night, and I went to the drum circle on the beach with my friend/roommate Lili. It's a clandestine gathering that happens every full moon where people bring their fire dancing props, drums, and other fun stuff. It was packed with people dancing around the drums and fire.

Lili and I stayed a bit away from the crowd and took a dip in the ocean. While floating in the water, we shared our personal goals. I told her about my dream of creating a conscious strip club—a space for all kinds of erotic performers to express their art. Unlike conventional strip clubs, this would be a space where performers are paid for their art instead of paying to work.

To make it happen, it would need to be super exclusive, with every guest carefully vetted to ensure there are no predators or disrespectful people. It would also be alcohol-free, offering high-frequency plant medicines and adaptogenic elixirs instead. I just can't stand drunk people—they make me feel uneasy and guarded. The whole point is for performers to feel safe, free from worry, so they can dance from their souls. I imagine this space fostering deeper interactions between performers and guests, moving away from the purely transactional vibe of traditional strip clubs.

After sharing our dreams under the moon, we joined the crowd to dance for a while. Eventually, the cops showed up and dispersed everyone, as they usually do. But when that happens, people just move a few blocks down the beach to another spot and keep the party going until they're kicked out again, over and over. We didn't follow the drums. Instead, we went home.

OCTOBER 20, 2023

Without planning it, I realize it has been exactly a month since I wrote in this journal. It has been an interesting month, to say the least. Where I stand today, I feel much better than I did last time. My body is healing, and the treatment for my bacterial vaginosis is working. I only have one more week before I stop worrying about what I put inside of me. I must admit, my sex drive has been at an all-time low these last couple of months. I did try self-pleasuring every now and then, but it was so hard to get out of my head. It's tough to go through this for me; the thought of my goals and aspirations alone used to be enough to send me off to orgasm land, and now it feels like I must run a marathon to even get me aroused.

So I started very slow. Leaving the big *O* out of the equation and simply doing things that feel good was the first step. Slowly caressing the skin on my face, my feet, my thighs, and simply feeling the gentle flow of energy left behind after each stroke. I did this until I was tired and then went to sleep. One night, I started my gentle, loving practice, and I found a spot that was extra sensitive right where my belly meets my right hip bone. I focused on this area until I felt the orgasmic energy building, I released beautiful tears of joy and love for my body. Going through this rebirth, I felt myself disconnecting from my body. I felt numb, and this was the moment of union between me and my body that I deeply needed.

～ ⌒ ～

I went to a cosmetic tattoo competition, and it was everything I needed it to be. I had no pressure whatsoever, I knew where I stood among all the other competitors, I had minimal experience in the category I signed up for, and I didn't practice at all. It was not my intention, I had the time to do so, but I didn't have the energy; I wondered why I even registered in the first place. But with the pressure off, I allowed myself to have fun and do my best. I loved how my eyeliner tattoo came out, but I didn't deserve to win. Real winners take the game seriously, and I didn't. But I learned a lot about myself. I learned that sometimes I would rather not go for it for real because of the fear of losing, so instead I play it cool and relaxed. But now that the lesson is learned, nothing is stopping me from doing it right when I'm ready and in a better place mentally.

During the weekend of the competition, I stayed at J's apartment since he's only a few minutes from the venue. It had been at least two weeks since I last saw him and asked for the break. We had spoken a couple times on the phone, but the conversations were very minimal and to the point. I knew that he had quit vaping and drinking energy drinks multiple times a day; he also started working out daily and even posted a video of his workout on Instagram. This distance had some funny moments: when he posted the video working out, the caption read, "Neglected things longer than planned, manifesting mode activated: get ready for J 2.0."

I couldn't help but feel so witty about it. In other words, the caption said: "Look at me!"

It was a playful moment, and I appreciated it. I enjoyed watching him from a distance.

Meeting him the day I arrived to his apartment for the competition weekend was a moment I anticipated. After all, I did find myself missing him. I pulled up to the side door of the building, and he was there, waiting to help me with my things. He was wearing gray sweatpants I had never seen him wear before. Was he aware of the effect gray sweatpants have on girls?

He opened my door as he usually does, and I got out of my car, all giggly and nervous/excited. We kissed passionately, and as we did, I noticed the energy currents down my spine and limbs. There it was, the kiss I wanted and needed, the kiss that showed me our story was still alive and worth working on.

We rushed to get to the venue before registrations ended; he saved my ass by printing some paperwork that I had completely forgotten, reminding me of the way that he is with me, so caring and supportive. Long story short, we headed back to his place and with no rush to get anything done. This was when things got a little intense.

We started kissing, which turned into an intense make-out session, the classic, hot scene in the movie where he was pushing me against the wall with my arms together over my head. He was kissing my neck and undressing me; my head was spinning. I knew I couldn't have sex without a protective barrier, but I also knew I was too weak right then to do what was right. I couldn't stop him; it felt too good. He threw me on the bed and ate me out. My mind was conflicted. I was loving the sensations on my body, but I couldn't let go of the worry, and it was keeping me from enjoying it to the fullest capacity, but I still didn't stop him. Even with all the worries in my mind, he still managed to make me orgasm using his hands. I love how he can do that to me; his hands are a gift from God to serve the Goddess. With his finger still inside me, he replaced it smoothly with his cock. I knew I had to stop him, but it just felt too good. The kinky side of me that thrived in the taboo had taken over; she was in charge of this encounter. I'd deal with the shame later, I was in too deep, and so was he.

Compared to our usual erotic encounters, this was a relatively short one. I guess he missed me. But I was perfectly happy with it. My vagina had been dealing with a lot, and I had already done too much this day. It was a short but very sweet romp.

The following day J and I tried sex with a condom, and I'm happily surprised that it didn't really feel that much different from bare skin. But it did come off a couple of times, so that made me a little paranoid and stuck in my head, which was not fun.

The day of the competition, we started a sexual experience with the condom, our usual intercourse involving anal play. Frustrated with the condom coming off, we decided to toss it and focus on my butt alone, play with a finger, then butt plugs, and then, well, you know...

I guess I had been receiving so much stimulation that by the time he started going inside my butt, I was fully open and receiving. He went in so slowly and carefully, and I just didn't feel an ounce of discomfort; everything was absolute pleasure. Our eyes were locked into each other's, and without words being exchanged, he knew exactly what I was thinking. I was shocked that this part felt *so* good. I mean, I love anal sex, but the first part can be a little daunting sometimes, yet this was nothing but absolute pleasurable sensations. We continued to have mind-blowing anal sex that reminded me how capable I was of feeling intensely.

The rest of the weekend was super busy, running around with the competition, then a photo shoot the next day at the beach, then the gala awards ceremony. It was genuinely a very hectic weekend. J and I did find time to talk about why I needed the break and the issues that took place for me to seek distance from him. We listened to each other and came clean about our errors and mistakes. He understood why I needed the space and agreed to give me more of it.

I wasn't completely satisfied with the weekend, to be honest. It felt a little draining, especially not being able to fully enjoy myself when it came to sex. But that's OK. Pleasure will be there for me when I'm ready.

NOVEMBER 6, 2023

At times, I have so much to write about that I get overwhelmed and don't know where to start, and other times I wonder why I even write in the first place. My brain is a tropical storm. There is so much going on in there, so many ideas and desires. I often shut down before I even try, and when I do try, it's so hard to finish it.

It's such a challenge to simultaneously find time and inspiration to sit down and pour my thoughts out. It was so easy when I first met J and had all those hot stories to tell, but that wasn't going to last forever. I knew at some point it would stop being so exciting and new. I really don't like having that limiting belief, but who am I lying to? It's the story of my life with everything new. I obsess over it until I'm done with it. If I like it, I can eat the same food for days on end, but a point will come where the thought of it alone will make me gag.

The exciting stories of J and me would have lasted a lot longer if we didn't have to deal with the consequences of a disrupted pH balance in my vagina. It really took a toll on our relationship not being able to have sex, but I learned so much in the journey.

Within just a few weeks of meeting him, I was certain this was the man I wanted as a life partner. He showed me the characteristics of the perfect husband: supportive, caring, open, and understanding, amazing father to his kid, best sex ever, and so much more. Even though I wasn't ready to jump into a relationship so soon after my breakup, I *had* to lock this man down. I looked past the fifteen-year age gap and extreme differences in dietary and lifestyle choices. The reality is that he fucked me good and spoiled me so well that I was intoxicated with the new relationship energy. It's a known fact that NRE is a drug, and no life-changing decisions should be made under the effects of drugs. It's when the drug wears off and we can see clearly that we truly understand what we're getting into.

Here is exactly what happened and what I learned:

When J and I took a break on our relationship, my goal was to finish my bacterial vaginosis treatment before reuniting, but having my cosmetic tattooing competition in South Beach and staying there for the weekend interfered with my plans. We talked about our problems and decided to continue our relationship without the sexual part that we had to avoid for me to get better.

We tried having sex with a condom since that was OK according to the prescription, but I was still in my head the entire time. What if it came off? What about sweat dripping and going inside of me? All these scenarios of what could go wrong and mess up the treatment would invade my mind and not let me be in the moment. Performative sex is not something I was interested in doing. Sex with J is never performative; if it hurts, I say it, and we fix it. So if I started feeling irritation due to the medication, I immediately would ask to stop.

Performative sex is something society has normalized and I practiced for a big part of my erotic life. It's counterintuitive and is based on the premise that there is a flow that needs to be followed for sex to be successful. It usually goes something like this: he eats her out for a little bit, and then she blows him, and then he fucks her in a position that she doesn't really feel pleasure in but she wants to impress him, so she takes it, and then they change to a different position, and so on. We often do this because that is what we see in porn, and there is no such thing as sex education in which we can learn how to do it right. Well, we are starting to see those kinds of workshops come up more and more, but they're still very difficult to find for the average folk.

We practiced other forms of intimacy while we waited for the treatment to be over. We made love energetically, we had anal sex, oral sex, we cuddled...but it wasn't enough to satisfy J's sexual needs. He was a fiend for something I just wasn't able to give him, not physically, not mentally, and not emotionally. I was unavailable from every angle, and his needs weren't being met.

I feel like this provoked some trust issues in him. There was a seed of doubt that I wasn't experiencing this issue, or that I was seeing other people. A few times, he made subtle comments about it, and a couple of other times, they weren't so subtle.

In the middle of a phone argument about something I don't even remember now, he straight up asked me if there was another man. I was in shock and responded with, "You know what, J? I wish I had the sex drive and mental capacity to be fucking some other guy right now, but no, I'm not. I'm genuinely not in a place where sex is even a desire."

If there is something I'm sure about myself and how I show up in relationships, it is that I can be avoidant, which will usually lead to finding a partner who is anxiously attached. What this means is that when faced with conflict, I need time alone to regulate my nervous system; otherwise, I start looking for reasons to use it as an escape. All while the anxious person is freaking out and reaching out to talk. This dynamic is very difficult to deal with because my need to be alone triggers my partner, and his neediness triggers me. Being aware of these avoidant tendencies, I find ways to work around the conflict. I've learned and utilized multiple tools to properly communicate my needs and reach a resolution, but if the tools don't work out, I hit a point of no return at which I completely disassociate and freeze.

That's exactly what happened with J during the last argument we had.

Last Sunday, we went to a festival and spent all afternoon and evening at a beautiful location with my friends. He didn't want to come to the festival, but I told him I wanted to eat mushrooms and that it would be so nice to have him there as a protective figure for me and my friends to be able to let go deeply. So he ended up making arrangements to be there with me. I knew of the possibilities of this backfiring and ended up insisting that I didn't want to force him to be there and that I would not mind at all going without him. But I also knew what I was doing when I told him this; I wanted him to come, and I was very seductive and manipulative.

I had an amazing time with him and my friends; I loved having him around because I felt so safe. I went skinny-dipping in the lagoon, I danced almost naked to the live music, and I just felt free and loved. I made sure to give him lots and lots of affection to repay him for the wonderful work of keeping us safe. We danced, we kissed. Everyone there knew without a doubt I was with him.

Toward the end of the night, we were waiting for the last party to start. I expressed to him how grateful I was to have him there and I asked if there was anything I could do for him. He answered by pointing at his penis with his eyes. Without thinking about it, I grabbed and squeezed it over his pants for a minute, and then stopped when my friend returned from the restrooms.

Soon afterward, they finally let us into what they called "the hangar." It looked like a mobile warehouse of sorts. There were some art installations, cool lighting effects, a silk hammock station, a lot of mattresses on the floor nicely decorated, and a portable pole, which was the main reason I wanted to be there. I was feeling some kind of weird vibes about what the theme of the party was going to be, but since he was there, I knew I was safe. I was massaging his back a little bit and asked if I could walk on it, to which he agreed. Shortly after trying, I stepped wrong, and I hurt him badly on his lower back. I could tell he was in pain, so I started massaging the area for a few minutes. While doing so, I was watching what someone was doing inside the silk hammock; it looked so fun, and I was waiting for my chance to do the same. When I noticed the hammock was free, I ran to it and started playing.

It wasn't until later in the night when we were walking back to the lagoon to find my sandals that I realized I totally abandoned him. I didn't mean to; I was just unaware of how long I needed to massage him for to feel better. I was selfish, but I could tell he was still in pain and not happy at all. I apologized a hundred times, but I knew my apologies were not enough to correct what I did. I hurt him, and then I abandoned him. I felt horrible.

Aside from apologizing, I was also telling him how sad I felt about the fact that I couldn't just grab him and sneak around with him and have sex in a bush or isolated area; this would have been the perfect time and place. The night before, he had stayed at my place, and I had such a hard time sleeping because I was horny and all I wanted was to rub up against him. We did enjoy amazing anal sex in the morning, so that helped relieve some of the heat. But since intercourse involving my pussy was not an option due to the discomfort, I didn't entertain any other options. Regardless, I was very sad that this was the reality, and I wanted him to know.

After a very awkward drive back home, we finally arrived at my place close to 4:00 a.m. I made him some tea and took a quick shower so he could go after me. I was exhausted, but I wanted to make it up to him for abandoning him earlier, so when he lay down, I followed his directions and gave him a back massage. I laid my body against his and caressed his scalp, whispering loving words to his ears until he drifted into deep sleep.

I didn't really sleep that night. I've noticed that I can't sleep when I eat magic mushrooms because my mind is in its own little world. On top of that, I had just experienced a day filled with interactions and stimulation, so my brain was still computing.

Immediately upon waking the next morning, he brought up a conflict. I was still half asleep, so I don't even remember how it started, but it turned out he wasn't just sad about me abandoning him after hurting him; he was disappointed about not getting enough attention. This took me by surprise because I knew that all afternoon and evening, I was all over him. I praised him all the time, I hugged him and grabbed him every second he was next to me, I went above and beyond to make sure he was taken care of and showered with affection. But apparently the one thing he really needed was sexual affection. It turns out even though we couldn't have sex, he would have liked it if maybe I gave him a blow job or at least squeezed his dick for a longer time when he asked me to. It really hurt him that I asked him if there was anything I could do for him, and when he told me what he would like, I didn't honor it for long enough.

Here is something about J. He loves blow jobs, but they're not enough to make him come. This is something I do for both our enjoyment and with no goal. The only problem is that I can tell when he wants more than my hands and mouth, and it's a big trigger for me not being able to give more. That was the reason even that was not an option.

We kept going back and forth about our disagreement. I asked if there was anything I could do to fix what happened, but he continued to spiral. I really tried, but I was so tired and drained that I couldn't keep up with it, so I shut down. He went to shower, and when he came back, I thought it was a brilliant idea to be vulnerable and share a story with him:

"The last time a boyfriend did something for me when he didn't really want to, I had sex with him that night, and it was 100 percent performative sex." He didn't take that well *at all*, and he interrupted my story. Then I elaborated.

"I was tired, and the only reason why I did it was because I felt like I had to repay him for what he did. I didn't desire him at the moment; I basically just lay there and let him fuck me as a form of payment. That is not something I'm interested in doing anymore, and you probably wouldn't want me to pretend to have sex just because I owe you."

This backfired big time on me because now he was outraged, and he didn't understand why I even said this to him.

"What makes you think I want to hear that? Who's a better boyfriend, him or me? It sounds like this dude who was nowhere near as good to you got some pussy, and I didn't."

I could tell at this point he was just seeing red, and no matter how hard I tried, he just wouldn't get it. In my eyes I saw a child throwing a tantrum. So I did what I do best, my preferred trauma response that kept me safe when my parents argued as a child: disassociate and go numb. My body was in the room, but I was not there. I left, and there was nothing he could do or say to bring me back. I might have been numbing, but deep inside, I was bracing myself because I knew it was going to hit all at once.

On his way out, he continued to yell out, and the last thing he said before slamming the door was, "Not a great idea to tell your boyfriend about all the sex you had with your ex."

After ignoring his calls and texts, I finally responded to let him know that I needed space and we would talk another day. Vero helped me navigate this conflict, and I found the space in my heart to set up a video chat date with J the following day to go over it again from a calmer place. But that didn't work very well. We both were still very hostile, and what he needed from me to move on was an apology that I couldn't give. I can't apologize for not giving sexual affection when my body is unable to; that is a hard boundary. Plus, I was still hurt about the way he reacted to the story I told him. I understand that it may have been the worst time and place for it, but I thought after calming down, he would get the point of me sharing.

About a week with minimal communication went by. We weren't upset, but we weren't OK. I needed space, and he did his best to provide. This conflict helped me confirm what I already knew in my heart:

When I broke up with my ex, my plan was to stay single and focus on myself again. J came in, rocked my world, and I immediately jumped into another relationship full throttle. I love J; I really do. I would hate for this to come to a hard end, but I just can't deal with the ups and downs of a relationship right now. I'm here for the good, but I have no capacity for the work that healthy romantic partnerships require. For the first time in my life, my career is a priority, and I'm willing to push all distractions to the side to focus on my big dreams. I can't focus on my dreams when I'm losing sleep over arguments.

J set the bar really fucking high; he showed me what men are capable of when they really want something. No motherfucker is going to get by with some bare minimum effort after this king came and showed me what I'm worth. It's going to be an interesting journey to find a quality man like him, but it's not going to be impossible.

From where I stand, a perfect resolution would be to continue seeing each other casually and enjoy the powerful intimacy that we are capable of cocreating. And I would love to continue working together on our tantra experiences and workshops. Who even knows? Maybe after some time taking it slow, it will end up working after all.

NOVEMBER 13, 2023
MORNING

After careful consideration, I talked to J. I shared my need for space and time alone. I told him I love our intimacy, and I don't want to stop sharing those moments together, that I want to focus on my career and that I don't want the typical boyfriend/girlfriend relationship. He took it so well, exactly how I expected him to.

His birthday is in a few days, and I promised him I would make him a nice dessert to celebrate. I'm making a new special dessert tailored to the things he likes. It's going to be a banana bread tiramisu. Sounds weird, but trust me, it's going to be exquisite. Aside from dessert, I want us to have an erotic experience like we used to share. I'll wear the outfit I bought at the porn convention that he gave me some money for. That was back in August, and I'm just now bringing it out to play, but it's OK. I believe in divine timing, and good things are worth waiting for.

I am a little concerned that a couple nights ago I masturbated and I may have pressed against my clit with the vibrator too hard, and now I have a tiny bump that bothers me a little. I've been avoiding touching it, and I'm applying ointment. I think there is enough time before Saturday for it to heal. I'm really anticipating this encounter. But I'd be lying if I said there's not a little bit of fear in me. What if *everything* is gone? What if everything we have gone through has killed the spark of our sexual chemistry? I don't want to be in my head again.

Last weekend, I was one of the speakers at my friend Kelly's first in-person event/retreat. Kelly is a *New York Times* best-selling author and rogue MD who has dedicated her life's work to help women get off psychiatric drugs. Her excellent work against Big Pharma has made her a member of the US government's disinformation dozen list, and she proudly speaks up for what she believes in.

This was a three-day immersion where over seventy women from all over the United States and even other continents flew in to be a part of. It was intense and beautiful to see the power we all brought in, the attendees, the speakers, the volunteers, and organizers—we all made magic.

Kelly took over the shadow work aspect of healing. Someone else took over family constellations, multiple-embodiment demonstrations like dancing, singing, acting, and so much more. The most impactful experience of the retreat for me the was the demonstration of Kimi.

Kimi has been a dominatrix for over twenty years, and you can see in the way she shows up that she is the embodiments of the bad bitch herself. The moment she took the stage, her presence was omnipresent. She did not stutter once; she was confident and elegant. Watching her move around the room with such grace had me almost drooling in admiration. Tears would come down my cheeks with the stories she told. The final portion of her speech was a demonstration in which she showed exactly how to ask for consent, how to establish clear boundaries and learn the pain tolerance of the submissive or receiver. This demonstration was different from what I imagined. When I think of a dominatrix, I think of a strong woman belittling their sub, but this was far from that. She works with praise instead of punishment.

Kelly was the muse for her jaw-dropping demonstration. She got spanked *because* she was a good girl and she deserved a good spanking; it was a reward. And when it *was* a punishment, it was for all those times she didn't believe in herself. They had not just me but all of us in tears. This is why Kimi calls herself a motivational spanker.

The curiosity I've had for this kind of work has been confirmed to be a new passion. I see how deeply healing this career path can be for me and for my clients. I *want* this; I want to learn all there is to learn about this practice.

I was the last speaker to go on stage right after Kimi. After beating myself up all weekend for not having anything planned, I finally put something together the night before. I created the playlist and picked my outfit. I decided if the entire weekend was about audacious embodiments, I must be audacious enough to get myself on stage wearing lingerie and stripper heels, so I did exactly that. I did, however, wear a loose dress over my outfit for the first few minutes of my speech.

I wanted to create a safe space, and the best way for me to do that is always by sharing a personal story. I talked about the shame that comes with dressing provocatively and posting pole-dancing videos with minimal clothing on social media and how it limited me for many years, making me wear basic clothing and play small because I was just not "that girl"—until I realized that dressing provocatively and being an unapologetically embodied sexy and beautiful woman doesn't take away my intelligence, my empathy, and talents. From there, I guided them through a sensual, hip-opening dance-movement class that made everyone there at least a little uncomfortable. I grinded on the floor and watched as they all followed my instructions. I completely let loose and showed them what it's like to love, praise, touch, and move my body like the fucking Goddess of seduction herself.

I'm still feeling the effects of this powerful weekend. For the last six months, I've been in and out of low-grade depressive episodes, but it's been a few weeks consecutively that I've been feeling a lot more energy in my body, and I feel like I'm finally out of this funk for real. This retreat has been a portal for me, the portal to the new me emerging from the shadows I've been in. I'm so excited about life.

The entire time I was down, I knew that at some point it would be over, and when it was, I would be going after life with even more passion and desire than I did before. Nothing lasts forever, and these down times are sometimes necessary to propel us forward feeling more aligned to take over our missions. I trust the process and take my time because what's on the other side is a whole new world I'm being prepared for.

NOVEMBER 13, 2023
EVENING

I was watching *Suits*, and our song came on, "Love and Hate," by Michael Kiwanuka. I normally skip it when it plays on my Spotify, but hearing it come up in the show brought up so many memories of J and I and the grief for the kind of relationship we were on the way to creating. My favorite memory is me lying down on the floor by his feet with my mouth wide open, him sitting on the couch leaning over me with his fingers dancing with my tongue to the rhythm of the song. That was the same night I cried in his arms and peed all over him. Every time I listened and danced to this song, I thought of him. He said it was his favorite song, and it quickly became mine, at least for a while.

It's an interesting place to be, feeling like I'm losing him when I'm the one that is putting the space between us. One day I'm crying for not having him, and the next I'm upset for having him and not be able to handle it. I guess it's true what they say about women not knowing what they want. But what else can I do? Fighting to push the relationship forward wasn't feeling right, and ending it completely feels even worse. J may have a thousand and one flaws, but he's a king in my eyes, and I really wish I could make it work, but not right now.

NOVEMBER 20, 2023

I arrived home from the beach last night so exhausted. My eyes barely stayed open during the drive. It was an adventurous weekend; it was amazing.

I finished making J's birthday dessert Friday night, so when I finished with work on Saturday, all I had to do was pack up and be on my way. I wore a cute outfit: a black miniskirt, black high-heeled boots, and a long-sleeve, see-through deep-blue top with my hair loose. All week, I anticipated this drive. Upon arrival, he was by the door of the building ready to help me carry my bags, grab the dogs, and move my car to a parking spot.

I waited for him on his balcony, watching a breathtaking sunset and unwinding from the long drive. I heard his footsteps approaching— well, I heard mostly Bella's cute little nails clacking with every step. I got to finally take a good look at him. He was wearing a classic unbuttoned beach shirt, revealing his defined chest; his chest hair was longer now, which I love (he shaved it off during our short separation, and I expressed how much I love his chest and belly hairs). He was wearing black jeans and Converse shoes.

I just wanted to hug him and feel his presence all over me. I missed him so much and so good. We sat down in his balcony, briefly checking in with how life and business had been and celebrating each other's wins. About thirty to forty minutes later, I could tell he was ready to start the experience I prepared for him. All he knew was that I made him dessert and, for sure, he was getting laid, so it was my time to unleash my inner seductress and show him what he was getting into.

He started by lighting the candles, playing music, and setting up the space while I changed in his room. This was the start of my turn-on. Undressing in front of the large mirror to the beat of the music, sensually removing every piece of clothing and feeling the fresh air caress my naked skin, I took my time dressing my body with the jewelry lingerie that I bought with money he gave me. A thong made of jewels and golden chains, and a matching V-shaped necklace that draped down my collarbone, chest, and in between my petite breasts. I was a representation of the Goddess in flesh and bones. Even I couldn't resist. I touched myself and even reached for the vibrator he kept for me in the drawers, teasing my vulva until reaching the edge of orgasm, and then I stopped. My personal erotic ceremony was finished, and I was ready to come out.

He was sitting on the couch facing the TV, I approached behind him and placed a mask over his eyes. I slid my hands down his neck, chest, and stomach, feeling the warmth of his skin against my forearms. I leaned my neck against his, then I kissed, nibbled, licked. I loved how sensitive his ears were when I hovered my open mouth over them, simply letting him hear the sounds I made when I twirled my tongue, breathing and moaning, teasing him and then finally licking and kissing his ears, his neck, his jawline, all while my long fingernails massaged his scalp and my other hand honored his chest and abdomen muscles.

I walked around the couch and straddled him. With the eye mask still on, I nibbled his lower lip while unbuttoning his jeans. I squeezed his dick over his pants but just a tease; my attention wasn't going there yet. I lifted the blindfold so he could finally look at the masterpiece in front of him. He couldn't see past my face right in front of him, his hands on my hips feeling the texture of my outfit. I rose and took a step back, giving him a show of my glistening body.

As I'm writing, I can feel my juices dripping on the chair, just remembering the anticipation we were both feeling in that moment. His face said it all; he wanted to ravish me. I moved my bottom piece slightly to the side and let him peek at my pussy, already so engorged. He bit his lip and reached over with his hand, but I stopped him—not yet. I knew he wanted to eat it, but the longer we played this game, the more I would want him.

Sitting on his lap again, I leaned over to the side, with my ass perked up in front of his chest. Now it was his turn to touch, squeeze, smell, and indulge his senses, focusing on my body. His touch felt warm and inviting. I couldn't help but sway my hips in ways that left my pussy right in front of his face. I could feel his breath on my skin and knew the moment his tongue reached out to lick me. Oh my Goddess, I really don't mind having pubic hair, but there is something about being completely hairless that intensifies sensations. I was throbbing and swaying my hips up and down to the rhythm of my own pleasure.

I knew he loved devouring me, but I stopped him to bring the focus back to him. On my knees in front of him while he still reclined on the couch, I removed his pants and appreciated his solid erection. I wrapped it inside my hands, one stacked on top of the other, feeling his girth, beathing in his scent, and licking the head. I pushed it down toward my face and slowly fit it inside my mouth, twirling my tongue around it while squeezing the base of the penis and testicles. I love how it felt against the back of my mouth. Right behind my top right molar, there was soft tissue that I pressed with the tip. I was scared that I was hurting him with my teeth, but he told me to keep going; it felt amazing for both of us. I kept going deep, breathing deeply when I could and holding my breath when he was in my throat, tears rolling down my cheeks.

I had enough. I reached down to feel my vulva, and she was so wet and slippery. I used the juice to rub on my clitoris and inner and outer labia; in between the folds was especially sensitive. I got back on his lap and took control of the penetration, first rubbing his hard erection on me and enjoying how nicely it glided against my skin, then bringing the head down to the opening and very slow and gently letting my weight down on him.

Our eyes locked onto each other, savoring each millimeter on its way in. I squeezed and relaxed my pelvic floor muscles with every stroke I let in until I was finally rested on his lap and his penis was fully inside of me. He felt big inside me. It took a minute to feel safe to fully rock my body. I grinded on him gently, my eyes still locked onto his, slowly picking up depth and speed in my movements. It didn't take long to feel the energy burst. My entire body was feeling so much energy running through. I couldn't tell where it was coming from, but it felt intense. I went faster and harder and deeper, and, oh my Goddess, this felt amazing. I loved this man so much, and I missed him so much. I wanted him so bad; I just wanted to merge into his body. I stopped riding him and lay on my side to feel the sensations emerging from deep inside me rippling down my limbs and my back.

From there, it was a blur. I don't remember how we got back into it after the break. I know we tried to continue with intercourse, but I started feeling a sharp and unpleasant sensation at the opening on my vagina that wouldn't allow me to enjoy his entire penis inside me. It was probably a minor cut, but I did find a way to ride just the tip that felt amazing. I can't explain how exactly I did it, but I loved it. We did that until I started to feel the sharp pain again and started getting in my head. So I offered some more oral sex, and as per his request, we did this right in front of the big mirror next to the TV.

He was sitting on the couch, and I was bent over so when I was deep-throating his cock, he could look at my legs spread open from behind. He soon had enough of looking at my ass and asked me to get on the couch and let him eat it. I never turn down a good ass eating, so I did as I was instructed and let him go to town. He grabbed some lube and started stroking his penis as he ate me out from behind. We both loved it, but he was having the time of his life. He was growling and moaning until he suddenly stopped. I knew he was about to come. He got up and released on my mouth and then crashed completely on the couch with his body convulsing in orgasmic bliss.

We praised each other for how amazing we did, sharing our favorite moments, positions, and sensations. We did that for a few minutes, and then I went to prepare the next part of the sensory experience, which was erotic eating of the dessert I made him with so much love. He told me some of his favorite desserts were banana cream pie and the cream from tiramisu but not tiramisu itself because of the coffee flavor. I made my own version of a tiramisu with the things he likes. I made a banana bread to replace the lady fingers and used Bailey's liquor mixed in with Nutella to replace the coffee liquor and espresso, and I kept the classic mascarpone cream with slices of banana in between layers. After blowing the candle, he took on the challenge of figuring out what he was eating. He knew of the Irish cream and he could kind of taste the banana, but I still had to share the secret ingredient and all the work I went through to make it without my electric mixer.

We slowly filled up each other's mouths, feeling the contrast in texture of the crunchy walnuts inside the spongy and succulent banana bread, the velvety texture of the cream and sweetness of the banana slices. Each spoonful was a moment of silence, and our palates the joyful receivers of this luscious delight. Not to toot my own horn, but that was probably the best dessert I ever made, and for it to be my first time baking in a while, I was really impressed to see that my culinary skills were still top notch.

After indulging in dessert, we went out for a stroll with the dogs and then to eat at our favorite Italian restaurant, which he'd introduced me to. We had a delicious meal while dreaming out loud about the amazing erotic experience we just had. We went back to his apartment so exhausted that I ended up falling asleep on his chest.

NOVEMBER 21, 2023
THE NEXT MORNING

Waking up next to J is always fun, especially when I'm connected back into my body. It was not my intention to make him horny or start anything; I just love playing with his penis. I love when it's fully soft, semi-hard, or super hard; I just love having it in my hand. He always says that he knows what I would be doing all day if I ever wake up in a male body, and he's right. I would be grabbing it all day! It's my little stress toy.

But, of course, it didn't matter that my intentions were not to start anything because the result was always the same. I woke up the beast, and I must deal with the consequences of my actions. Luckily it didn't take much for my curious play to turn into adult play. The morning haze made it hard to remember how exactly it started, but next thing I knew, I was having sex with him. I just know it felt amazing. The poor neighbor had to deal with our noise, but I didn't care. I love when we can be rough, and I genuinely wonder how I can still walk after how hard I asked for it to be.

I could tell he was reaching a point of no return, and normally I would intensify my movements to send him over the edge, but I was enjoying it so much that I demanded for him to keep going. Like the warrior soldier that he is, he put his orgasm to the side and changed positions. I love when I'm bent over on the edge of the bed with my bent knees with him standing behind me, grabbing my wrists and using them to pull me into his hips as he thrusts, making the impact even harder and deeper. I couldn't tell when the orgasm started and finished; the entire time, I was feeling it flow throughout my body and ripple with each thrust.

But here's when the sexy-time story turns a little not so sexy.

We took a short break, and while he was in the bathroom cleaning up, I grabbed the butt plugs and placed them under the blankets, then pulled them out when we got back to playtime. His face when I passed them to him was priceless. Anal play is his favorite due to the dominance factor. For me, it's a love-hate relationship. It requires a lot of preparation for the experience to go smoothly, but when done right, it's genuinely such a pleasurable game.

We went from the small plug to the medium one, and from that to his penis. We went slow and controlled, but I kept experiencing some discomfort until it was completely inside me and hitting the right spots; that's when it's all pleasure. Usually when I reach this point, everything feels amazing, but this time, I kept experiencing an equal amount of pleasure and pain. It's so interesting; it's a pain that I don't necessarily want to stop, but I do at the same time. It's like when you have really been wanting to take a massive shit, and you finally can let five days of constipation explode out of you. It's an intense feeling that may not feel so pleasant, but it is at the same time.

Now I'll share something super vulnerable because that's what this writing is all about.

I could smell something not so pleasant, and it was clear that I was not squeaky clean in there. I also started to feel the sensation of pooping intensify a bit. When we stopped, we were both dirty, and we just wanted to go clean up. I got up from the bed and walked toward the bathroom, where he was cleaning himself up and preparing the shower for me. I was walking like I'd just gotten the shit fucked out of me...as I had. I was in between worlds and weak to my core.

The beautiful thing about this is how much of a bond I've created with J that at no point did I feel embarrassed or ashamed that my poop was all over us. It's just part of it, and there is always a risk of that happening. What's important is that you trust the person you're with to not see you as any less than. Besides, most of the times we have anal sex, I happen to be clean without doing an enema. I'm not sure how I feel about doing those; I've heard mixed comments about whether it messes up your microbiome, and it's not a risk I would like to take. For now, I'll take the risks of being dirty, though I'm not opposed to trying it before a hot weekend adventure maybe?

Aside from the messy butt sex, this was truly an amazing weekend. I got to show him how much I genuinely desired him and that our spark was still there.

NOVEMBER 26, 2023

Last night, we went to a sex party. My head is spinning with images and snippets of the night. Two days ago, I called J and told him I had a fantasy of riding him at a party, just wearing a short dress with no panties. I also told him that we should take advantage of my still–freshly waxed kitty, so it needed to be soon. He did his homework and found this sex party. We had to go through an application process that was based solely on looks; this community was for young and fit couples.

The cover picture of the party was two topless girls with very revealing underwear. I didn't love the vibe of the cover photo—you could tell this was a *sex* party, and it didn't necessarily give off the highest and cleanest energy. But as long as I'm with J, I know I'm safe, and I could leave at any moment if I wanted.

The night before, I had erotic dreams about the party, and all day, I was mentally preparing myself for the night. The topic even came up while working on one of my client's eyebrows. She told me that she enjoys the lifestyle, and she goes to Mexico often to a sex resort called Desire. From what she said, it's more of a high-end place and not the kind of raunchy parties that happen often.

I had the hardest time getting ready. My hair was dirty and difficult to style, but I didn't want to wash it because...well, women and dirty-hair dilemmas are a whole book on their own.

I didn't have a cute and sexy outfit. I realized I had a lot of sexy lingerie but nothing nice to wear over it. I could just wear lingerie, but it was kind of cold out, and I wanted to feel comfortable.

I finally made my way to J's apartment feeling a little frazzled about the traffic, my hair, and my outfit. I guess I was a little more overwhelmed about this sex party than I thought I would be. It didn't take much at J's apartment to start feeling sexy and desired again. I'm always impressed by how this man is so turned on by the mere sight of me. On the drive to the party, we set some common ground rules and expectations. We knew we weren't interested in having sex with other people and that we just wanted to be in the environment and have fun. Ultimately, it was all about me having this experience for the first time. We realized that a casual friend and her man were also going to the party. Part of me was happy that I knew someone there, but I wasn't sure how it was going to turn out. I knew they were into the lifestyle but I'd heard some unfavorable remarks from multiple people about her boyfriend that made me a little reserved around him.

Upon arrival at the property, we noticed a couple that was just also being dropped off by their ride and confirmed that we were here for the same party. They were young, good-looking, and friendly, but I still showed no signs of interest because all I wanted was to be invisible until I was settled into the space. We checked in and walked through the property. It was full of nature, and that made me feel more grounded immediately. Walking into the crowd, I saw it was just like any pool party, nothing weird or intimidating. We ran into my friend and her man and said hi. It was nice seeing her face, and that also added a level of comfort. We found a place to sit down and just look around the place, not really interacting with others but still open to talking with anyone that approached us.

Sitting there, we met the person that runs the property and the DJ of the party. Nice people and a good connection to have for when I plan my events. It's always good to have options. I saw at least two people doing drugs, which is always at least a little triggering for me, but I also knew it was very common in these gatherings. I removed some layers and stayed in my cute little lingerie outfit, belly chain and a silk blouse over the top to give me some comfortable warmth. I felt sexy and classy.

J and I went to the back of the property where the "fucking tent" was and went inside to take a peek. There was an inflatable mattress, S-shaped furniture, and something else on the other corner, with the only light coming in from the entrance to the tent. In the comfort of the private space, we made out and teased each other for a bit. He ate me out on the edge of the mattress, and then I played with riding just the tip. Nothing crazy, just building up the excitement and then going back to the pool area.

After feeling comfortable for a while, I decided to give the Shabari experience a try. The gentleman performing it was part of the first Turn On Miami experience where he did a demonstration on me. Without much negotiation, I lay on his table facing up with him on my right side. He placed my feet together with my soles touching and my knees wide open; he tied my knees to the massage table and my hands back and over my head. The rope part took about five minutes, and then he started playing with a mild electric tool and other props. It wasn't intense except in some areas that were quite sensitive. I told him that my right nipple was sensitive and to stay away from it. He teased my privates over my panties in a way that I really enjoyed. But then he teased me with something that felt sharp; I told him that I was sensitive down there.

He pulled out a vibrator and asked me if I was OK with it, to which I said yes. He wrapped a condom around it and started tapping on my pussy with his palm, starting slow and increasing the speed, then pressing with his fingers. He pressed the vibrator over my panties and stimulated my clitoris. I orgasmed loudly; the people all around me became hard to notice. As I orgasmed, he covered my nose and my mouth to stop my breathing. After just a few seconds, I would push it off with my right elbow, then he would take it off and choke my neck. He did this a few times throughout the orgasms, and I enjoyed pushing his hand off my mouth. I was tied up and immobile, but this was the one little thing I had control over, and it felt like I was putting a fight that added to the experience. I felt something go inside me; I liked the sensation, but I was conflicted. We had not agreed to this. I was under the impression that I would just be tied up; everything else somehow just happened. In the moment, I really enjoyed it. It was euphoric and intense. I cried, I laughed, the classic massive release I'm used to but had no idea was about to experience.

He quickly untied me. I told him that I was OK, to which he said he knew. He kept telling me to just breathe and relax, that he'd been doing this for twenty years. I think he was concerned about what the people around us would think, since to most people, I probably looked like I was having a bad time. But this was not my first rodeo, and relaxing like he kept telling me to do was the opposite of what I wanted to do. J came to support me, and the not-so-gentleman asked him to go get water. But J knew that I needed him there, so he kept trying to stay. I could feel the tension in the space taking away from my experience. I tried to mitigate the situation by asking J myself to go get some water. I sat up and started to breathe deeply, waiting for him to come back. I was feeling cold, and this guy was not good at all at providing the nurturing I needed. When J came back with water, I just melted in his arms as he carried me away to a bench.

Sitting there with him, I immediately started feeling calm in his warmth. But I could feel he was upset. I told him I was OK; I was just going through my process.

J asked, "Did you know that was going to happen?"

"No, I didn't."

"His fingers were inside you."

"I know. I'm not happy about that, and I will be telling him how I felt about that. I wish I would have known exactly what I was getting myself into."

"But you make me wash my hands when I—"

"I know, trust me. I got carried away, and I didn't set a boundary with him like I should have. I'm already beating myself up for that, and I really would like to talk about this later."

"But you don't want to go home already, do you?"

"No. I just need to ground myself again, and we can keep playing."

"I'm OK with everything. I thought the experience was nice to watch. What upset me was that you both ordered me to get you water when I knew you needed me there."

"I know. I think in that moment, I was just overwhelmed with both of you talking over me, and it felt like the easiest way to stop it. But I did wish you would just be the one taking care of me. He didn't really allow me to *feel* like you always do. But please, let's talk about this in more detail later. I just need to go pee and clean myself."

We got up and walked by the crowd of people that now seemed indifferent to us. There was a woman bent over a man's lap getting spanked. Now that made sense because I kept hearing a pattern of claps, but I couldn't tell what was going on.

About twenty minutes later, the rope guy came around to check on me. He did this multiple times throughout the night; at least he got that part of aftercare right. Already feeling much more grounded. I told him my point of view about the experience. I told him although I did enjoy the sensations, I wasn't expecting it to be such a deep experience, and I would have appreciated more clear negotiation and boundaries. He seemed confused and said that he asked J and me. I said that I didn't know he would put his fingers inside me, and then he tried gaslighting me by saying that he didn't. I mean, I felt it, J saw it, and on top of that, it was on the video that J recorded with my phone. I didn't really feel like getting into it at that moment because I wanted to enjoy the rest of the night and not dwell so much on this, but I did tell him that J and I did this all the time, and he's very aware of the process and how deep I can go, that his presence was the reason I was able to fully surrender and I needed him there.

This made J happy, and most importantly it gave me peace of mind. I really loved the way J was so composed while the guy said that he had twenty years of experience and so on. He could have easily shown off that he's also a master in the art of touch and let him know about how skilled he is. But instead, he stood in his confidence, knowing that he's sure of what he's got. It really made me realize that J's confidence is just part of his branding and not something that he needs to rub on people's faces. He had many chances to show off, and he didn't.

Things were starting to get wild at the party. Looking behind us, we saw people having sex, and I noticed that I was not turned on at all by what I saw. I mean...I was turned on but not from seeing the people having sex. J and I walked around the property and found a spot that didn't feel too exposed to make out and, well, you know. I started by feeling how hard and big he felt in my hands, and I just wanted to put it in my mouth, so I did.

I gave him head and somehow ended up on the ground getting pounded from behind. I was not worried or even looking around to check who was watching. I was just loving how he felt behind me and how he was making me moan loudly. It did feel good to be loud and know that people could clearly not just hear you but also see you, and it's totally safe and judgment free. I knew when J was about to finish because he likes to grab my hips and push me into him. This is when I squeeze and say dirty things to increase the sensations. He pulled out and ejaculated on my back, then collapsed on the ground with me. I could feel my vagina pulsing even after the fact. It was fucking amazing. Every bit of it felt so delicious.

Chilling in our almost-hidden spot, we took some time to observe the party from our point of view. To our left, we saw two guys standing next to each other getting blow jobs and asking a couple nearby to join. Ahead of us, there were other people making out and having sex. I guess you could consider this an orgy? It didn't really look like a pile of people having sex together, just separate couples doing their own thing.

We got up to go back to the restroom to pee and wash myself again. Right outside the restroom, there was a bed and waiting area. And on the bed was the same couple that was doing the spanking earlier. He was fully dressed, and she was fully naked and wearing a butt plug. He was fingering her and looking outside at the voyeurs. It was, in my opinion, not a very pleasant or hot thing to see. There were people waiting to use the restroom right next to the bed. It just looked very performative and not like they were having fun.

We went back to where we had been sitting earlier next to the property owner, who was just chilling with her partner and her dog, and we chitchatted for a bit. I noticed to the left of us there were a guy and two girls doing dirty things. One of the girls was standing against a wall with plants, and the guy was fucking her from behind. Both were wearing clothes and only revealing enough to get the work done. Now *that* turned me on so much. I realized that I enjoy the kinky and taboo part of sex more than fucking in open space for everyone to see. It's why I felt so indifferent about the people having sex in the open, yet these people found a spot that was open enough to see but private enough to make it risky. Also, I happened to really love that position they were in.

We went back to the tent area, and we saw the same people that were swinging earlier continuing their oral sex party. It was kind of hard to see, but we stood there for a second watching them. As we were walking away, one of them invited us inside, and we respectfully declined. We did stay right around the tent, right by a beautiful tree where I invited J to get me from behind again. At this point in the night, I was just wearing my silk blouse and belly chain; all it took was bending over and welcoming him in. J was as hard as he could possibly be and again made me orgasm over and over as he thrust deep inside me. I could hear the people in the tent moaning, and I wondered if they were being turned on by our sounds. I sure was turned on knowing that there were people having sex right next to us but not being able to see them or them us.

I really wanted to ride him, but the only spot that was around us didn't feel very secure, so we kept doing it in the same spot until I'd had enough. I started to feel hungry and tired, and as much fun as I was having with J, I knew my body, and it was time to go. Oh, but he was so hard. He really wanted to keep going, but we already learned the lesson of not pushing my vagina too far. As we walked back to our spot, he was proudly parading his erection for everyone to see, and I didn't mind at all. We got dressed up and silently left the party.

As we were waiting for our ride outside, something funny happened. A woman was asking for a lighter, and she complimented J on his cock, but I didn't really hear her that well and I just looked confused. So I asked her to repeat what the compliment was about.

"Oh, I hope you don't mind. It's just not often that one can compliment someone on their cock. By the way, you are so beautiful." That part was directed at me. "When you were walking around earlier, I couldn't help but notice you have a beautiful cock."

J was loving the compliment, but I genuinely didn't understand what she was saying until she walked away and J clarified for me. I was so tired and ready to leave. I felt so silly just standing there, not really understanding what was going on, and I probably looked like I was jealous. I really wasn't jealous, and if I was, it would be more about me not being the one getting the compliment. Otherwise, I would have continued the shower of praise for my lover.

On our ride back, we ordered food that arrived right on time after I showered. We took some time to decompress and share about how the night went, without really going much into detail.

Here is what I learned: Sex parties are fun, but they can be quite overstimulating. While I was there, I was engulfed in the turn-on energy, but after leaving, there was a slight feeling of dirtiness that didn't feel quite right. I'm a sexually free person, but I'm not as open as I thought.

I don't have any issues with orgies, threesomes, or bringing any crazy sexual fantasies to fruition. I would love to experience those things with people I feel a deeper bond with, but I wouldn't go to a party with the sole purpose of finding someone to fuck, and that was the vibe I got at this party.

It turns out that I value sex and who I lie with more than I thought. I don't see myself capable of performing any kind of sexual acts with someone I just met. First of all, it's hard for me to be attracted to someone right off the bat, and secondly, I need more than physical attraction to be interested in a person.

I've had my fair share of sex parties for a good bit of time. I'm a curious being, and this was something I wanted to experience for a while, but I don't think it will be something to do often. For now, I need time to process everything that happened, especially the lack of boundaries in the bondage experience. It sucks that this experience would have been a total success if only I knew what I was getting myself into. It's tough to admit, but I feel a mild level of violation was done to my body. It was a big lesson on boundaries. I could have done better. But he could have done much better at creating a safe space for me. After all, for someone who's been doing this for over twenty years, he should know better.

DECEMBER 23, 2023

Today is my ex-husband's birthday. I would say happy birthday, but it feels weird, plus he's probably with his girlfriend, and I wouldn't want it to start a fight. It's crazy how someone you cared so much about becomes a nobody in your life. It kind of sucks.

I've been super stressed and anxious, and the worst thing about it is that I'm addicted to it. Sacred Ink had a busy November, hitting over $10,000 for the first time in a while! But December became a little slower, which I guess is a good thing since I've been busy doing other stuff.

Finally, my conscious strip club dream is going to materialize! I'm working with Meli and Lismany, the organizers of Kelly's Audacious Embodiment retreat, to help me put this night together. It's costing a lot of money. I haven't finished paying off the debt I got myself into during the slow season, and it really doesn't make sense to invest all this money, especially when my goal really is Sacred Ink. But I don't care. I've been putting it all on a credit card, and I know I'm going to make my money back and then some.

This is such an exciting project, manifesting what I envisioned when I decided I wanted to be an erotic dancer. It's funny that a lot of people ask me what is conscious about the project. Clearly, I have thought about this for a long time and forget I live in my own world, so I explain: It starts with an invite-only filter for entry, where guests need to apply to join and go through a vetting process in which I make sure they want to join for the right reasons. Instead of alcohol, we serve adaptogenic plant elixirs. Our performers get paid directly and don't have to depend only on tips to leave paid. A lot of people don't know this, but at strip clubs, the strippers have to pay a house fee and tip everyone and their mothers on the way out. This is such an exploitive aspect of the industry because, as a performer, it doesn't feel fair to pay to dance. One of my favorites is the rose petals tipping currency! Guests buy rose petals from us, and that's what they use to make it rain on the dancers. At the end of the night, all profits from roses are split evenly between the dancers. I first saw this initiative at Zen & Kush, an event hosted by music artist Lizzy Jeff where I performed last year, and I absolutely loved it! I don't think there is anything wrong with cash. I love real money, but it gets passed around, used for drugs, etc., so it is physically dirty. With roses having the highest frequency in the universe, it feels like such a treat to be showered in rose petals while performing.

Just to give you an idea of how big this production is, it's costing me around $10,000 just to put it together, between the venue, videography and photography, event management, marketing, stage rental, talent, and so on. All of that before I get to see how profitable it's really going to be. Based on Meli's calculations, in the worst-case scenario, I should at least break even, and in the best-case scenario, there may be up to $8,000 in profit!

I really hope it's profitable. Otherwise, I fear the possibility of this being too much for me. It's all I've been thinking about from the moment I wake up. And it's hard to fall asleep with my head spinning. I've had a mild headache for a few days now, and I'm really starting to feel my body's message: stop worrying and let go.

After all, that's what I hired help for, to be able to let go and not carry this all on my own.

But there is still a little feeling of guilt about not investing all the energy and money on Sacred Ink. And that inner dialogue about me not committing till the end of my projects and relationships.

I'm currently going through a fast for tonight's ayahuasca ceremony. It was J's Christmas gift. I've been mentally and physically preparing myself for this experience. I have tremendous respect for the medicine, so naturally there is a level of concern. But it's not my first rodeo, and I'm hopeful that tonight's experience is going to be exactly what I need to hit a reset button and surrender.

DECEMBER 25, 2023

I feel refreshed and energized. My roommates are both out of town, and I have the place to myself for the next three days. Having my roommates around doesn't necessarily stop me from doing my own thing, but it feels nice to be in my own energy.

Ayahuasca was beautiful and mild. My first ceremony in Costa Rica two years ago was so deep and intense that I blacked out completely and the shamans had a really hard time bringing me back to my body. From what they said, apparently while I was blacked out, I looked like I was giving birth from how intense my experience was. I don't remember any of that; I just remember waking up choking from the tobacco smoke on my face and Agua de Florida being spilled all over me after peeing myself while astral projecting right outside of the earth, looking down at where I live and where my body was in the moment, all while experiencing the most intense and long orgasm of the universe. The next day, I was exhausted and my body inflamed. So naturally, I was a little fearful that this time would go the same way.

There were roughly twenty of us, but the land was big, so it didn't feel crowded. It was a chilly Miami night, but there was a big fire in the middle of the circle keeping us warm. Spread out around the fire were our beds and chairs. To the left were the men, the women to the right, all of us coming around to the fire to dance and sing as we pleased. The shaman was kind of funny; I couldn't take him seriously but still came from a respectful place. I liked that he had a sense of humor while keeping us in check. The crew was composed of the shaman, his wife, a couple of other ladies, the fire man, and three musicians that blessed us with their melody all night long.

Going up to drink the tea, my heart was racing. I held onto J's arm as we approached the shaman one by one. The cup was just like a shot glass, easy to drink in just one gulp if you don't think about it too long. The taste of ayahuasca is extremely unpleasant; just thinking about it makes me want to vomit. I drank it fast, followed by a cup of water to help it go down. From there, we all went to our beds and held silence for ninety minutes, waiting for it to take effect. A calming voice said to me that it was going to be an easy journey.

I sat straight up on the ground, meditating and setting the intention for the night. After about forty minutes, I started to hear people going over to the purging holes dug into the ground about fifty feet behind me. I was holding it in pretty good, but hearing the people gag and burp was triggering my gag reflexes. My stomach felt weird, and I couldn't tell if I had to run to the porta potty or the purging holes. I went to try and poop first with no success, then to the purging hole but still nothing. So I went back to my bed and lay down with my back leaned against my duffel bag and pillow, and about fifteen minutes later, I had to get up and finally purge.

It was an intense feeling but very necessary to the process. On my knees, hands on the ground, looking down into the hole, a deep breath in and out it went, intentionally letting out all that no longer serves me as vomit projected powerfully out of my mouth. With the pressure in my head, I could feel my face becoming that of a demon and then returning to normal while I waited for the next impulse to come in. I cried and spat out, trying to get the taste out of my mouth. Writing about it, I feel like the demon face every time I threw up was me letting go of that evil fear that had been consuming me this year. It was the demon in me letting it all out.

I must say vomiting is not fun business, but I've learned to use it intentionally to my advantage. I used tantra to feel every single part of it, especially the unpleasant sensations.

After my purge, I went to my bed and curled up inside multiple layers of warm and comfy blankets. I felt like I was floating in the clouds; everything was perfect.

One of the first visions I had was that of what seemed like massive spider legs hovering over me. My initial reaction was fear. Was this where my brain was going? But then I sank into it, and it disappeared. I didn't really have many visions; my eyes kept fluttering open and looking up at the sky. There was a beautiful rainbow around the almost-full moon, the sky was starry for a big city, and the tall trees were swaying and dancing with the wind. My senses were enhanced, and the nightly sounds were very soothing. I was fully conscious and aware of my surroundings while immersed in my own experience.

Another vision I had was me in the form of some sort of gigantic jellyfish or octopus with multiple legs floating in the middle of the Milky Way. It made me giggle, and then I realized that it was me and the multiple legs represent my multiple interests. A mastermind puppeteering all my different passions. Right before the ceremony, this was the main thing weighing on my mind, and I immediately felt so much relief when I saw this.

After feeling warm in my bed for a while, I decided to go get some fresh air and join J by the fire. Coming into the experience, his main concern was that at this tribe, they didn't provide a lot of medicine, and in his experience, he usually needs a lot of it to feel it. I could tell by his face that he wasn't feeling much, and I asked him if he already went for the second round of medicine, but he had no idea we could already do that. So we went over to the shaman and asked for our second cup. He remembered J having a hard time connecting from previous ceremonies and gave him a generous cup, then gave me half a cup as I asked. I must say, the second cup is always harder to swallow.

They gathered us all in two straight rows, females on the left and males on the right, side by side. Then they walked around us, singing prayers and spraying us with what they called lotion; I believe it was Agua de Florida mixed with their own blends of healing elements. This ritual took about ten minutes, and once finished, J was fully immersed in the journey. Apparently, this was the portal that he needed to go through.

We continued to enjoy the fire as the live music started to play. The singer's voice was so angelic, and the instruments sounded so beautiful. Until I felt the urge to purge again. I got up and walked toward the holes and let it rip once more. The smell of the medicine and vomit from the hole triggered my gag reflex, just one deep breath in and the same feeling of the demon in my face letting it all come out. From there, I went to rinse my mouth and went back to my bed. I expected to go deep after this second cup, but I just continued to have a nice, mellow trip inside my blankets.

Lying there, I had a vision of the same jellyfish/octopus thing inside my tattoo studio. This time, it represented me again as the mastermind, but the meaning was different: I didn't have to do everything here, just direct, a confirmation that delegating tasks is the next step in my career. I think that was it for the missions and messages, confirming things I already knew in my heart.

I remembered it had already been over twenty-four hours since I last ate. I was starving, and they were not serving us fruits and snacks until the sunrise. Then I remembered I packed an orange in my bag! I pulled out the switchblade and sliced it into pieces, hoping the fragrance didn't divulge what I was up to.

It was not enough to save me from my hunger, but it would at least help me through the sunrise. I saved a slice of the orange, and I walked over to J's bed all the way on the opposite side. I brought it to his nose so he could take a whiff, but instead he devoured it. He was so happy to see me all giddy about sneaking around with the orange and made some space in his arms for us to cuddle.

Not too long after that, we went back to the fire and continued to enjoy the music. Then we went back to our beds until the colors of the dawn appeared in the sky.

I'm so amazed that I can remember so many details of the night since my Costa Rica experience is nothing but a blur to me. I guess you really do have a different experience every time, like they say, and ayahuasca gives you what you need and not what you want.

JANUARY 1, 2024

I just ended things with J. My feelings changed, and staying was starting to feel unfair for both of us. This had been coming since we took the break, and I really gave it a fair shot. He was such an amazing boyfriend and passionate lover. But it just wasn't right. I woke up next to him yesterday, and all I wanted to do was find a way to get out of having sex with him. I couldn't stand staying next to him anymore; my body was rejecting him, and it was a very unpleasant moment. The night before, he opened up to me about some of the downloads he received from ayahuasca that made him aware of his deep fear of abandonment. As I was facing the hard truth about the ending of our story, I knew that the timing couldn't have been worse and that I would abandon him at a time that would be very painful. It really made me wonder if a deep, shadowy part of me that I'm not conscious of gets off on this. And if a deep, shadowy part of him gets off on the suffering.

A big part of me was beating myself up for not wanting to stay with this perfectly attractive, healthy masculine figure. But I can't hear that voice when my body is screaming so loud. I have nothing bad to say about him except he gave too much, trying to control something that was inevitable.

I feel numb, but I know it's a water dan waiting to explode any moment. Right now, I don't have much to put in words except that his scent is still lingering in some of the belongings he's left behind, but slowly dissipating as I put them in a bag. And soon the moment will come when there will be none of his essence around me.

JANUARY 9, 2024

After feeling numb for a couple of days, I finally broke down while eating breakfast earlier last week. I had sent him an aftercare text with words of affirmations about our time together, and he left it on read. I wasn't upset about that; I knew he needed the time to process. But when he sent me a screenshot with the information for a stage rental company (for the Conscious Cabaret event) that he was able to get me through one of his clients for $300 less than what I was planning on paying, I started feeling again. We weren't together anymore, but he still came through with his word, and that reminded me of the man I left behind. To make matters worse, the neighbor started blasting music, and the song playing was "Amargura," by Karol G.

When the part about how hurt she feels about being left on read came on, I just bawled, grateful that my roommates weren't home so I could really let it all out. All day after that, I felt very sensitive and had low energy. And the next few days, the feelings of emptiness would come and go, but always with the good conscience that I had done the right thing for the both of us. It's okay to feel sad after doing the right thing.

On the bright side, the event has finally launched, and ticket sales are slowly coming in. I'm really hoping enough sales are made during the early bird so I can continue to fund what I'm missing. So far, I must still pay for the stage, seating, and the other half of the venue and event management, and when the time gets near, I have to pay for the food and the performers' fees.

I'm not going to lie; I am freaking out a little bit. After getting myself in debt starting my cosmetic tattoo business and struggling to pay it all off, seeing my credit card balance is bringing back old feelings I'd hoped to never experience again. I've been refreshing my email constantly and checking my Instagram page nonstop. I must admit, I've been trying to control the outcome when I know that it's time to surrender. I had the inspiration to make this happen because I know it's in alignment with my purpose. All I must do is make the right moves and let the universe take charge. Let go and let God.

That's what I did this morning. Instead of checking my email and messages first thing after waking up, I thought of all the things I was grateful for, got up, and made my morning beverage, and after feeling aligned, I checked my phone and noticed I had a message from Meli celebrating two more tickets being sold! That was exactly the confirmation I was looking for, and I will continue to do my best to chill the fuck out. So, as of now, we have sold five tickets and have ninety-five more to go.

JANUARY 19, 2024

What I feared kind of happened. When I decided to launch the cabaret, I knew I didn't have the finances to sustain it. I just kind of looked
at my bank account and thought, *Yeah, fuck it, somehow the money is
going to come in and make it happen*. I was paying for things in parts
in order of importance, but when my marketing team for Sacred Ink
sent their invoice and my credit card was maxed out, I panicked. I made
some payments, deposited some cash, and prayed that somehow things
would work out. The next day, I opened my statements, and my credit
card balance had just what I needed to make it happen! I don't know if
it was a miracle or some old payments had finally posted, or a glitch in
the matrix, but I didn't even question it. I paid my team, and it was all
good from there!

I did, however, panic enough to create an account on a dating site
called sugardaddy.com.

I just think it would be so nice to focus all my hard-earned money
on my goals and get a little spoiling on the side for maintenance. But
it gets tough when most of the sugar daddies out there are very unat-
tractive, old men, and I just can't see myself comfortable being intimate
with someone I don't feel a connection with. However, I did find just
a handful of men on the site that were younger and interesting to look
at. I'm currently talking with one of them, and I'm having a fun time.

He's thirty-six, slim, fit, Italian from New York, and he travels too
much and is not able to sustain a traditional relationship. We jumped
on a video call, and he looked exactly like he did in pictures. His energy
is serious and focused but easy to break when I flirt. We were trying to
meet in person yesterday, but work got busy, and he was only in town
for a couple of days before leaving again. We might meet in a couple of
weeks when he gets back. I did try to get him to spoil me a little, even
though he hasn't met me yet, but he said he has rules and must meet
me first. I'm really enjoying the flirty chase. Of course, I'm not doing
any chasing; I'm just playing along with it and being super adorable and
bratty. He's absolutely loving it. I just must be careful not to over-give
just because I'm having fun with it.

I did some research last night about how to be a sugar baby, and there are a few ways to do it. From what I learned, apparently you can either make them pay for every single interaction, even if it's just a video call or coffee date as part of the vetting process, but this will most likely only work with that they call "John type" daddies, which are more basic and transactional. Whereas if you skip making them pay just to meet you, this may lead to a "whale," which is a daddy that is very generous and loves to spoil for no reason.

I'm going for a whale; I don't like things feeling transactional. In an ideal scenario, I find someone that I am attracted to enough to play along, he takes me on dates, trips, and business gatherings, he spoils me, and I get to focus on my career and projects while he's busy with his work. I'd love someone who can play along with my brattiness and tame me when need be. Someone who is rarely in town and rewards my entertaining and playful texting when he's gone. I want to be the courtesan to a busy and successful man who craves to be in the presence of a beautiful and smart woman—but I want it to feel natural. Just thinking about having to kiss someone for money makes gives me the ick.

I wrote this for the site:

I'm an ambitious, independent, fun, and bratty baby. I love flirting and being silly, but I'm also an amazing listener and space holder. I'm an entrepreneur, a cosmetic tattoo artist with my own studio. I am also a professional dancer and enjoy producing my own entertainment events. I'm looking for a daddy that loves supporting me so I can focus on my endless projects and business ventures. To me it's important having a playful support system that feels aligned, respectful, and generous.

Of course, there is a lot of shame that comes with these kinds of dynamics. I'm putting that to the side for now and allowing myself to explore this area where I have a lot of curiosity.

JANUARY 20, 2024

Today was a tough day. I just felt tired and low energy at the studio and tried to take a nap after coming back home, but it didn't happen. I masturbated and felt better after but still very low energy and sad. Yesterday, we had rehearsals for the cabaret, and we were finally able to try out my shibari suspension from the pole. It's likely that the experience triggered my grief, and I'm just going through the motions.

Everything erupted just about thirty minutes ago. I'm much calmer now, but I felt so alive in the moment. Here is what happened...

Yesterday, J wanted to have a conversation for closure, but I didn't read his last message because I was busy all day, and he took that as the closure that he needed. So when I called him today to see if it was a good time, he said that he didn't need it anymore. Only to send it via voice note. When I heard it, I was livid. He was blowing up in my face about how amazing he was to me and that the quality of love that I give is shit and that he will never settle for someone that doesn't match his effort. He then proceeded to send me a screenshot of my OnlyFans account, and he said:

J: I know a woman's gotta do what a woman's gotta do, but just keep in mind this is the exact same low-frequency energy that you experienced at the strip club, and the entire reason you're starting the Conscious Cabaret. Just seems like a step in the wrong direction to be funding such a glorious event with that energy.

I know I'm an evolved being, but I'm also a fucking human being, and in that moment, I ravished in the mundane human I am. I went off on him.

"Oh, was this the closure you said you didn't need anymore? You just sent it in a voice note like a fucking coward? What happened after ayahuasca telling me that I am an amazing girlfriend? I've been here before. When a man doesn't get the love they want, they much rather get hate than nothing at all."

Just one of the things that I remember saying. I was fully aware that I let it get to me. And I still don't regret any of that. I felt so alive and present. The best advice I have ever heard was not to let my mindfulness get in the way of my humanness.

It just really sucks because this entire time I was so happy that the breakup was easy and drama-free, and then this had to happen. I guess that's just how I like it sometimes.

JANUARY 21, 2024

It's an interesting time for me right now. I'm spiraling and probably not making the right choices at the moment. I can see this whole sugar-daddy thing ending up just like stripping. I'm very curious about a lot of things, and I'm not afraid to try it, but it doesn't mean I will always like it. I know right now I'm grieving the loss of a relationship that felt very supportive, and I feel like no one is there for me to love me and spoil me. So I'm looking for someone that can fill that gap.

I'm realizing so many patterns and shadowy aspects of myself. I have a tremendous amount of self-love. I have worked very hard to get to this point, and I know I'm a gorgeous, sexy, intelligent, and emotionally mature woman. So when I first meet someone that I like, I expect them to see that right away and I look for ways to get their attention. I learned the exact word to describe what I go through, and it is *limerence*: a state of involuntary obsession with another person. This is especially true when I don't get the attention I want right away; I obsess over ways to get it. When the attention is finally on me, I love it, but soon enough, I get over it, and it's basically the end.

I can already see myself doing that with the guy from the sugar daddy site. We had a FaceTime call, and I saw him as a potential limerent object, and his withholding was exactly what I needed to send me on a quest for his attention. After just a day or two, I caught myself doing it again. Constantly thinking about the possibilities of where this could go and what kind of avatar I want to play with around him. Basically, how can I make him obsess over me? Just so I can have fun with it for a while and leave him when I've had my fill. I guess Carolyn Elliott, author of the book *Existential Kink*, would agree that this is one of my relationship kinks, and therefore the kink of all the men that were collateral damage of my seduction.

I'm still unsure whether this is a pattern that I'd like to interrupt or keep exploring, but I am aware of its existence, and that's already a step in the right direction. At the very least, I can now explore it in a mindful way.

FEBRUARY 6, 2024

I'm freaking out. I'm losing my shit right now. I just finished punching and screaming into a pillow and letting rage take over me. Where do I even start? And can I even make sense in my writing when the tears in my eyes are blinding me? I'm literally just hours away from getting my period, and all emotions have taken over me. The cabaret experience is only four days away, and I'm nowhere near the number of tickets I need sold to break even. I need to sell at least forty more tickets to make my investment back. So I've let fear consume me.

To add gasoline to the fire, I had a heated phone conversation with J. He keeps on playing the victim and telling me about the good man that he is. The last thing he said after the argument over the phone was, "Good luck with the cabaret. We both know you don't have the license to run this."

I was shook. "What do you mean?"

"A cabaret license, baby."

I lost my shit completely. "Is this a threat? Why are you even saying that? You know what, J? I don't have capacity for this right now." And I hung up.

What the fuck does he event mean by license? I'm hosting an experience. I am not running a fucking brothel. He's pathetic, and I hate that all the glory I ever saw him in has crumbled in front of my eyes. I can't help but feel gross about his sorry ass being all, "Poor me, poor me, I was nothing but good to you, I would move mountains for you, and this is how you treat me."

All this time, I'm thinking this grown ass man has the capacity to deal with the breakup, and he's acting like a little bitch.

I already feel so much better after putting all of this into writing. I finally just took my first deep breath of fresh air and can start to think clearly.

I'm an emotional being with an immense capacity to feel. Love can take me on a never-ending joyride, but this capacity to feel is not limited to happy moments; grief can feel like breaking bones. And although experiencing rage is not common for me, when it takes over, I let it consume me.

I accept it all, and I love it all. I stopped labeling my emotions as negative or positive when I realized they all feel pretty good in the body if you stop blocking them and let yourself experience them. Because the relief of letting it all out makes it all worth it.

FEBRUARY 12, 2024
THE CABARET

I'm just getting back into my journal today and reading what I wrote the last time. After the raging episode and writing down my thoughts, I felt so much better and lighter. So much so that creativity came back into my body, and I created an amazing graphic and text to promote the cabaret. It was so good that I couldn't stop reading it and feeling the message resonate on so many levels.

"This night is for those craving to experience more depth to the often shallow and shadowy adult entertainment industry. Don't get me wrong, I love a human experience with all its aspects; we're not just love and light. Lotus Exotic is where the light shines through the cracks of our broken pieces, to illuminate the deep, dark desires that live hidden in our minds."

The cabaret was a memorable experience. It was absolute magic. Almost everything went as planned or even better, except for leaving me about $3,000 in the negative. When the day came and I made peace with the fact that I wasn't going to make a penny from all the hard work I poured into it, I realized I had no choice but to enjoy the fuck out of it. My mindset went from trying to make money to creating an experience for myself.

I had a huge team of volunteers that were punctual and eager to help. I directed everyone to their tasks and noticed myself just standing around, not knowing what to do. This was the moment I realized that my support system is rock solid and I could just relax. I went to the greenroom and started working on my hair and makeup with my friend Alex. My energy was calm and collected; crew members would come into the room to ask me questions, and I would calmly answer and direct them where things were. I felt so in control while at the same time relaxing in the makeup chair, like the queen of the cabaret.

OMG, something hilarious happened that I can't stop laughing about. My makeup was almost done, and I had to go poop. I ran to the restroom to do my business, and when I flushed...well, it didn't flush. There was no time to panic; the doors were opening in less than an hour, and we couldn't have this problem right now. This was not my problem to solve, and I'd better move fast. I came out of the bathroom and found Andrea, who was the person in charge of the venue for the night, and I let her handle it. I ran back to the greenroom, internally giggling and wondering if people knew it was my shit they were dealing with since I did it so fast. Long story short, Isaeah (who is stunning, tall, strong, and masculine, who also happens to be my Acro partner for my performance; everyone loves to see us together, but there is totally nothing more than a friendship) fixed it, and we were back on track.

When the door opened for the guests, I couldn't help going outside and checking out the space. I didn't even realize that I had forgotten to put on all my jewelry, but I was so happy and excited to say hi. Ten minutes till showtime, the crew met up in the greenroom. A quick check-in, and we were ready to rock. Meli was on stage welcoming everybody, and I was on the side, watching how everything unfolded. She called me on stage, and I don't remember what she was saying about me, but I was trying to hold my tears back. I was totally not grounded in this moment, and if there was one thing I would change about this night, it would be the way that I presented the experience. I totally forgot everything that I wanted to say and how I wanted to say it, but it's OK because there will be plenty of time for me to do it again. I don't beat myself up too hard.

As the show went on, I would watch from the back seats, blending in with the audience and tearing up at the beauty I was witnessing. Seeing the performers enjoy themselves and the rose petals land on their bodies was the highlight of the night and the reason why I put this together.

My performance went exactly as planned. I danced to "Palm Trees," by Teo; it's a song about being in a relationship and loving the person while simultaneously wanting to go away and be alone. This song perfectly represented what I was going through in my personal life. Everything worked out perfectly with minimal preparation. I came up with the idea just four days before the event, and we only rehearsed it a handful of times. When the song finished, I stayed on stage, crying and feeling the roses on my skin. The audience was cheering louder with every second, and the feelings of love and gratitude filled me completely.

The night went by fast, and I was floating around like a fairy in la-la land. When everything ended, we had extra help to clean up from some of the lovely guests that volunteered. We picked up fast, and I was home by 2:00 a.m. There was a feeling of accomplishment mixed with a bittersweet feeling of "Now what? It's done. What's next?" I confirmed that the best part about accomplishing something is not hitting the goal itself; it is the feeling of getting there. The goal is the peak, but it comes down from there.

Two guys who are known in the tantra community snuck into the event and sat down in the VIP section. Since I had to personally vet all the guests in the room, I realized their names were not on the list. I was too busy that night to deal with it, and I gave them the benefit of the doubt. I reached out multiple times to one of the guys to show me proof of ticket purchase, and I was very polite about it, but when he ignored me after three days, I reached my limit and sent this text:

"You're not responding which to me confirms that you somehow managed to break multiple barriers of entry. I consider this a violation of our space and all the women that you watched perform on stage that night. Extremely disrespectful to everyone in that room and the tremendous amount of work that we put into this experience. You have two options: Redeem yourself and pay for two VIP tickets and your reputation will not be tarnished by this (I'll let you do that yourself if you continue down this path) or I'll make sure everyone in the community knows what you did. If I don't hear back from you within 24 hours I'll make a public announcement and reach out to everyone you've ever worked with and plan on working with and they all will know the kind of person they're dealing with."

He responded shortly after and acted a fool. After some back and forth, he sent me the money followed by this text:

"My friend was extremely disappointed when I showed him your texts. Is this how you treat your other VIPs? The level of retaliation over not seeing your text was really uncalled for, unprofessional, and out of character for conscious producer. As representing your whole team, you've left a sour taste about your "conscious cabaret" by threatening guests."

I said "You guys are ridiculous. You have some nerve thinking you could get away with sneaking into a private event like that. You're lucky I didn't have security escort you out and actually gave you the chance to make up for what you did. Don't come at me with the BS of not seeing my texts after reaching out three days in a row."

I don't understand why people think that because I host a conscious event, I am going to let them walk all over me. I am very proud of the way that I handled the situation and would do it again in a heartbeat.

I am grateful for the experience and everything I have learned about myself in the process, and I am excited to do it again when the time and finances feel right. The first one was hard to market because I didn't have the footage, testimonials, and content to advertise. But now that I do, launching the next one will be much easier. At the moment, we have so many people waiting and asking for the next experience, and it feels like a good confirmation that I am, indeed, following the right path.

FEBRUARY 14, 2024

So much has happened in my life that I haven't even had the chance to write.

I met a guy in the world of BDSM, James. He is a shibari rigger and dominant. I met him at a sex-positive event in which we played with bondage and suspension. I liked that as part of the planning process, we went through my medical history, my boundaries, and my intentions for the experience, the total opposite of that other bondage guy that made me orgasm in front of a bunch of people without my explicit consent.

My boundaries were to not insert anything inside me and to allow him to use a vibrator but only over my panties. Before jumping into the suspension, he wanted to play with me on the ground to get to know me, so he tied me up to a spanking bench facedown and used a few toys to see what I liked. He started with a flogger. (That just made me realize that J didn't put the glass dildo that he'd gifted me in the bag with all my things. Why would he do that? Would he keep it to use it with other people? That's just gross.)

But anyway...I didn't love the flogger, and I asked him to stop. I guess I'm not into impact play? So he used other toys and a vibrator. He put the vibrator straight on my clit, and the sensations were too intense to take in. I asked him for less pressure, and he just left it in place for me to adjust as I needed. I had, like, three little orgasms; they were nice, but I could tell I wasn't fully surrendered by their intensity. After I asked to stop, he untied me from the bench, grabbed me by the back of the rope harness, and picked me up in the air. I wrapped my arms around his neck as he went to put me back down on the nearby sofa where I ended up sitting on his lap like a big baby. We stayed there for a few minutes while he caressed my legs, and I cried and laughed on his shoulder until I came back to my body. What I loved the most about this experience was that I was able to communicate when I didn't like or wanted to change something.

Later in the night, I danced on a pole that they had. I met some new, interesting people and genuinely had a great time. It was so much better than the other swingers' party I went to a few months ago with J; this felt so much more respectful and friendly. There was a big room for orgies and exhibitionists, private rooms, a public shower, and the main playroom in the front, which was where the suspension rigs were. I didn't hang out in the back too long, just peeked in every now and then to see what people were doing. For the most part, I stayed in the front learning how to use impact toys from a seasoned dominatrix.

After hanging out in the space for a while, we started the actual suspension part. He created a harness around my body and slowly suspended me from the rig made specifically for this. He kept it basic because he was just getting to know me and didn't know my capacity for suspension. I felt comfortable in the suspension except for the cold AC hitting my feet. After he put me down and held me in his arms again, we chatted about how neither of us were swingers or slept around with random people. He said he can't really do the casual thing, that he can do friends with benefits and even polyamory, although he's not poly himself. It was hard to hear with the loud music in the space. I was reading his lips and looking at his face when I realized I really liked him. Like, I just wanted to make out with him. Which is an amazing feeling to experience since I rarely felt that way about J.

The following days, he checked in on me multiple times, and we continued to talk throughout the week. We made plans to meet that next Sunday at his place for a more intimate experience in the privacy of his home. This was perfect timing since it was the week of my birthday and every day that week had a special celebration of some sort, and this would be the grand finale. I was really anticipating this encounter and feeling excited about the possibilities of where this could go, but I was also aware that there is a high chance that I might not like him at all when I got to know him. He lives over an hour away, but I was happy to do the drive if it had the promise of a fun experience.

Upon my arrival, he immediately gave me a tour of his house and showed off all the work that he had put into it. He showed me the play-room/dungeon; it was very impressive. One of the walls had a lot of rope hanging, floggers, and all kind of sensory and impact play tools. Another wall was a full mirror, and there were four different kinds of BDSM furniture, most of which he made from scratch or fixed himself, a leather couch, and another shelf with more toyboxes.

While he was showing me around his house, he was sharing so much about all the work that he'd put into the space, so I thought he was just very proud and happy about all the renovations, but I soon realized that he's just very talkative in general. He brought up his exes and other play partners, like, fifteen times throughout the night, and I barely felt like I could share much since he was the one doing all the talking. At times, he would tell me long stories that I couldn't keep up with, and the entire time I was unsure why he was even telling me the story.

I was feeling very friendly vibes and not any kind of attraction to-ward me. I couldn't tell if he was playing it cool or if he was just genu-inely not that interested in me. Or maybe he was kind of nervous in my presence and all he could do was talk? I don't know...I sometimes catch myself doing that when meeting new people and later wonder why I talked so much. But the bottom line was that I didn't get any indication of this being anything more than just a play partner.

Before we started playing, we went over my boundaries again, and this time I was more comfortable being fully nude and even allowing him to use his hands and toys inside me. He asked me to choose a few toys from his room. I picked a vulva suction device that makes your vulva plump. I was curious about this one. I also chose a vibrator, a glass dildo, a pinwheel, and a machete for sensory play. I told him that I was extremely paranoid about things inside me that were not clean, so he promised he would keep his hands clean and showed me how he cleaned his toys with surgical scrub, assuring me that his toys are cleaner than brand new out of the package.

It was playtime, and I was undressed under the rig, all the toys by the side on top of a towel. He started by creating a harness around my torso, and then he was quiet and focused; we both were. As I stared at him working the rope, I was taken back to when I first met him at the party. When I went to say hi, I was eager to meet him, and he gave me an intimidating look that made me feel like I interrupted something. As bratty as I am, I love when a man can easily put me in my place. Watching him get back into that dominant role immediately put me into surrender. He was so close to me and smelled so good, the perfect ratio of cologne and pheromones, and every time he pushed his hair back out of his face, it made me want to make out with him, especially when he was holding the rope with his teeth.

When he finished the harness, he laid me down on the mat, on my back with my knees bent close together. I was not feeling comfortable enough to open my legs, but I knew it was going to happen eventually. He pushed on my knees to spread my legs open and started using the suction tool. I was not a fan from the start because it felt like my insides were also being sucked out. He assured me that was not the case, so I went with it for a couple of minutes, but I think more than anything, I was just being shy. Then I realized that the whole point of this tool was to bring blood flow to the area to make it more sensitive, and I was already sensitive enough without it, so I asked him to stop.

He suspended me in the air on my back. I loved the way his hands felt when they went over the tight ropes against my skin. Then he tied my right foot to the top of the rig, making enough space between my thighs to place the vibrator on me. The sensations were too strong at first for my clitoris; he said he liked to torture me in that way, but I don't think he understood how sensitive I really am. Eventually, my body became more welcoming of the intense vibrations, and I started to sway my hips to find my own pleasure. The rope felt so tight around my body, especially my collarbone. I'd lost track of how long I'd been suspended, but what he was doing felt good. While in the air, I had a couple of ghost orgasms, the kind you feel creeping in that make a quick wave without much of an explosion. Then he started to slowly bring me back down.

"You're putting me down?"

"Yeah, but we are not done."

I was lying on the mat, and as he untied parts of the bondage, it felt amazing to be liberated from the tight grip of the ropes. I can't describe it with words, but there was a current flowing through my body, and I felt so happy. He lay right by my side and cuddled me for a few minutes while I went through the motions of the scene, which for me is usually crying followed by giggles. After my emotions settled, we started to play again, and he reached for the glass dildo. I was still feeling a bit shy in his presence because I was not as wet as I knew I could be, but once inside me, the toy felt great. The dildo was not shaped like a penis; it was made up of ball-like textures, and every time it went in and out, each of the balls massaged my G-spot and I love it. Paired with the vibrator, he made me orgasm multiple times, one after the other until I was shaking.

We took a break, and he lay down to my left side facing me, my eyes still showing pleasure as I looked up at him. He wrapped his left hand around my neck, and putting pressure on it, he brought his lips so close to mine. I wanted to kiss and bite him so bad, but I was immobile, and I was scared he wouldn't let me.

"I want to kiss you," I said. And I don't remember exactly his response, but he didn't let me. I hated and loved it at the same time. I giggled.

He started caressing my pussy again, and suddenly he slapped it hard.

I said, "Ouch, no!"

"Start counting."

"What do you mean?"

"Three?"

"Three."

"What do you say?"

I said, "I don't know. What do you mean?"

In a demanding tone, he said, "You say thank you."

I was so confused. I just stayed quiet. Then he slapped it again just as hard.

He said, "Two?

"Two."

He waited for me to say it.

"Thank you?"

And lastly, he did a gentle tap that felt so delicious.

"See what you get when you're a good girl?"

Apparently, this is a common thing to do in BDSM, but since I'm completely new, I just didn't know what was happening. I'm sure he loved the fact that he was the first to show me.

He got back up and started playing with the vibrator and dildo at the same time, and after just a couple of minutes, I was starting to feel the big wave building up inside me. I kept my eyes locked onto his. He was so focused and serious. The way he looked back at me and then slowly back down into what he's doing, absorbing all of me with his eyes, was all I needed to make the wave finally erupt. A full-body, brain-shattering orgasm that turned my body into weird shapes and my voice into loud echoes bouncing off the walls of his spacious house. As the orgasm settled down, he kept on pushing buttons, made me orgasm again, and this time it was even more intense than the last one. Playtime and all the orgasms I had before this moment were amazing, but these were the reality-bending releases that I love and crave.

Once finished with our scene, we went outside to sit in his hot tub for aftercare. I was still processing everything that just happened, and I was back to my shy and reserved self. But he was just like normal, talkative and nonchalant. I was paying attention to him talking but, at the same time, wondering why he was telling me all these stories. I was so bored. I just wanted to go home. I was dreading the drive and feeling a little deflated about the night in general. Our scene was fucking epic. I loved to see him in his role; it was so hot. But outside of that, he wasn't what I expected. Funny how I can be so creative and assign roles based on minimal interaction and then be disappointed when they don't follow my script.

FEBRUARY 25, 2024

Things with James have been developing slowly. We decided to give dating a try. Earlier this week, we went out to eat with some of his friends. Dinner was chill. His friends were a little too plugged into the matrix for my taste, but it was still a good time with good conversations.

After dinner, we made out in his car, and it was so hot. He came prepared with rope and a vibrator. He pulled my tight jeans down and used his fingers and vibe. It was a relatively busy avenue, and people were passing by the car, which made the experience more exciting. At one point, I was getting so close to climax, but then a car pulled up to the right in front of us. When the couple stepped out of the car and walked toward us, I had to hold it in. James looked at me with wide eyes, watching how I would react, and I was looking back at him like I wanted him to stop what he was doing, but I didn't really. The couple totally noticed we were up to something, and they looked a little awkward as they passed by. It is my hope that they felt inspired by what they saw.

After they passed us, I leaned over to unbutton his pants and feel his erection, and then I gave him head for a few minutes until my thigh started hurting from the seat belt buckle that was digging into it. I get that we were both very limited by the discomfort of the car, but it was such a fun and hot experience that my pussy was throbbing from the pleasure the entire drive back home.

Then, yesterday, he was hosting a community rope workshop at his place. I couldn't make it in time for the actual workshop, so by the time I arrived, most people were gone and the few left were just hanging out...pun intended?

Eventually, it was time for everyone else to leave except one of the girls that was staying because the next day was the community party and she wanted to stay in the area. She asked James if it was OK for her to park her van in the driveway and just camp there for the night, but he offered for her to stay in the guest room instead. I was not happy to hear that.

All signs had indicated that we might have sex for the first time that night, and I really didn't feel comfortable knowing that there would be someone else in the house limiting our privacy. On top of that, I know this person is very flirty and would love to get into his pants, but he won't do that because he doesn't like that she sleeps around with a lot of people.

I knew I looked like I was not enjoying myself. I was thinking about going back home, but then he picked me up from my chair, carried me into his room, gave me a fuzzy blanket, and offered me snacks. I told him I was feeling overstimulated by all the people and that I wasn't feeling great. I was also feeling super emotional because on the drive up, I saw a dead dog on the side of the road. I couldn't help but cry about it with him. I really needed to let it out. Then he put some funny videos on his laptop. After laughing for a few minutes, I started to feel much better about staying in his bed. Now that we were alone in his room and his friend was out there doing her own thing, I didn't care so much anymore. As a matter of fact, knowing that someone could hear me get something they wanted was one of my biggest turn-ons later when things started to get hot.

We started making out. One thing led to the other, and then next thing I knew, we were having sex, and I had to ask for permission to orgasm every time I was getting close. I didn't want to do it at first when he told me to, and I did have an amazing orgasm without asking, but he said if I came without his permission again, he was going to put lidocaine on my clit and I wouldn't feel anything after that. So I followed his directions, and the next time I approached climax, I asked.

"Can I come?"

"Come for me."

Something about the firmness of his tone and dead-serious face when he said it just made me explode. It made my orgasm so much more intense than I anticipated. I was moaning and shaking for what felt like ten long minutes. It was so good that I needed a break after that. But he didn't let me rest for long before putting his dick in my mouth and pushing it deep in my throat. He could go for a long time, but I was just feeling so exhausted. All I know is that he made me come another couple times, and he didn't come at all. But that was nothing new; it's been all about my orgasms every other time we played anyway. In the relationships I had early in my life, the men almost always left me wanting more. The fact that the tables have turned, and I am the one getting more than they do, is not something to complain about.

I used my long drive back home to feel grateful that the sex was as good as it was, but I also felt confused about it all. This man does not have what I need in a relationship. He is not affectionate, and although I know he likes me, he doesn't show much interest in me. I would love to keep him as a play partner or a friend with benefits, but I know myself, and eventually, I'm going to want more than what he can give. It's very confusing because I know at my core this is not the person I will want to have something serious with, but the heart is an interesting organ, and feelings are not rational.

FEBRUARY 28, 2024

I'm reading back what I was writing about around this time last year. It's crazy how feelings toward a person can change. When I first met J, I saw him so differently than how I see him now. He really left a bitter taste in my mouth after that last call when he showed me the worst of him. What's interesting is that his worst was always part of him; I just didn't always have access to it. I wonder if I would have perceived his worst in a different light if my love for him was enough to work through it. The truth is, I loved the idea of him more than I loved him. I loved how he treated me, I loved the good father he was, and so much more. But deep inside, it never felt like it was sufficient. It was missing a deep knowing that I've never experienced.

I've done enough internal work to know that what I am about to say is not rational, but I do wonder if I ever will find that person that I could see myself loving for a long time. A life partner, a person that I will want to build a home with. Someone that I look up to and see as my rock. Someone that I look forward to seeing at the end of the day. Someone that will love me for who I am, including my past and endless curiosity. Someone that I find attractive even on their worst days and want to jump their bones at the mere sight of their body.

I'm approaching the end of an era in my life. I only have a couple of months left in the place I have called home for the last five years. I recently learned the meaning of a new word, *énouement*, which describes the feeling of knowing the end of something is approaching, and that's exactly what I'm feeling right now. It feels unstable, like I need to spend more time in nature, grounding with Mother Earth.

I'm also starting to feel a little numb to all the new adventures I'm living. What most people would consider hardcore feels so normal for me now. It's kind of the story of my life, right? Feeling so excited and eager about new things, relationships, and projects and slowly losing the enthusiasm when the newness wears off. I'm really worried about what people would think if I put my writing out there like this. Would this be an issue later to find a life partner? I wonder if I can make this anonymous. My body is feeling very turned on by that idea. I know the attention whore in me wants to share with everybody, but the thought of no one knowing where this came from really excites me, even if eventually it comes to light. How does one even launch a book anonymously and make any sales? I don't know anything; all I know is that I was feeling down when I sat down to write, and this has sparked some joy in me that I will use to make myself a delicious and nutritious dinner.

MARCH 5, 2024

I just got back home last night from a weekend at James's house. I was really looking forward to an amazing, sexy weekend, but I got my period the night before heading up. He doesn't like blood and made it clear that he wanted nothing to do with it but that he still wanted to see me and spend time with me.

Something else that makes us very incompatible: I am obsessed with my blood. I take pictures of it, I use it as paint for art, I collect it and feed it to the earth, and I love admiring it, so the fact that he is grossed out by it is a big no for me. He says it's because he's in the medical field and he's trained to see all blood as infected blood, but I don't care. It's a mismatch in my eyes regardless. I warned him that since I was on my period, I was going to be the biggest baby and that I may need some alone time, and he said it was OK. This time, I took the dogs with me since I was going to spend the night.

Upon arrival, we spent the first hour or so watching how they interacted with the space and his bird. After that, it started pouring and we just chilled by the window, watching the epic hailstorm. A few hours had passed by, and we still hadn't shared a moment of intimacy, not a kiss, hug, or cuddle, and we were talking like I would with a regular friend. I was being very observant of his behavior and what my triggers were teaching me.

When we talk, it's mostly him doing the talking, and when I finally have the chance to speak, I don't feel heard. I don't have his undivided attention; he looks away, checks his phone, or changes the topic. He doesn't have follow-up questions about what I say or show much interest in what I share, and I honestly feel so unseen in his presence. I know exactly what this brings me back to, and it's the relationship with my mom, where I try to get her praise and attention but I'm never good enough to get it. My mom speaks highly of me to her friends, and so does James, but what good does that do when I don't know how they feel?

Life has an interesting way to bring back old traumas, and at this point, I already know better than to follow the same pattern, so when I see he's not paying attention, I just stop talking and wait to see if he even noticed I stopped in midsentence. He sometimes notices, but I don't take it personally; it just confirms what I already know: that my needs will never be met in a relationship with him. And it's not even about "If he wanted to, he would." It's just not in him. Like my friend Kelly says, I will not try buying eggs from the hardware store.

He had been wanting to do fire play with me for a while, but I always hesitated due to my fear of it. This time, I was ready for it, or so I thought. I went outside to smoke while he set up the space for fire play. When I walked into the dungeon, it looked like I stepped into a ritual. He was squatting down, and in front of him on the floor was a big, black fire safety blanket. To his left side were a small candle, a glass with a clear fluid, and two fire torches. There were other things lying on the floor around him, but I don't remember what they were in detail.

He asked me to undress and lie on the blanket. He went over fire safety and assured me I was safe. But the moment I felt the heat of the fire over my body, I freaked out and asked him to stop. I was feeling so disconnected from him, and I really needed a moment of intimacy to be able to surrender. With tears in my eyes, I sat on his lap facing him with my legs wrapped around him. We gazed into each other's eyes, and he held me in his arms. I needed him to tell me that I would be safe, so he did.

Feeling much better, I lay back down, and I closed my eyes. He was bringing the fire torch close to my skin to warm me up, then touching me with it, quickly followed by the caress of his hand. I was able to take it in if I made the mental effort to do so, but every now and then, it scared me again. He started to drag the torch at slower speeds, and I felt the sensations lingering on my skin. He let me know that my skin was then catching on fire and asked me to open my eyes to watch it. It went out fast, but it was cool to see it, and when he did it on my lower belly near my pubic mound, it felt arousing.

From there, he made a ring on my chest with some sort of hair mousse. I was terrified because it was so close to my face, but he brought the torch to the mousse slowly, and I saw the flame go back and forth around on the surface of the circle. After that, he placed a loose piece of cotton on my left thigh and lit it. This one scared the shit out of me because it made a loud sound and a big flame, but it lasted less than a second, so I just laughed after it went off. Then he did it again, but right on my chest, and he made me watch it. Knowing it was going to be a sudden sound, I was bracing myself for the flame. I was breathing heavily, and I screamed when it finally went off. I was really enjoying this, and I'm glad I didn't let my fear get in the way of trying a new experience. Lastly, my favorite was the fire knife; he lit it up at the base and dragged it all around my body. I was watching it as the heat followed the sharp sensation of the tip of the knife, and I loved how it felt when he came close to my inner thighs and privates.

Done with the fire, he brought out the magic wand vibe and started playing with my pussy. I loved the sensations, but I didn't see myself having orgasms. The fire was fun and exciting, but I wouldn't necessarily say that it was enough to feel turned on. However, at one point, he did hold me down with his body and force the vibrator against me while I put up a little fight. I liked it. I wanted to tell him to stop to add to the fight, but we had not negotiated this, and he would have actually stopped. This was interesting, and I'm curious to explore it more in depth at another time.

The next morning, I knew what was coming—anal play. He prepared an enema and administered it himself. I was so nervous because I had never done one before; I always just kind of hoped it was clean in there, and somehow it worked most of the time. The way I see it is, if I am having anal sex with you, it is because I trust you and feel comfortable with any embarrassing things that could happen. I was in the bathroom for, like, thirty minutes with horrible cramps. I couldn't even tell if they were coming from my period or the enema, but eventually I started to feel better and ready to play.

He started with the vibe on my clit and massaged my asshole for a few minutes. Then he tried to put it in, and I was like, *Nope*. I may love anal, but I still need levels of preparation. He got the butt plug and put it in. He played with it. He would pull and hold on to it right at the edge, and then I would push it back in like a game of tug-of-war. Once I was ready for more, he replaced the butt plug with his erection, making its way in very slowly and pausing to keep it in place until I was ready for more depth. I reminded myself to be open and not to clench for a painless insertion. It's just that first one that can be painful if done too abruptly.

I was lying on my back with my legs open and with him in front of me. I guess that would be missionary style but with the focus on my ass. When everything started to fit nicely and feel good, he placed the magic wand on my clit and started fucking me in the ass just how I love it. The way his penis is shaped was making it so easy for him to hit all the right spots from this position, and in just a moment, I felt the urge to orgasm.

"Can I come?"

"Come for me," he said firmly.

The way he nodded his head up as he said it with such assertiveness and a dominant attitude was so fucking hot, and it just made me so weak every time.

The orgasm was so strong, and I felt it everywhere, from my clit to my ass, with his cock pushing onto my G-spot from my ass. I didn't even know what else is being stimulated there, but it felt so good, and it ran through my entire body.

"You really do love anal, huh?"

"I really do," I said while still feeling the orgasm lingering on my body. "And I need a break from the intensity."

After a few minutes, I hopped on top of him and started riding his cock in my ass with the vibe on my clit, and before I knew it, I felt another orgasm creeping in.

"Who's my little anal slut?"

I don't think I was able to answer.

"Can I come?" And I just knew he was going to deny it.

He softly shook his head, brows raised, and said no calmly as he looked into my eyes tearing up trying to hold it in. I was really trying, but it was just too late. My face was doing a good job at hiding it, but he was inside me, and he could tell I was lying by the way I was throbbing. I was staring at him with puppy eyes, trying not to come but failing miserably.

"Come for me now."

And I could finally vocalize what my body was feeling.

I must admit, it diminished the intensity of the orgasm, but it was still so fun and exciting to give it a try. I don't remember how many times I came in this scene, but every single one of them was so delightful that the enema was totally worth it.

Later on, we took the dogs to the park to play, and I started to feel so disconnected again. It's so crazy how outside of the bedroom or playroom, it feels like we are strangers. I asked him a couple of questions about his life goals, and it got the conversation about compatibility started.

James said, "We still haven't had the compatibility talk."

"Yeah, I know," I said in a low voice.

"So do I have what it takes? You can be honest; it's not going to hurt my feelings."

I don't remember the conversation in detail, but I told him that I don't see my needs being met in a relationship with him, that I don't feel desired or seen around him, and that I'm not here to change anyone into who I need them to be. The conversation was brief and to the point, and it helped me be less in my head and more into my body the rest of the day.

Later in the evening, we started another new experience for me; he had just bought an anal hook and had never played with it before. I had seen it in some images before, and it looked hard core, but when I saw the hook in person, I really wanted to try it. It's honestly not as scary and painful as people perceive it. It has a ball at the end of the hook, so instead of a sharp end, it's more of a butt plug with a curved metal rod, and if you are an anal slut like me, it's all pleasure.

We were outside in his yard, and he started by creating the chest harness on me, and then we proceeded. I was leaning slightly forward on the table, and he was standing right behind me. He licked his fingers and massaged the excess saliva on to my asshole, then started pressing the ball of the hook against it. Right after noticing that I was tensing up, I relaxed my ass and did as if I were pushing out slightly, then the ball swiftly went in. At first, it felt tight in there, and as he was tying the hook to the harness, I felt every little movement. Once in place, he helped me get into the hot tub.

My back was stiff, trying not to make any movements that pushed the hook further in my ass, but the longer it was in there, the more comfortable I started to feel. I started to get curious about the sensations by grabbing the hook and pushing it down toward the floor, playing with the edge of almost pushing it out completely and then back in. At some point, my back became a lot looser, arching and curling. My back pushed the hook deeper when I curled and then back to the edge when I arched. While James was telling a story I don't even remember right now, I was distracting myself with self-pleasure. I wasn't even trying to hide it; my eyes would roll up, and a moan would escape every time I hit the right spots. At one point, I asked him to take a picture of me, and when I got up and leaned against the wall of the hot tub, the hook hit it first, and it reminded me of how careful I had to be. It was not painful. I liked it, but it was a strong sensation.

I loved it so much that I didn't want to take it off, and I asked him to please always put the hook in my ass every time I stayed over. And it even inspired me to draw one of the pictures that he took of me wearing it.

Before this moment, I didn't know that I could draw, and it helped me unlock yet another talent I didn't know I had.

MARCH 20, 2024

I am a firm believer that before taking on this human experience, we make a conscious decision about the kind of life we want to live. I wanted to have multiple passions. For me, that looks like growing a cosmetic tattoo studio, producing events, dancing, writing, and so much more. Time management is a tricky thing when you're self-employed because personal and work time collide and it becomes a blurry line. I'm always working, but I'm grateful to have created a career from the things I enjoy. Sometimes it feels like there are not enough hours in a day to do all the things I want to do. Yet, taking the time to slow down and connect with my body and mind is nonnegotiable. I simply cannot function without a morning routine where I check in with myself before engaging with the outside world. Sure, I can get up and go, but my day would just feel like it didn't even belong to me. My mornings are designed to explore my mind and listen to my thoughts.

Today, after dancing, I did some sunset yoga at the park, and it reminded me that connecting to my body in this way helps me feel so grounded and grateful to be in nature and feel the sunshine on my skin. I'm human, and sometimes I let the urge of the world get to me, but making the conscious effort to honor my basic needs has always rewarded me exponentially

MARCH 27, 2024

This last week has been a roller coaster. There are so many moving parts in my life, and it's hard to keep up. I'm saving up for and looking for a new home to rent, preparing for taxes, treating Tammy (my large dog) for a resistant UTI, dealing with car problems, and being busy with clients. At times, life can be challenging, but I'm grateful that at least business is thriving, and I can keep up with everything else. I was in a retreat this past weekend from Thursday to Sunday, but since it was just about thirty minutes from home and I didn't have the budget to rent a room or camping gear, I decided to stay at home and drive back and forth every day. The retreat was exhausting because of all the driving and all the work it required, but it was deeply transformational and profound.

The event was called Sol y Luna, it was focused on tantra, BDSM, personal growth, and relationships. Every day during the day, there were classes and experiences to join, and in the evening, we had a party followed by some performances and a sample taste of the Conscious Cabaret. Every night for three nights in a row, I performed, and although by the end of the retreat I was exhausted, it was so worth it.

One of the most profound experiences I joined was an exercise called Puja. It was led by someone that I already hold in such a special place in my heart, Priestess Francesca Gentile, a wise woman with the most spectacular sense of style and fashion. It started with an explanation about what she calls the inner aspects, also known in the world of personal development as "parts work."

This is based on the belief that we all have many different parts of us that live within our consciousness. We have the inner child, which includes all the ages we have ever been up until the present moment. We have an inner primal part, an inner protector, and many others. In my case, some of the parts that I can easily recognize aside from the ones mentioned are the entrepreneur, the peacemaker, the romantic, the author, the artist, the healer, the seductress, the manipulator, the submissive, and the dominatrix, along with other parts that have not been labeled. The main purpose of working with our inner aspects is to give them the space to be seen and honored. The way she describes it is something like a roundtable where there is the leader or higher self making the calls and giving all the other parts the chance to be heard. Ultimately, it is always the loudest part that takes charge, so it is the job of the higher self or integrated adult to be aware of who is leading and take control of the situation.

For example, let's say my inner six-year-old child gets triggered because someone didn't invite me to their party. It is totally valid for me to experience rejection and even throw a fit in the privacy of my own home or perhaps with a friend. Then my inner nurturer would come around and give my six-year-old part the loving support that she needs. All while my higher self holds the space by staying grounded and not letting the protector give my friend a call and rip them a new one.

Get it?

Anyway, I would say there were about fifty of us, and after the introductions, we formed two circles, one on the inside looking out and one with the outer circle facing the inner circle. We had a three-to-seven-minute experience with the person in front of us, and then the outer circle moved to the right to face the next person. With each person, we played one of our inner aspects—the primal one, the animal, or whatever the leader would guide us into. In one of them, we tapped into our twelve- or thirteen-year-old selves, and the instruction was to feel curious but suspicious about the person in front of us. We were supposed to get near them and then back up to enact this dynamic, but the person I had the experience with was smiling the entire time, and it was hard to feel scared. I mentioned this, and when he was able to get into the role, his energy changed drastically. His expressions turned serious, and his stare penetrated my eyes. Immediately, I stepped back, and tears started rolling down my face as a memory flashed into my mind.

I was about thirteen years old living in Cuba when my mom made one last attempt to send me to English lessons. I always hated school and any type of learning environment that I had no interest in. This was not the first or even third time my mom attempted to make me learn English, but the time to finally leave the country was approaching, and she wanted me to get a head start on the language.

The first class I took with this teacher, there was at least one other student in the room if I remember correctly, but this second class was a private one. We sat at a round table with the professor sitting to my right, slightly in front of me. Underneath the table, I felt his hands touching my right thigh. I was confused and completely frozen; I was acting like it was fine because I didn't want to make a scene and make things worse. I thought if I just played it cool, it would be no time before the class was over and I had to head back home. Nothing happened after that, but I remember the walk back home and how uncomfortable I felt. I didn't know how to tell my mom. I had already dropped out of so many classes, and I feared she would think I was making it up so I didn't have to go back. But my mother trained me well and always warned me about these kinds of situations, so I told her, and of course I never went back. The crazy thing is that until this point, I had never thought about this, and the exercise brought to my attention something that was shoved deep into my memory.

I joined a couple of other talk circles about polyamory and relationships in general, one about understanding men, and a very profound one about our suppressed inner shadows. All of these were great, but the best circle I joined was one that started spontaneously at a beautiful and delightfully decorated tea temple in which I got to meet Francesca in a more intimate setting. As the rain poured outside the tent, six of us stayed bundled up around her, listening to her words of wisdom and sipping on a variety of meticulously prepared teas. We could stay there forever hearing her talk about navigating our inner aspects, relationship advice, and the definition of the word *priestess*. We even skipped the other activities that were going on because the container we created was so powerful. When it was time for us to start getting ready for the show, she invited us to use her private room to change, which was a luxury since the night before, I had to go back home to change. At some point in the conversation, she told me that she used to teach sacred sensual dance, and one time she even won a striptease competition without even taking all her clothes off, and that she was playing with the idea of performing a song for the cabaret. Immediately, my eyes perked up.

"Oh my God yes! It would be such an honor to have you perform!"

I don't think she expected me to be a *fuck yes* about this judging by her expression, but I could tell underneath the nervousness, her inner diva was cheering up and down with anticipation.

"We are all about inclusivity, and having talent of all shapes, sizes, and ages is one of the pillars of the experience we create."

The show went great, the one from this night and all three nights combined. I am feeling so grateful about the experiences and connections I created in this retreat.

MARCH 31, 2024
4:00 A.M.

I just had a great time at a sex-positive party from a community I belong to. I will journal about it tomorrow in depth when I'm feeling right about it. But while I did enjoy my time there, I have some feelings I need to put into writing so I can go to sleep and not let them roam freely in my head. I can't put a name on this feeling or exactly what part of me is experiencing it, so I'll just start by saying what happened.

James took a friend to the party. She is a beautiful and hot dom, probably in her thirties. She only bottoms occasionally for the right top, and James is one of the few. He is always so proud of that, and he's repeated it multiple times. I told him I really wanted to play in my dominant role at the party and found people that would let me do impact play on them. After inserting the hook in my ass, we were in the kitchen and he asked his friend if she would bottom for him while I helped him co-top (both of us doing impact play while she bottoms). I could tell by the look in her face that she was not down for it, and quite honestly, I wasn't down either because I had already agreed with a few people to have scenes with them. I said something like, "Well, but she only occasionally subs for the right person so—"

Before I finished my sentence, she cut me off. "I *never* sub for anybody." And before they even corrected me, I realized I used to wrong vocabulary, and what I meant to say was, "She only bottoms sometimes."

That's when I reminded her that I was new and still getting to know the right terms.

I broke the awkwardness by saying, "I want to do what I want and with the people that I want." I was very firm, and he immediately understood. I appreciate him wanting to help, but I don't know what he was thinking by making that proposal to her when she doesn't even know me. Of course, she was not going to be down for that.

While we were outside and I was topping one of my bottoms, she and James started a fire scene, and I'm not going to lie. I felt some kind of way. One moment, he was showing me how to use the floggers, and the next, he was setting up the fire stuff and undressing her to start a scene. So I just kept doing my thing and paying attention to my bottom, occasionally looking to the side to watch their scene. From my periphery, I noticed how she would look either at me or in my direction, and when I would turn in their direction, she would keep eye contact. She was so perfectly still for a fire scene, and I genuinely found it impressive since in my experience with fire, I was jumping like a lizard. I made a comment about how calm she was, and I felt like I was wrong for saying that. She just stared back at me. Everyone around was commenting, so it's not like I was interrupting. At one point in their scene, something on the side table caught on fire and started a big flame; everyone kind of freaked out a little bit. After James put out the fire, she (or maybe it was someone else, but if I remember correctly, I think it was her) said, "That could have been on me!"

And I said, "OMG, yeah I'm glad it wasn't on you." Obviously coming from a caring place because it would have burned her badly.

She thought about it for a second and then said, "I would have come immediately!"

Again, I felt like I said the wrong thing when I was genuinely just trying to connect and interact from a wholesome place.

Then toward the end of their scene, he tried doing impact play using the flogger that set on fire, but the fire kept going out. He kept trying for a few minutes, but nothing was happening. I playfully said, "I don't think you're doing anything there. She's not even moving."

She just looked at me and said, "I am enjoying myself," but this time in a more firm and domineering tone.

I stepped away after a moment because I was feeling uncomfortable. I needed to pee, and my hook was feeling like it needed to be checked on. I wondered if this was just kind of how it goes with scenes and I just shouldn't take it personally (especially because nothing ever really is according to *The Four Agreements*), but I don't know. It just didn't feel like a very friendly interaction, but then again, my judgment may be clouded by some underlying, unconscious, territorial inner aspects.

I shoved the feeling of not belonging to the side, and I continued to play around with James. We did a short fire scene, and when things got hot (and not from the fire), we went to a private area where we had amazing sex. After finishing up, he said something like, "We have to make moves. You're driving all the way down to Miami, and I am my friend's ride home. It's so late; her kids are going to be pissed."

That's when it all really hit a soft spot. A couple of nights ago when we were figuring out the logistics for the party, which was in the middle point between Miami and Boynton, I had invited him to come to my place after the party, and he said he'd like to see how the night went before deciding. I was OK with the answer since that would also give me wiggle room in case I wanted to come home alone. I intuitively knew that it was very unlikely for that to happen, but I wasn't totally sure. The fact that he made the decision to be her ride home without telling me that he wasn't coming down to my place hurt me. At first when I was processing it, I felt like this was just a confirmation of where we stand in our relationship. He's not my boyfriend, I'm not his girlfriend, and this will never lead to anything serious and long term because of how incompatible we are. But then the narrative changed to, I have high standards for communication from everyone in my life, including friends, lovers, and serious relationships, and this hurt in a way that will need to be communicated and repaired.

APRIL 2, 2024

James and I had a two-hour-long conversation about our experience at the party. The first part of the conversation was sharing our favorite moments and a recap of how much fun we had. The second half, I openly shared about the moments at the party that I didn't like and how I was hurt by him not telling me that he wasn't going to come to my place. He told me that he didn't think coming home with me just to sleep and then leave the next early morning was a great way to spend time with me, that he would have rather make an entire day out of it, especially because he doesn't sleep well outside of his home. Then he openly explained how his avoidance of conflict got in the way. He felt like if he had told me that he didn't want to come home with me, it would have prevented us from having a fun night. But he realized that sometimes his fear of doing the wrong thing leads to him doing exactly that.

I guided him through a conflict resolution exercise that I learned at Sol y Luna that I will do my best to explain. One person starts with their perspective of the conflict, and the second person must repeat it back to them, followed by their point of view. Then the first person repeats it back, followed by anything else that they need to add. This process is repeated multiple times until they both feel clear on the issue. Here is a demonstration of how I explained it to him. I hope I don't confuse you.

I would start by saying, "If you really knew me, you would have known that what I really needed was to be clear on whether you were coming to my place or not, so I'm not left wondering if it's still happening or not as the night goes by."

And then he would say, "If I really knew you, I would have known that what you really needed was to be clear on whether I was coming to your place or not, so you're not left wondering if it's still happening or not as the night goes by."

Followed by something like, "If you really knew me, you would have known that I was afraid if I told you I didn't think it would be a good idea to go to your place just to sleep; it would have ruined the night."

And then I would say, "If I really knew you, I would have known that you were afraid that if you told me, you didn't think it would be a good idea to come to my place just to sleep; it would have ruined the night."

Then I would say: "If you really knew me, you would have known that I didn't care if it was just to sleep because I would have preferred to spend the rest of the night in your arms after such an intense party."

From there, he understood the exercise, and we continued to go back and forth.

"Why am I tearing up right now?" James asked.

"Is it because instead of yelling at you and blaming you for everything, I'm actually trying to have healthy communication?"

"No, it's because everything that you have said had me feeling heard and understood, like you genuinely get me. No one ever gets me."

With this conflict out of the way, I explained something else I learned in that class called the marshmallow rule. Really, it can be called anything that the couple wants, but the marshmallow rule is used when a person involved in the conflict or conversation has reached capacity and needs space away from the other. Calling "marshmallow" is a way to end the conversation with the promise that they will be back when they feel right; this way, it brings peace of mind to the other person. There is no need to say how long the time will be, but some couples may choose to set up a time for check-in where they simply will come together and the person calling "marshmallow" will honestly say if they need more time or if they are ready to talk, but it's important that the person needing the space is left to make the first move. In the case that the person that first needed the space reaches out, and now the second person needs to call "marshmallow," it is now the responsibility of the second person to be the one reaching out.

After explaining the marshmallow rule, I told him that was exactly what I needed, that a couple of days felt right, but I wasn't sure exactly how long I would need. All I needed was space from him and for him to know that he would be supported in his process. It was such a beautiful way to navigate this conflict, and I made it known that I was happy with how we communicated and that I was really looking forward to sharing more quality time with him again when the time was right.

It has now been two days since we had this talk. I miss him, and everything reminds me of him. But I'm also really enjoying the distance and coming back to myself. I feel so much peace knowing that he's not going to text me or reach out because it keeps me away from checking my phone in hopes that he does.

I had another interesting conflict with my friend Vero who was at the party as well. James and I were doing our shibari suspension scene, and she missed it. By the time she came around, we had just finished and he was about to untie me. I was feeling a bit dizzy because this suspension included some interesting acrobatic moves. The way that I was suspended was as if I were both the puppeteer and the puppet, changing positions and directions on my own as opposed to a static position that is changed by the rigger.

When she arrived and saw we were done, she asked me to do it again, and I pushed myself so she could see it. On the drive home, I gave this some thought and noticed an unpleasant feeling that I was able to interpret. Since I consider Vero almost like a mother, this was a trigger of my mother wound. In one way or another I always wanted my mom's approval, but somehow she always had something to say about how whatever I did could have been done better. One time, my mom missed a pole dance competition because my father was going and she didn't want to run into him. So when Vero missed my scene and I pushed myself to do it again for her to watch, it came from a wounded place.

Trusting that she had the emotional maturity to navigate this conflict, I told her how I was feeling. We both cried over the phone. She apologized, she told me that she loved me, that she is proud of me and that I never have to do anything to please her. She added that she was really upset to have missed my scene because she was navigating a conflict of her own on the other side of the property. It was truly amazing being able to express how I felt and feeling heard and supported.

APRIL 4, 2024

I spoke to James today. Part of me wanted to keep my distance for a bit longer, but I just reached out without giving it much thought, and I feel good about it. We video chatted for about twenty minutes while he was getting ready for a business meeting. His hair was brushed back sleekly, still wet from the shower, and his face was looking so bright. It was very refreshing for my eyes to see. I don't understand why I like his face so much, but I do. I have learned to love his facial expressions, especially anything he does with his mouth and tongue, his barely noticeable lisp, and the air coming out of his nostrils when we kiss.

It feels good to feel this way, and, at the same time, conflicting with the fact that he and I don't match at very basic compatibility needs. It's hard not to fall into the trap of wanting things to change, but I do remind myself that we are enjoying the new relationship energy and that it's best to enjoy the ride for as long as it feels good. With that being said, the call gave me the inspiration to share about some hot stuff that happened at the party. Every time I think about it, it makes my heart skip a beat and my lady parts tingle.

Arriving at the party was a little chaotic. I came straight after a very Zen and intentional tantra-focused event, and the energy contrast was a bit overwhelming. At first, I couldn't find James, so I decided to hide in the bathroom line, but everybody kept saying hi and interacting with me, and it was too much. Eventually he found me. We went outside, and after being cradled in his arms for a few minutes, I felt much safer in my body to go back inside. We had agreed that since he was going to be my protector for the night, he was going to put a collar on me, and I was genuinely happy to oblige. But when I saw the size of the collar that he pulled out, I had second thoughts. This thing was huge, and it did not look decorative at all. I behaved like a total brat while he was putting it on me. In my head, I thought, *If I want to explore my dominant side, wouldn't the collar make it the opposite?* Eventually I wore it for a bit, but not proudly as one should. Apparently, from what I learned, being collared is a big deal in the BDSM community, especially when it's done by someone with a great reputation.

We had our shibari suspension scene, which was unique, and a lot of people were really impressed by the acrobatic twist that we gave it. The inner attention whore in me loved it. From there came my favorite part—the hook! I told James that before putting anything in my ass, I needed at least two orgasms to loosen up, and, well, he did more than that.

He took me to one of the rooms in the party that was used as the dungeon, and he started by creating the chest harness that the hook would be attached to. As he was doing that, I was looking around trying to understand what was happening in front of me. About twelve feet in front of us was a sex swing, and there was an old man dressed in schoolgirl clothes, his back comfortably rested on the swing with his legs spread open and feet on each side strap, holding a bottle of lube on his right hand and occasionally pouring it on his ass while getting pegged by a woman. At first, I wasn't sure if it was a transgender woman because I couldn't see a strap on her hips, but then I learned that there are silicone panties that you could connect a dildo to, and that must have been what she was using. It was a bit of a mind trip and not necessarily anything that would turn me on, but I did like the openness of the environment.

Upon completion of the harness, James bent me over, squatted down, slid my thong to the side, and started to eat me out while grabbing my hips. His tongue felt amazing against my pussy, and I loved the way he was getting every bit of it, licking and running his tongue on my outer labia and in between the folds, then sucking on my clit as I felt the warmth of his breath coming from his nose on to my ass. It was so hard to stand, and I put my hands on the floor for stability. He stopped for a second and stood up. Then I brought my upper body back up, just to be pushed back down again. I was anticipating what was next. He was about to fuck me, and oh, how I wanted it.

All I could see was the floor when I feel his kilt come up and his rock-hard cock rub on my clit and slowly open me up, getting deeper inside me with each stroke until I felt all of him in me. I was gushing wet, and the position was making everything feel extra tight. My moans were getting lost in the music. He fucked me so good and hard and it was like a never-ending orgasm that built up with every stroke.

That served the purpose of opening me up. He put away his cock and proceeded to insert the hook in my ass. Walking out of the dungeon and around the party, I was super casual, but he was walking right behind me and making presenting gestures with his hands pointing at my ass. It was fun to see him and other people's reactions to the hook; most people didn't even notice right away because I was so nonchalant about it, but when they did, it was always a fun surprise.

My favorite thing about the hook is that once it's been in there for a few minutes, I forget that it's even there, but a tug or pull will make me stand on my tiptoes. At some point in the night, while I was topping some people with impact play, I would rest the weight of my body on their backs, and the act of curling my back to climb on theirs would immediately remind me of its existence. Same would happen if I were to sit down or lean against something, and it was so much fun!

After playing with some people, I asked James to do some fire play with me on my thighs, and I was pleasantly surprised to see how much calmer I was compared to the first time. The fire was nowhere near as scary as I remembered it to be, and it was fun to watch. After finishing the fire scene, he sat behind me, and we made out while he played with my pussy. My legs were open and facing the pool, and I could see from the corner of my eye that his friend was watching us play, and I wondered what was going through her mind. James grabbed me by the hand and led me to the back of the house, where they had tents designated for private interactions. In there, I got to finally get his dick in my mouth. I could taste my juices from earlier, and I was just so happy to be sucking on it. I loved the way it felt when it was in my throat and against the back of my tongue. I loved pushing it deep and kissing it and gently biting it. It made me so wet to have it in my mouth, and I love to make him come.

He grabbed me and put me on top of a massage table, then started to fuck me again. I could feel the ball from the hook in my ass from the inside of my pussy, and I could tell he felt it, too, by the way he was moaning. I never heard him moan like that before, and it was the biggest turn-on. With my mouth wide open and tongue sticking out, I asked him to do something I'd never even considered in the past.

"Spit in my mouth."

He looked confused, then leaned forward and slowly let it drip inside it. It was so fucking hot! I asked for more, then tasted it in my mouth as he continued to fuck me for a few more minutes. Then he got me down on my knees, and he leaned against the table. I was sucking his dick again, but now with an end goal. I knew he was getting close to the edge because his legs started to twitch and his moans grew louder. I was working hard to earn his delicious cum, but reminding myself not to go too fast or grip too tight and to maintain a steady rhythm. Using the thick slobber that he dug out from the depths of my throat as lubricant, I ran my fingers through the top and sides of his cock when I stroked upward and then sucked and swirled my tongue around the head when my hands stroked down. I was enjoying this so much and feeling how wet and throbby my pussy was when I felt him tense up, his cock starting to pulse. Time to decide. Do I eat it, or do I watch it explode? I really wanted his load all over my face but ended up sucking it right out of him and savoring every bit of his sweet, rich, and generous ejaculate.

Aside from the little bit of drama that was easily resolved, the night was a success. I like this community of people because they're open minded, nonjudgmental and consent/boundaries oriented, which puts me at ease.

APRIL 8, 2024

Today was a low-energy day. I spent last night at James's and came back home today. I had some properties to check out that I wasn't looking forward to. There was a little house that I fell in love with, and my application was rejected. Ever since then, I kind of lost enthusiasm for moving, but I still had to check out more spaces. I'm not sure how I feel about the one I liked from today. I love that it has a huge backyard for my fur babies, but I think it's shared with my duplex neighbors. I love that it's only ten minutes from the beach, the price is reasonable, and I really think I can make it work here, but I'm not bending over backward to make an irresistible offer on it. If it's meant to be, it will be for the price and move-in date that I choose, and if not, well, thank you, next.

After visiting the properties, I went to the beach and sat down with my feet in the sand to watch the spectacular sunset, thinking this could be my new sunset spot. And realizing how much I miss my ex-husband. We had such a stable relationship, no drama, steady day in and day out. We would go on mini vacations every couple of months and longer vacations whenever possible. Although there wasn't much excitement and spark, especially toward the end, I was taken care of. All this moving stuff wouldn't be landing solely on me; we would be a team, and it would just be so much easier. The brat in me is annoyed at the fact that I must deal with all this alone. She thinks, *Why do I have to prove that I am a responsible adult who can take care of myself without a man? I don't wanna! I just want to be a princess and focus on princess things.*

Another thing that had me down was yet another realization that James and I can't be a thing. I know this is going nowhere, and I've made peace with that, but I have reached a point where it's more energy draining than energizing. He's fun, and I have learned to be around him in a way that works for me, but the drive up north and then down south is too much. If there were other incentives, like him being more affectionate or perhaps offering to help with gas and tolls, it would be a different story, but we are basically friends with benefits, and it's just a weird dynamic.

James has a lot of female friends, many of which apparently would love to fuck him, but he is very selective with who he sleeps with, and he doesn't go past the point of having kinky/sensual scenes with them (this includes tying them up, using sex toys, fire play, impact play, and other BDSM games that are not necessarily sexual for him). Judging from the way that we hang out, I feel like another one of his friends with the exception that he reaches a deeper level of intimacy with me. Part of me feels honored that I am the one he chooses to do that with, but an even bigger part of me is not getting her needs met, and she's getting bored. From where I stand now, a perfect scenario would be to keep having fun with him at parties and events that we go to, perform together a gig here and there, and continue our friendship, but the long drives are not feeling right for me anymore.

Lastly, my fear of rejection and not being able to please everyone with my writing is bubbling up. In the writing of this journal, I have learned a lot about myself, and it is my intention to keep it real and raw in between these lines. But I would lie if I said no parts of me want everyone to love my writing and to be understood perfectly. I know I can't control people's perceptions of me, no matter how much I try to project myself clearly. Understanding that I will be misunderstood by many feels like a big obstacle. While I know that it won't stop me from sharing, it's got me in analysis paralysis. I'm not sure where to go from here, but the moment will come when I will feel ready to make the moves in the right direction.

~ ◦ ~

Eroticism transforms into art through the lens of the right observer, while in the wrong eyes, it appears purely carnal. Except for a very small percentage of the human race, sexuality is a significant part of living. Yet it is treated like a dark shadow to keep in the confines of our bedrooms. Having this kind of attitude toward eroticism has led us to experience it in very extreme ways. On one far end of the spectrum is the puritanical view of it, where we pretend to be godly creatures and reject the human nature. And on the other far end is the hyper-sexualization of everything and anything.

Often, many of us go from one end to the other without a middle ground. It's actually very common for folks that shame sexuality to be the ones that see it in absolutely everything. It's why a girl in the West is sexualized in school for wearing clothes that reveal their shoulders or legs, and women in certain regions are not allowed to show their faces and hair. What is sexual is merely in the eye of the beholder, and how it's interpreted depends on their view of the world.

APRIL 13, 2024

Last weekend, I drove up north to spend some time with James. He had offered to come down to Miami to visit me, but I was more in the mood to go up. Yeah, I know what I said. Life is nothing but a paradox, right? I have been so busy and anxious lately. I've had a lingering mild migraine for weeks now. I really needed an experience where I could surrender control, and I knew he could do just that. I've finally reached that point with him where I can let my guard down and be totally me. It's so interesting; he's kind of like the annoying brother I never had with the exception that we are intimate with each other. I've learned to go with the flow and interact with his clever remarks. He gets on my nerves sometimes but in a wholesome way.

He created a new experience for me that I loved a lot more than I thought I would, and we learned a lot about how pleasure and orgasms work for me. He set up his dungeon with cool red and black lights, music, and lots of toys. He strapped me down to a bench on my hands and knees with my wrists and legs tied down to the sides and my body rested in the center (this is so hard to explain with words!). My options were to look down at the floor or the large mirror in front of me. Of course, I was watching him through the mirror and admiring how good my body looked in this position.

We were starting with wax play, which was totally new to me, and I was giggling with anticipation as I saw him holding the candle in his hand. He let a drop of wax land on my butt, and I screamed and arched my back off the bench. It was hot when it landed, but the intensity lasted less than a second, and the moment it cooled down, I felt my body waiting for the next drop. The best part was in between pours because I didn't know when or where the next drop would fall, and all I could do was wait for it. He kept pouring the wax on me, and each time, he poured more and more as my skin became desensitized to the heat. The longer he went in between pours, the more wax accumulated on the candle. By the end of the scene, I could take a big splash of hot wax on my skin and enjoy the burning sensation without screaming or jumping.

When we stopped the wax play, he scraped it off my skin using a knife. I loved this part, and I could tell he enjoyed it, too, by how careful and intentional he was with the knife. The sensation felt like a long scratch, but it was not sharp enough to cut me unless he tried.

At some point, he walked by my side and grabbed my pussy. It felt so fucking good, and I moaned, wishing he would keep touching me like that with his hands. Then he grabbed the vibrator and placed it directly on my clit. I have told him before that the vibrator is too intense for me, but I still don't think he understands just how sensitive I am. He says he likes to do pussy torture and see me squirm, and honestly, I'm OK with that. I don't mind it at all. But what I have noticed is that everything turns numb, and reaching orgasm is hard. I am OK with not having orgasms. It's not necessarily the end goal of sex or play. It can still be a super fun and hot scene without it ending with a big explosion.

At some point, the vibrator started feeling less intense, and I started enjoying it. It felt good, and I started moving my hips in ways where I could control the pressure and placement of it. I was riding the vibe, and I saw him through the mirror getting the fucking machine ready. I was kind of scared. It sounded so intense, fucking machine...

"That thing is not going to be jamming into my vagina, right?"

"Just get lost in it."

He strapped my torso on to the bench tight and placed the machine right behind me. He inserted the dildo, and it felt so big!

"Oh, no, no, that's too deep."

Then he pulled it back out a bit. I'm pretty sure it was fine, but I had the fear of the machine destroying me. When he turned the machine on, I was pleasantly surprised about how good it felt. It was on a slow setting. It had a very steady rhythm, and it made a little wave as it went in and out. He slowly started to add speed to it, and I continued to enjoy it. I kept looking back at the machine and noticed myself getting even more turned on just watching it work and feeling how I was getting fucked by a robot.

While getting fucked by the machine with the vibrator on my clit, I had a couple of little ghost orgasms, and then I asked for the butt plug. When he put the butt plug in, combined with the dildo from the machine and the vibrator, it was just too much for me to handle, so we stopped. We went to his bedroom and cuddled in bed until he fell asleep.

He was wondering why I didn't orgasm, and I told him I felt like I disappointed him. He said he was the one who felt like he disappointed me. I know how much energy and thought he put into the experience for me, and I felt like my way to have a fair energy exchange was to have massive orgasms for him to witness. But just because I didn't have crazy orgasms doesn't mean that I didn't absolutely love it.

It took me a day or two to integrate the experience, but now I feel like I understand my needs and pleasure map even more. It was such a hot scene! I loved the wax, the knife, the machine, and all the toys he used on me. I loved watching him walk around me, and the way he was holding the candle above me was a huge turn-on. The only thing that would have taken this experience to the next level was slowing down. Perhaps putting the vibrator around my vulva first for a while before putting it on the clit or using his hands to massage my vulva gently before the vibrator. This way I don't reach the point of overstimulation that sends me over the edge without orgasm.

I communicated this to him, and he understands me better now. I think it's so important to know that sex and play are all about communication, and if both partners are willing to communicate, learn about the other person, and adjust to their needs, things will continue to grow. Nobody knows our bodies like we do. Everyone has different tastes and dislikes, and what works for me doesn't work for everybody.

For example, my last two exes liked when I slapped their limp penises, but when I tried it with James, he didn't like it, and I did it a few times before I understood that he just doesn't like it. Some people love having their balls grabbed and played with, but others are very sensitive, and it's too much to handle. I love that we can talk about these things and work toward even more pleasure in a healthy way without taking it personally.

In past relationships, I didn't know how to speak up about my needs because I didn't want them to feel like I was criticizing their skills. But now I understand that a person who is confident and genuinely invested in learning will always be happy to hear feedback. Both of us knowing this about my body has me excited to play with the machine again and just continuing to play with him in general.

APRIL 14, 2024

I went to the skate park across the street from my apartment complex today. It was my second time going there, and I can't believe I didn't go sooner. I don't know what it is about places like this. I think it may be a high school trauma from feeling like I don't belong with the cool kids. I used to always be so intimidated by skateboarders at the park, and that always stopped me from going, but I guess now that I've gotten decent at roller skating, I got the confidence boost to show up.

So today, I strapped on my skates, and since I was already nervous going in, I decided to take it one step further and added my pink heart-shaped glasses to match with my pink skates and pink hat. I rolled in like I owned the place. I tripped a couple of times from the pressure, but before I knew it, I was easily flowing, doing tricks, and skating backward like it was my job to look good doing it.

These are the kinds of uncomfortable situations I love putting myself through because once I overcome the fear, I feel a big boost of self-esteem. It makes me feel like I could really do anything I want because even if it's minor for most people, the fact that I got through the discomfort is something to feel good about.

APRIL 15, 2024

I have made a big decision for myself for the next few months. At first, I was very resistant to this, but right now I feel at peace and like a huge weight is off my shoulders. I'm going to move into my mom's efficiency apartment. It's tiny, and I won't be able to have my pole there. It's basically just going to be my bed, my love chair, probably something to eat on, and the tiny kitchen. I'll probably be cooking at my mom's big kitchen, and she's probably going to love it since she rarely ever cooks at home. Honestly, I'm not even going to count on that because my mom is the pickiest eater and impossible to please.

I won't have enough space for my pole studio, so I'll have to set up the pole stage in the backyard anytime I want to dance. I'm kind of bummed about that, but maybe that will be the push I need to start going back to classes since I haven't been to the pole studio in over six months.

This feels very humbling but like the right move for where I want to go next. I didn't want to make a rushed decision and put $8,000 on a rent deposit when I would rather invest it in my business. So the money that I had been slowly saving up for moving just went toward nine months' worth of marketing management today, and I feel so good about it.

I know being so close to my mom is going to trigger the shit out of me often, but I'm taking this as a chance to build on my patience and possibly strengthen our relationship even more.

I don't love the place, but that's going to be my motivator to continue to pour into my business and be able to move into the place I want and not just what I could afford.

APRIL 16, 2024

I just came back from a fire dance class, and I must say...I'm officially taking on a new hobby/talent. I love it so much, and I'm seeing myself shake the fear of fire slowly. I was able to balance the fire staff on my head and do a spin with my body while keeping the shaft in place, and from there, I did some air spins (I think that's what it's called?). I'm excited to continue learning more about fire and slowly start collecting props.

Since I won't have a pole studio at my mom's house, I will take this as a chance to play with fire props in her spacious backyard.

APRIL 18, 2024

I'm so fucking annoyed right now. This week has been extremely slow. I've had no clients at all. Since I made the decision to go back to my mom's house for a few months and didn't need my Realtor's services anymore, I still wanted to compensate her for the time and effort she put in helping me find a place. So I gave her a free brow service. She was the only client I had scheduled today, and I really didn't feel like driving to work just for her. I even had dreams last night in which we rescheduled for a later time so I could spend the morning writing. I called her an hour before the appointment to make sure she was still coming in hopes that she would reschedule. But she confirmed, so I closed my laptop and got ready to go to the studio. Only to get a call from her saying she was running thirty minutes late.

"I got caught up with something at work, and I really needed to take a shower before leaving, and I'm gonna be late. Do you still want me to go, or do you want to do it another day?"

In my head, I'm just like, *I just fucking got here* just *for you*. That's time that I could have used doing something I was feeling really inspired by.

I hate when shit like this happens. I could have followed my desires and told her that I needed to move the appointment to a later time. But I didn't want to be "flaky and irresponsible," so I told her I would wait because I'm already here.

I hope she's not wearing that strong perfume like the last time I saw her that left me with a throbbing headache all day. I don't understand people and their need to smell like fragrant alcohol. I hate colognes and perfumes. I don't mind it when it's super faint, but I would much rather smell a fart than those pungent scents.

Well, I guess I could be grateful that she gave me something to write about, which is what I wanted to do all day anyway. She should be getting here any moment. I'm on the rooftop of my building venting into my phone's notes. I feel much better now after journaling. Wow, this is such a powerful practice; it really helps release intense emotions.

~ ᵔ ~

I just finished my client's brows and I have to say: venting and allowing all the negative feelings I'm experiencing toward a person or situation really helps clear out the energy and allows me to see things in a better light. Normally, if I didn't do that, I would still be professional, but with a slight passive aggressive-attitude toward the client. However, when I came downstairs and ran into her, I smiled and greeted her. During the appointment, we ended up having a genuine conversation about life that probably wouldn't have happened if I had not taken the time to have an emotional release through journaling.

APRIL 24, 2024

I'm so annoyed right now. Can you tell me why I just got a notification saying that J just subscribed to my Patreon account? Isn't he supposed to be getting over me? Why is he sticking his nose all over my business? I have blocked him from all my social media accounts, yet somehow, he found a way to get the link to my Patreon. What this tells me is that he either created a new account or used someone else's account to see my stuff. On top of that, he acted like he's not hiding anything by subscribing using his full name and even a profile picture.

I didn't know how to deal with this, so I just blocked him from there too. Then I got a message saying: "Hey, was notified about your post yesterday. Hope you don't mind but my curiosity got the best of me. Thank you for all the reflections and kind words. Hope you're doing well, and I just wanna let you know that I hold no hard feelings toward our situation and wish you all the happiness in the world."

What the fuck does he mean, he got notified? There is no way he would have found this unless he looked for it. This is getting kind of creepy at this point. It's making me reflect on which part of me likes this. Why? Why? Why? Why did it have to end like this? I can totally see the part of me that feels like "this pussy must be fire to have these grown ass men obsess over me," but I can also see how this pattern needs to end sooner or later.

I feel like responding in any way to his behavior is only going to make things worse. My game plan is to continue to ignore him until he gets bored and stops trying to get my attention.

This past weekend, I hosted a small gathering to say goodbye to the place I called home for the last five years. It was just a couple of friends and James, but it was an amazing evening filled with experiences and memories to add to my collection. James brought his rig and massage table to do some suspensions and fire scenes. He also brought nitrous (laughing gas) for me to experience for the first time. My friends and I ate some mushrooms, and James stayed sober all night except for a whippet here and there from the nitrous can.

We played with energy orgasms, then danced for a little bit while waiting for the mushrooms to take effect. Then we went on with our rope and fire scenes. We keep working and perfecting the suspension in which I am my own puppeteer and make beautiful shapes and movements by pulling on the ropes with my hands and feet to change positions. We have done this now a total of four times, and each time, I have been able to make the transitions from shape to shape more sensual and intentional. There is still one transition that I keep making a little too harsh, but I have no doubt that I will figure it out. My friends took videos of the scenes, and it's so lovely to watch how sensual the energy was between us. The way we looked into each other's eyes as he caressed my skin and held my head while I was completely restrained and helpless was so beautiful to witness.

APRIL 26, 2024
2:00 A.M.

I really should be sleeping right now, but my brain is going a thousand miles per hours thinking about the endless possibilities of Conscious Cabaret. My friend and roommate Lili got a burlesque gig at this very popular bar in Wynwood, and I went to help her out. I did her makeup, drove her, filmed, and collected tips for her. I guess I can be a good friend? I feel like this is a side of me that I don't explore often because I don't have many close friends. But anyway, one of the reasons I wanted to go there tonight is because I had a talk with my cabaret team letting them know that I was ready to plan the next one and that I was jumping into finding a venue ASAP. I had been hearing more and more about this place, and it was about time I visited.

Upon walking into the place, I immediately fell in love. It had a chill living room vibe with lots of couches and a seating area with tables to the left side and a beautiful bar to the right. Toward the end of the room was the stage, and if you kept walking toward the back, there was more seating and even a cute little garden on the outside part. Lately, I have been asking the universe for a sign of its support to keep me in the right track, and this one was so clear that my jaw was on the floor for a good minute and a half. In the search for tables and high chairs for the first cabaret, I saw these barstools on alibaba.com (an online wholesale site from China) that I really liked because they were really pretty and only about twenty dollars each, depending on how many I got. Well, I was sitting at the bar filming my friend's performance when I looked down in front of me, and there were those exact same chairs! I couldn't deny that this was a clear sign. Perhaps it had nothing to do with this location specifically, but it meant that I was making the right moves.

Before leaving, I asked the manager if they ever rented out the space for events, and she connected me with the owner himself. I told him what I was looking for and a little bit about my concept, and he was excited to talk about it. He invited me to come back the next day (technically today) to check out the kind of shows that they do there.

APRIL 28, 2024
3:00 A.M.

Would I ever actually be happy with my partner after a party? Somehow there seems to be a pattern of something upsetting me at parties and leaving me feeling like shit. I just got back to James's home from a party, and although I had a really good time playing and learning to use impact toys, I'm really upset that I didn't get the attention I wanted from James. I really wanted a sensual scene and to have the hook in my ass again. But he was busy all night having scenes with other people, and I felt like I was chasing him the entire time to do a sensual scene. We did have a spectacular scene at the start of the night, and it ended with a massive energetic orgasm, probably the most intense I ever had. I beat myself up for not loving that and focusing on what went wrong instead of the good. Although I'm upset, I can recognize that shadowy part of me that enjoys playing the victim for not getting what she wanted and him feeling bad about not making the extra effort to have the sensual scene with me.

I can totally trace this back to my childhood and how my father somehow was always upset after a gathering. It's almost like I'm so used to it that I will find anything to cling on to feed that part of me that yearns for that familiar feeling.

OK, I'm coming back to this with a well-fucked woman's perspective. Last night, when I was writing that entry I was sexually frustrated, and I couldn't go to sleep at all just thinking about how under-fucked I was. I literally did not sleep at all. I got up with the sunrise and sat outside to drink my morning beverage, then I went to the play room and grabbed some toys and tried masturbating. It was interesting because I was so horny, but masturbating did nothing for me. All I wanted was his cock.

I went back to sit outside with my blanket and just let myself cry it out until I heard James coming out. I tried to hide it, but I'm pretty sure he could tell I was crying by his expressions. He checked in on me and invited me to go back in with him when I felt ready. When I joined him, I told him exactly how I was feeling, and he immediately took care of business. He went down on me, then fucked the frustration out of me. He felt so good going in, like water after intense thirst. All the time I was frustrated just made everything feel extra sensitive and amazing. I got on top, and I started riding his dick like I had just gotten nine hours of sleep and had energy to spare.

Now that I am a well-fucked woman again, I see how small the issue was. I decided to join the party at the very last minute, and he already had all those scenes planned ahead of time. We were both sad that we didn't get to do our sensual scene, and yes, that's a bummer. But a lot of times, things did go exactly as planned, we still had a great time, and there will be plenty of parties to do that and even more. It also doesn't help that I'm close to my period so I'm more sensitive to stress than usual.

APRIL 29, 2024

Shortly after the cabaret, I was invited to a yacht party by an event producer. On the boat, I got to meet some elite performers that I have always looked up to. Some of them were nice and sweet, and others seemed a little reserved and guarded. I was talking with one of the sweet girls about the cabaret, and she was telling me how she's been wanting to do something like that herself for a while. Every idea she was sharing with me was something that the cabaret had, and we were bonding over this.

About a week or two after this, the event producer posted an event announcement that looked cool. I congratulated him, then he told me that he wanted to weave me into it and that he would be reaching out soon. Time passed, and he never did. When I saw that someone I knew from a community I belong to was going to be doing shibari at the event, I started to feel left out. I noticed I was feeling negative emotions and decided to get off my high horse. I reached out, saying this: "Congratulations on your upcoming show, I know it's going to be spectacular and that theater is such a dream venue! I remember you mentioned that you wanted to weave me into the event. I know sometimes things don't exactly align as we want, especially when there are multiple decision-makers involved. But I wanted to let you know that I have been working with a shibari rigger who is phenomenal. We've been incorporating a lot of aerial acrobatics in our suspensions and have been performing it at parties and other events. Anyway, all of that to say that I'd love to be considered for future shows and gigs. If you have any cool ideas, I'd love to collaborate!"

The reason for me sending that message wasn't to try and take anyone's place or to plug myself in somehow. It was to acknowledge the fact that he wanted to make me part of it but he didn't. He said that we connected too late in the process (I call BS) and that he would love to add me to the guest list. I was happy for the invitation, but as the days approached, I realized I didn't want to be there, and I also had another commitment that I had forgotten about.

Anyway, last night after having dinner with James, we started getting messages on the group chats of the community that we belong to. Some friends sent a few videos and said, "The center of the table of goddesses is similar to the finale of the Conscious Cabaret." When I opened the video, it was a stage with women caressing and dancing with each other like the final scene of the cabaret, and to the side was someone throwing rose petals on the dancers.

I didn't want to be there because I knew there was a high chance I would be incredibly triggered that I wasn't part of it, and I wouldn't have known how to act. But when I saw the video, my trigger was so beautiful to experience. This is something that happened at the cabaret fully organically and without planning. Before the show ended, I walked around and asked all the performers to slowly add to the puddle of sensual touch and dance, and it was truly magical. So when I saw this, of course, my ego felt like the idea was replicated. But underneath the burning feeling of betrayal was a strong fire inviting me to step up and continue to innovate even bigger. I realized that good things will be replicated, and that's an honor. Our ideas are not ours to own; they're for the collective to experience.

The idea of rose petals as tipping currency wasn't completely original since I had seen it before at Zen & Kush, and I had probably seen the bed with women somewhere as well. So I didn't have any hard feelings and simply felt inspired.

Right now, I feel so motivated to plan the next show, and I feel like everything is aligning beautifully. I have a meeting with the owners of a bar on Wednesday to discuss hosting the next show there. I really, really, really want this to work out. But I also have some leftover trauma from the rental property that I really wanted that rejected me, and this is making that resurface.

MAY 1, 2024

I just got back from the meeting. I couldn't meet with all the owners, so the meeting was just with one of them. Before the meeting, my mindset shifted from really wanting to make it work there to, *How will they make it work for me?* I walked in feeling confident that only the best outcome was possible and carrying zero attachment to the results.

It's totally doable, and just like everything, there are some things to consider. The options are either going fifty-fifty on everything—where they put the venue and I bring the show and we split the profit evenly— or I rent out the space for the time of the show and keep all my profits. I don't love that one of the core values of the Conscious Cabaret would be lost here since they prioritize alcohol sales, which makes me nervous.

Aside from that, the venue is stunning and intimate with a cozy vibe. It has a 420 smoking area, great location, and good reputation.

Since they have never seen the show before, they want to see a demonstration of the entire show from start to finish, and they want it to be as close to the real show as possible. I do find this a little hard to do because part of what makes Conscious Cabaret is that it's not scripted. Performers get to have the stage to create from within and not stick to a boring routine. It's funny because he was telling me how the burlesque shows that they have are not selling as well as they used to, and I think it may be because people don't want to come back to watch the same acts more than once. Which explains why my shows being organic make a big difference in the performance art industry and has the guests wanting to come back for more. But how do I help them understand that people love my show because it is different when they have such a calculated structure to their events?

Since they clearly don't understand my concept, they don't know how successful it's going to be. It's hard for them to see how much they can really get from it, but I have so much confidence in what I got that I offered to just do the space rental where they make a set amount of money, regardless of ticket sales, plus all the food and beverages they sell. This feels better to me because the cost of the venue is comparable to the cost of the last one if we count the fact that on top of the location, we also had to rent out the stage and seating and add most of the decorations. It comes out to about the same, and the best thing about it is that there is no extra work to be done. The stage, lighting, music, seating, aerial rigs, and everything we need to run the show are already there. We just have to set up the poles and plug in the show.

My mind is running so fast with numbers that I haven't even stopped to process the way he was flirting with me the entire time, asking if I would do a private dance for him. I didn't necessarily feel uncomfortable or like he said anything too far out of line. But it's funny how different this conversation would have been if I were a man. I guess I've just learned to live in this female body and have dealt with enough of this bullshit to let it roll past me and not take it personally. As a matter of fact, I have learned to use it to my advantage. Being smart by playing pretty and dumb is the secret.

MAY 2, 2024

Where I am at right now is the junction of taking this offer and making it work to my advantage and putting aside the whole alcohol situation or continuing to look for a place with the same perks and no alcohol. I feel like having alcohol available is not necessarily a big deal because if someone is not a drinker, well, they don't have to drink. I think what I am dealing with right now is an ego thing. In the process of promoting my first cabaret, I talked about why no alcohol was important for the environment we are creating, and it feels like having alcohol as an option now makes me a hypocrite. But I also recognize that sometimes we must adjust to our environment, even if it's uncomfortable for a while, until we are ready to create the environment we want.

MAY 4, 2024

I have been feeling so emotional these last couple of days.

I've been taking little sobbing breaks throughout the day, and any little thing has me breaking down in tears. Tonight is my last night at home, and tomorrow I'm moving all the big stuff, including my bed. I still have another week to come back and slowly clear the smaller things out. But the pole and mirrors will be gone. I really wanted to take the time tonight and have one last dance in my home studio, but I can't even find the strength to get up on the pole right now. My body feels so heavy, and all I want to do is curl up into a ball and grieve this pain. I'm so grateful for James coming over and helping me move tomorrow and for my friends supporting me from the distance. But I still feel so emotionally alone in all of this.

MAY 9, 2024

It has now been four days since I moved out all the big stuff, and I'm slowly starting to feel like home in my new place. I still have a few things left to pick up, but I have been doing it slowly because moving is stressful enough, so I'm taking my time.

I'm not going to lie; I really like my new space! It's small, and I thought I was going to hate it. But I made it look and feel cozy and cute. I have everything I need, and I'm learning how to live in a simple way that doesn't require a lot of space. Of course, that doesn't mean that I will settle for smallness. I have big ambitions in life. But this feels like exactly what I need for the time being.

I like that I am back at home and close to my family while still having full independence from my mom's side of the house. My grandparents live just blocks away, and they visit every day. They all get on my nerves often, but I think it's a great opportunity to start practicing my boundaries and communication skills. My grandmother has been slowly forgetting things for some time now. She is still very healthy, but the early signs are showing, and I am grateful to be spending more time with her.

MAY 19, 2024

Life has been thick lately. It's just been one thing after the other nonstop. Starting with the stress of moving and still not having everything completely settled, then my car breaking down, still not being able to have a good dance or skate flow sesh, and having the worst day ever yesterday.

First, I didn't get enough sleep before waking up, but luckily, work went smoothly and the clients were a breeze to get done. Shit went downhill when I got home ready to take my time making a good lunch, pamper myself, load up the car, and slowly start getting ready to go to Turn On Miami for the show I had been practicing the entire week for. Then the sharp metal gate closed on the back of my left ankle right where the Achilles tendon meets the heel bone and made a deep cut. The pain was bad, but the worst part about it was that I was dealing with this situation alone. I limped my way inside the apartment and allowed myself to cry like a baby, watching the blood drip all over the floor. It was a lot of blood, and I noticed part of me wanting to bleed more just to see how bad I can take it. My mom and grandma casually passed by my window and came to help me when they saw me. I lay down for a little while, hoping I would feel better, but although it didn't get worse, it also didn't get better.

When I got to the venue, I was so frustrated because it was close to one hundred degrees (it was a record hot day), humid AF, and on top of that, the ground had this black dust that was making my feet feel sandy and gross. Luckily, I had help unloading the car, but for me even just walking around was extremely uncomfortable. Even just leaning on the foot would feel like my skin was ripping apart because of the location of the cut. I sat down outside feeling soggy and emotionally overwhelmed when I broke down crying once again. At some point, I went back into the property and lay down on some cushions next to a couple of acquaintances. They were so kind and helpful, and I realized that what I need the most in these situations is outside help and attention. The inner princess in me comes out to play and she wants all hands on deck. I used to get so overwhelmed when loved ones would gather around me when I'm down and ask me if I need anything, and I realized why that is. I wasn't comfortable saying what I really needed is to receive caring energy. That it is not about the medicine they would bring but the act of being there to serve me when I'm in need.

Anyway, I was very irritable and wasn't very nice to a lot of people there. I'm usually very intentional with my words and do my best to have clean and meaningful interactions with other people. But when I'm feeling irritable, it's easy for me to snap and let the little bitch out. Surprisingly, everyone was so kind to me, and it was almost like they knew I was just having a hard day.

My night got better when James got there and blessed my eyes with his cute face and a gift he got me from the BDSM conference he went to. He got me my first toy! And it was a riding crop, my favorite. I felt bad that it was just his birthday the day before, and I was the one getting the gift with nothing in return. But I was thrilled to have the first toy of my collection, and it was a nice one.

My show was the last on the list, but there were other erotic dancers throughout the night that were doing a great job entertaining. A big part of me was like, *OK, now I have no choice but to perform through the pain and potentially cause further damage.* This was because I was feeling very competitive and felt like I had to prove who the real deal was that night. Nothing wrong with my competitive inner aspect. I love and respect her desire to be seen and validated. But I decided to listen to my higher self and take care of my body. Luckily, Lili was there and helped me entertain by doing a burlesque act. I still did a little something on the pole as part of the transition into the fire scene that James and I had planned as part of the performance. But even the simplest moves felt like a mission, and I ended up feeling disappointed that I even tried.

The fire scene was amazing. I'm feeling more and more comfortable around fire, but I love how it always feels like a challenge when I encounter it. At the end of the last flame, I broke down crying like I normally would. But I had never felt this kind of release with fire before. I was feeling extremely sensitive in general all day because of the cut and the frustration that came with it, and this release felt delicious in my body.

James and I are concerned that we may have confused the audience with all the crying because later in the night, people came around asking if I was hurt. That's when it dawned on me that this crowd was relatively vanilla to understand that what was really happening was a beautiful phenomenon that occurs when someone surrenders complete control (especially with something they fear) to a trusted person. We haven't heard back from the organizers to give us feedback as they normally would, even though I reached out to ask.

I even got into a minor disagreement with James because of the crying. He was saying that I need to control my emotions more when it comes to performances (compared to personal scenes) to adjust to the audience and give them a good show. But he got the point when I explained that, for me, a big part of giving a good show is to demonstrate the real and raw beauty of conscious movement and the full range of emotions that humans can experience without shame or limitations.

The most important lesson I learned today is that caring for my vessel is always a priority, and that I can't perform at all if any part of me is not there 100 percent. It's like making a mediocre chocolate cake for a friend just because chocolate cake is their favorite when you could instead make the most decadent *flan de coco* that will blow their minds.

MAY 27, 2024

I just finished the busiest weekend of my life! This entire month, I have had gigs every weekend in a row, and now for Memorial Day, I performed Thursday, Friday, Saturday, and Sunday. All of that on top of a relatively steady week at the studio. *Abundance alert.* I'm grateful and very much looking forward to readjusting my internal clock again after going to sleep past 4:00 a.m. and sleeping during the day.

The first three nights were for a luxury swingers' lifestyle event where they closed an entire hotel in South Beach just for themselves to party and fuck all day. They were nice people, and I made such great connections. They treated me so well and went above and beyond to ensure I was having a good time. They paid more than I asked, paid for my valet parking, and gave me money for gas every night. I absolutely loved it.

I'm still not a fan of the swingers' environment compared to the kink environment because consent works differently there than in the kink community. There are a lot of consent-oriented swingers out there, but for a big part of them, consent is implied unless you specifically say no or refuse. I can still work around it, and it doesn't bother me a lot, but I must keep my guard up and my boundaries clear, which can be draining.

The last night was for Fetish Factory Weekend, where James and I did a couple of suspensions. This was a lot more chill, even though it was so much more hard core. Everyone in that room was dressed in outrageous fetish costumes. There were people dressed in all leather and latex, some of them wearing dog masks and rubber masks. Everyone lets their kinky, weirdo self shine, and I fucking love it.

James and I had the entire VIP session to ourselves where we performed the suspension from. It was elevated from the ground, and we were parallel to the main stage. The suspensions went great, and I think this was the longest I have ever been able to stay up for. While finishing the second suspension, I looked over to the main stage and was surprised to see how far the show went. On the pole to the right was a very handsome and athletically built man doing a split on the spinning pole wearing nothing but a steel chastity cage on his penis (ass and balls out), and to the left of the stage, a naked woman was doing a shoulder stand with her legs wide open and another woman behind inserting her with a dildo in her pussy with her hands. Like I said, outrageous and crazy.

Since I'm not much of a partygoer myself, I wouldn't necessarily go out of my way to be here. But since I was with James, I felt safe and I had a great time in our little VIP area with our friends. We were pretty much doing what we usually do at our community parties but getting paid and praised for it.

Today, I woke up around 2:00 p.m. and have been chilling at home with family and resting my body from the crazy week I left behind. This week, I have some important moves to make in my business, and I am feeling excited for it.

Today, while eating, I allowed myself to get lost in my food. The combination of creamy, crispy, and silky textures swirling around my mouth, releasing flavors with each slow grinding of my teeth had me salivating into another level of consciousness. The food itself was not an exquisite chef-made dinner. It was a poorly cooked mix of rice and red lentils that I put too much water in and cooked for too long turning it into a ball of mush and a frozen veggie burger that I threw in the air fryer and topped with artichoke spread. But it was well seasoned and cooked with so much love that it was the best little meal I've made for myself in a while. If I would have perfectly measured the water-to-grain ratio, I would have just gotten the classic rice and lentil medley, but instead I was surprised with this new favorite recipe.

While eating, I also got distracted with thoughts of the past and the future. But when I noticed, I brought myself back to the present moment, reminding myself that I may never again have this exact same combination of grains, legumes, and veggies, cooked the exact same way, with the same appetite. And I easily found myself back into my mindful eating practice. It reminded me that life can be a little salty sometimes, but I can still enjoy the other delicious flavors that it brings. There is pleasure in the mundane, but it's impossible to feel it when we are distracted by the noise of the world.

MAY 30, 2024

I'm fucking exhausted. Physically, mentally, emotionally overwhelmed to the point of burnout. On my way to work, I stopped by the park and lay down by a tree to cry and pray to Mother Nature for loving support. I'm carrying so much on my back, and I have so many projects going on that I just can't focus.

My main project now is my cosmetic tattooing trainings for beginners. I've created a program that is literally the best thing that has been created for beginners. All the trainings out there are so vague and short that it's just impossible for a newbie to learn everything they need to know. But since they are cheaper, most people gravitate toward that. This really hurts me because I made the same mistake when I first started learning, and it cost me so much more money in the long run. But the real reason why it hurts me is because I feel like no matter what I do in this industry, it's like no one can see the value in it. I've questioned so many times if this is even the right path for me. And the answer somehow always seems to be yes.

Don't get me wrong, my career pays the bills, and I'm comfortable where I'm at. But I know there is so much more potential that I still haven't unlocked. I've read so many books about personal development and listened to so many entrepreneurial podcasts, and I continue to stay stuck with the same income, no matter how much work I put into it, and I know why. Everyone I see succeeding significantly in PMU has all their energy completely focused on it. But I can't do that. I have so many extremely different passions, and it's so painfully hard to just stick to one thing. I love tattooing, and I also love performing, I love writing, I love producing events, and I love the world of tantra and conscious kink and everything related to sexuality work. It's so hard and frustrating, feeling like I'm stuck when I have so much to offer. I don't know what kind of kink or energetic blocks I have that I haven't figure out yet, but I'm done trying to figure it out on my own, and I'm praying to the universe to have my back and push me in the right direction.

Now I'm really holding myself back from diving into the world of conscious kink and learning how to be an intentional dominatrix because although I feel intense passion and attraction toward that, I'm also extremely fearful that it's just going to be the next shiny object until a new one comes along.

There are times in my life where I'm happy to be the way I am, and I'm grateful for the never-ending options to choose from. But sometimes reality hits, and I have bills to pay, that's when it gets hard for me.

Here are some post-*perreta* (tantrum) downloads.

After feeling sad and mopey all day, I got home from the studio and prepared myself a little bowl to smoke with the intention to numb the feelings for a little bit. I'm not one to hide from the intensity of life, so for that reason, I allow myself to consciously detach from time to time. I have been doing a little more of that than usual lately, and I was feeling a bit of shame for it. I also allowed that for the time being, fully accepting where I am now. Then, slowly, things started to look better when I received the down payment deposit from my first student for the program I'm teaching in a few weeks! Suddenly hope started to crawl back in and ideas started flowing. Earlier, I asked source and the tree I sat next to, to show me a sign of encouragement. I prayed for help, and this was a clear sign that my prayers were heard.

Root Chakra (Muladhara) – Grounding, stability, survival, basic needs, security.

This is one of my favorite pieces that I've created. When I stare at it during meditation, I find myself completely lost in its intricate details, as if it's pulling me into a deeper state of presence. Whenever I feel flustered or overwhelmed, I sit in front of this painting, take deep breaths, and imagine myself being drawn into the earth through this portal. Almost instantly, a sense of grounding washes over me.

Interestingly, I wasn't consciously intending this effect when I painted it. But after spending time with the piece, I started to notice something fascinating—hidden within the patterns are countless faces. So far, I've counted 16! It feels as though ancestral wisdom and unseen energies are woven into the design, watching, guiding, and reminding me that I am always supported.

If you ever feel disconnected, unsteady, or in need of balance, I invite you to meditate with this image. Let it anchor you, reminding you of your roots and the unshakable foundation beneath you.

JUNE 1, 2024

Today was a good day. Last night, I had a gig with James that was fun and well paid. It was another swingers' party! I didn't realize there were so many of those going on all the time. I guess we have a lot of horny people around, and I like that. Let people have their fun as long as they're being safe and responsible.

We did our usual aerial acrobatics suspension and wowed the entire crowd. It was so funny how they all would cheer whenever I would change positions. The reason it was funny is because in the kink community, these kinds of scenes are seen with reverence and respect, so people just observe quietly. But the folks at this party were not all necessarily kink aware, so in their eyes, what they're seeing was a performance, and they cheered when they liked what they saw. I thought it was such a fun contrast from the crowd we are used to, and I couldn't stop smiling while hanging.

The best part of the scene was the end. So the theme of the party was the forbidden fruit and Adam and Eve kind of vibe. So for the last pose, he had me hanging on my back looking up, my hands behind my back and head leaned back, with my hair tied up to my heels and an apple in my mouth placed by James. Everyone went crazy! Then he bit a chunk off, leaving us both breaking the one rule we were given—eating the forbidden fruit.

We hung out for a bit before packing up and leaving. I was sitting on his lap sniffing him and admiring him. He looked so good, and I'm just so physically attracted to him and the way he smells. I don't even know what it is about him, just an average guy with a pretty face. But I just like him. At one point, I said, "I wish you liked making out." Then, next thing I know, we're kissing like never before. Literally, our best kiss ever. It was gentle and soft at first, then it built with more passion, my heart beating faster and my inhales getting deeper, indulging in the sweet scent of our breaths and the very faint smell of his cologne and sweat.

After the show, we went to eat pizza, and we had a good time being silly with each other. At one point, he looked at me and said, "Can I tell you something?" Then I was literally saved by the bell when they called his name for the order. I feel like he was just about to say something vulnerable, and the moment was killed by the garlic knots. Later in the night, he told me that at the last gig, he saw my breath coming out of my mouth during a suspension and that it was interesting for him to see. I asked him if that's what he was about to tell me earlier, and he said yes, but I don't think that's true.

On his way to drop me off from the gig, we had a conversation about how I struggle to stick to a routine when I'm working with him and how that is most likely due to me being so independent and always performing without a partner on the pole. We both agreed that I have some improvement to do in this area. I am very flowy and easygoing. I figure things out as I go. But he is a lot more structured, and he likes to know where the flow is going ahead of time, so we butt heads here. I totally see his point, and I told him that I would make a conscious effort to be more collaborative and work as a team. I also realized that this has been a pattern for me because it's not the first time that we have had this conversation. So I made it known that there was a high chance that I would do it again unintentionally, and that moving forward what I need from him is to know that I would never consciously do something that would harm him, us, or the performance, to please not take it personally or think that I'm neglecting him or his input, and to let me know how he's feeling in the moment so we can reach a compromise.

In partnerships, there is usually a constant battle that never ends. And I think sometimes we must accept that the other person is going to have traits that annoy the shit out of us. There is no such thing as a partner that doesn't trigger you. It's about learning to navigate these triggers in a healthy way and accepting and loving this person for all that they are.

After he dropped me off, we cuddled for a bit before he headed back up north.

This morning, I managed to wake up early enough to have my morning routine before heading to work. I wore a new, cute bright-pink athleisure bodysuit that got me compliments from all my clients. I had the energy to set up the pole stage outside by the pool and had some nice bonding moments with my mom too. Somehow, I ended up ordering two identical bodysuits, and we were matching and taking photos. Then, after setting up the stage outside, my mom decided to give it a try and learn how to use it. My grandparents were in the house, too, and they also joined in my party. My grandpa took a hit of my bowl to alleviate his back pain, and my grandma jumped on the stage as well when she saw my mom and me having fun.

Lately, I've been taking it day by day. I've had a lot of two-to-four-rated days lately, so I'm grateful to have had a solid seven of a day today, and I'm hoping (while detached from the outcome) that I keep the momentum going.

JUNE 2, 2024

I just had a powerful moment playing with my crop. James suggested that I practice my aim with a pillow by making sure I always hit the same spots. I felt myself getting into a rhythm and loving the sounds I made. I missed a few times and hit myself, which is what they call earning your mark, but for the most part, every whip was right on the money. I decided to play with my words since that's something I've been struggling to do. For some reason, I feel my throat chakra completely blocked when it comes to the role play part of BDSM. I feel so weird and cringe when I try to say even the simplest things, like, "You're such a little pain slut."

So I followed some advice I received once of tapping into a memory of someone that really upset me and to let it out on the submissive. I went through my old text conversations with J and immediately felt the rage building inside of me.

I played the song "Paint It Black," going with the beat, softly spanking my pillow and building up the intensity. At one point, the music changed beats, and I was hitting the pillow with the pulsating baseline of the song. I started cursing out the pillow and allowing things I would never actually say to him in real life to come out of my mouth. I allowed that inner angry misandrist to come out to play in a way that wasn't harmful to anybody. I don't remember exactly what I said but something along the lines of, "You just love pain, don't you? Is that why you went out of your way to please me and now are feeling sad that I didn't reciprocate that? So you can be the sad victim? So everyone can see how good you are and how poorly I treated you? Get off your fucking high horse. You're not perfect, you fucking peasant."

Phew, it was intense, but I felt so powerful. By the end, my hands were shaking and tears filled my eyes. Even my mom called me to see if I was OK since she heard me screaming over on her side of the house. I answered the phone, cracking up telling her, "It's all good, just spanking the pillow." You know, just one of the things I could be doing on a random hour of a Sunday evening.

I started looking more into the Shamanic Kink Immersion by my fairy godmother Francesca, happening at the end of the month in upstate New York. I really want to do it, but I'm saving to pay off some credit cards, and I'm not sure this is the right path for my finances now. It would be a nice getaway, which is something I'm in huge need of, and I would gather some skills in a field that I'm really enjoying.

So I've asked myself something that Francesca taught me. What else is possible and how can this happen?

I have two or three weeks to think about it and see how the universe conspires in my favor.

JUNE 6, 2024

So I just had a funny moment. I was outside doing my usual morning routine, drinking my lemon water and playing with Tammy by the pool. I was just wearing a shirt with nothing else, sitting with my feet crossed and legs open, going through some emails on my phone, when I looked up and realized the pool maintenance people had just walked in and probably saw everything! I immediately put my legs down and did my best to hide the fact that I was fully naked from my hips down. The worst thing about it is that I wasn't planning on staying there much longer since I had to get ready to go to work, but if I got up, my ass would be all out. It was a funny moment, and I was feeling so giddy just sitting there waiting for them to finish. This is just the kind of situation I put myself in without thinking. Now I know they come every Thursday.

JUNE 7, 2024

What an interesting day. I had so many realizations and downloads of information about the right path in life and career. I had a conversation with a new client that helped me realize I need to adjust my pricing to the current economic situation. Two years ago, I was able to see three to five new clients in my studio happy to pay my full price of $555 for a set of brows and $150 for the touch-up. But these days, I'm lucky if I get two or three in a week, and some weeks, I don't have any new sets. I'm still making enough with the lash extensions and brow-shaping services to get by, but I had much better days in the past. This client was so kind and such a great communicator that I made a decision right there without giving it much thought. I lowered the price from $555 to $388, and I feel good about it.

Then in the evening, I went to an ecstatic dance event called Expasion Ecstatic Dance Miami. I got invited by my friend who was hosting, and it was fucking epic. I honestly didn't have any expectations going in, just the intention of letting go and moving my body. I parked right in front of the venue, but since I had never been there, I got confused and ended up going all around the block until I found the back door. I felt so silly that I got so lucky with the perfect parking spot and still went for a long walk. When I walked in, I saw some familiar faces, so from the start, I felt comfortable and sat down next to a friend from the acro park and started stretching with her.

Right when everybody was gathering in a circle to start the class, I saw J's new girlfriend (or whatever she is to him, if they're even still a thing) walk in. Immediately, I looked behind her to check if he was there, too, but thankfully, she was alone. I felt my body contract and my back hunch over. How do I act around her? She knows me from previous events. We have had conversations, and she knows about me and J, and she knows that I know that they have or had a thing. It feels so awkward to be in the same room knowing that we both know.

And then I realized that I don't have to pretend that I don't know that she knows that I know. I can simply acknowledge the fact that something happened and that I don't care enough to let it get in the way of having a great time. Immediately, I felt my body expand with a big breath and a giggle. Then when the dancing started, and I found myself in front of her like I was bound to do at some point, I simply smiled and nodded. She responded in the same way and then looked away, and we both went about our own experiences.

And then there was the dance. Wow, what a magical experience! It started with a guided movement practice where we would dance to the rhythm of the music while embodying different elements one at a time. We started with water by making circular and wavy movements, then moved on to air, where I spun around and took space with my body, then fire and earth. All were great, but the fire element really activated me. We started building up the heat in our bodies with movements that made my muscles burn, accentuating my movements and repeating the same patterns over and over until I found myself in a trance that I didn't want to stop. The trance was so strong that I felt like I had no control over my body. I was moving so vigorously that I fell on my knees, and my upper body continued to do the same movements. I even hit my forehead on the floor from how rough I was moving. Then, without even thinking about it, I screamed at the top of my lungs, then stayed down for a second, and when I brought my head up, I noticed all the space that everyone left around me. This was such a powerful experience because although I'm used to these kinds of things, they are usually done in my own private environment, and I was able to let go in such a beautiful way in an environment that had a lot of strange faces.

At one point, we were guided to form pairs, and I didn't know what to do. I don't usually like following directions when they tell me to find a partner. This guy that I had seen at other events before was signaling to be my partner. At first, I didn't want to, and I didn't know how to avoid this. I felt like it would be awkward because I had a feeling that he was attracted to me, and I'm not attracted to him. So I had two options, and both were hard. One was to set a boundary and say no thanks, and the other one was to look past the discomfort and practice bonding with him even though I don't reciprocate his intentions (fully aware that he may not even be interested in me and I may be imagining all of this). This is one of the biggest obstacles that I'm faced with when it comes to working with other people in tantra and BDSM. It's easy for me to connect with a lover or friend, but I struggle with the feeling of bonding with people that I'm not close with. So I decided to dance with him. We looked into each other's eyes, our bodies rolled on each other, we played, we laughed, and when it felt right, I disconnected from him.

I danced my heart out, and I took breaks when my body wasn't resonating with the music and needed to cool down. While on the couch, I realized how hot and sweaty I was, and I played with the idea of taking my top off. I noticed a couple of guys took their shirts off, so I followed. I was a little shy and uncomfortable at first, as I usually am when I'm topless in public. I told myself that it was fine, they were just breasts, it wasn't sexual, I was just hot and this made me feel more comfortable. Guys don't have to worry about this like girls do, so I do my best to let go of the fear of what people think. I love this feeling of discomfort, and I love when I can get past it and be free in my own body. At some point, I completely forgot that I was topless, and quite honestly, I don't think anybody else even cared. The whole point of the experience was to be free to be yourself without judgment.

While dancing, I had an interesting moment. Somehow, I found myself on the floor with the music very slowly turning down, like when you go underwater and everything goes quiet. My body felt wavy, almost as if I were on psychedelics. I turned inward and moved slowly with the music. Someone dancing near me gently grabbed my feet. I normally would have preferred to stay alone in my world, but I wasn't bothered at his touch. From there, I leaned back, and somehow my upper back landed on him— I think on his knees, but I'm not sure. He tapped my chest, and my upper body went forward again. I wasn't aware of my movements, but somehow, they were in perfect synchronization with the way he was guiding my body. This interaction felt like it lasted at least three minutes, and then the music started to sound normal again, and so did my body. Such a strange and new sensation, especially when the music tuned out just like they do in the movies.

At the end of the event, we all gathered in a circle again and shared about our experiences. It was such a contrast from the typical style of partying that we are used to. Especially here in Miami, the clubbing scene is filled with superficial people that want to get drunk and fuck around; people can be so competitive and go out just to show off. But here, everyone is sober, dancing for the good of it and connecting with each other, and that is something to cherish. I'll be making ecstatic dance part of my life more often.

JUNE 10, 2024

What a weekend. Starting with the ecstatic dance on Friday, then a fire play class on Saturday, followed by playtime after, then shibari Sunday with James. I just woke up and finally feel rested and excited to take on the week ahead of me.

Let me tell you about Saturday. Throughout the day, I kept feeling this weird vertigo that scared me. It must have been triggered at the ecstatic dance class, but thankfully by the end of the evening, it was gone, and I got to enjoy the fire play class and party. On my way to the venue (which was interestingly the same from the night before), I was thinking about how sex with James had been feeling a little empty and that I didn't want that anymore. I wasn't sure sex was something I wanted to do today, and I was feeling kind of conflicted.

The class was interesting, and I learned some more about fire and safety. The party after the class was great. There were not that many people, so it was the perfect kind of intimate environment that I love. There was a couple that have been in the lifestyle for over forty years, and it was so nice to meet some of the elders of the community. James and I played with rope first and then impact, and I ended up having a better time than I imagined. He tied me up and suspended me from the ceiling and played a funny joke on me.

So the day before, we were talking on the phone about how anal play often comes with, well, you know...there is stuff in there. And he was referring to it as Hershey's kisses. So while suspended (fully naked), he spread my legs open and ate my pussy and ass. I was sinking into the sensations, and then he got up abruptly and said, "You have to be fucking kidding me," with a dead-serious face.

I was so confused. I knew I was clean because I'd showered right before, but I didn't know what he was talking about, so I felt self-conscious for a second. Then he leaned forward and gave me a kiss and passed something to me. I was hesitant to take it at first, but then I tasted the sweetness and realized it was a Hershey's kiss. This was so clever! We both just started cracking up hysterically. I couldn't even tell if there were people watching, but we were in our own little world with our inside joke. After that, he had me fully inverted and placed a vibe on me. This was so fucking hot! Normally, the vibrator is too much for me, but I think he has learned how and where I like it. I was moaning, and I could feel how wet I was getting from this, and then he stopped. I loved that he stopped. I love delayed gratification, and he knows that now.

After the suspension, we had some cuddles for aftercare, and then I asked for impact, which is unlike me. So we went to the bench where I leaned on and let him spank me. He knows I'm not into pain, so he went gently with toys that are not harsh. I could tell that he was slowly increasing the impact, and I was able to take it in. He placed the vibe on me again for a couple of minutes, then continued to spank me. At the end of this scene, I was turned on and feeling kind of drunk, which tells me I went deep there. Who would have known, right? I guess I'm slowly starting to like impact play.

From there, I went home, and he followed a few minutes behind me. I was exhausted and starving, so I made us a quick dinner, and then we went to bed. Getting ready to go to sleep, I started playing with his balls with no intentions of starting anything, but then he started getting hard and moaning, so that quickly activated what we had started earlier in the night. We had such amazing sex; this was literally our best sex to date. The room was completely dark, and I think that added a layer of intimacy for some reason. The sex would probably be considered vanilla, but it was so wonderful. I felt like we were finally connecting and making love. I was also feeling a lot more comfortable being vocal, and at one point, I started saying his name over and over, and it was such a turn-on! I love this sex so much, and two of the main reasons were the way foreplay started hours before it happened and the fact that I wasn't planning on having sex and it just escalated naturally.

Going to sleep with James requires at least ten minutes of adjustments. He sleeps with like five pillows, two behind his head, one between the knees, one by his feet, and one under the arm. Then I have to be the small spoon under his arm with the pillow. I love cuddles, but when it comes to sleeping, I need to have space, so when I finally heard him doze off, I tried to slowly sneak out of the cuddle, but the second he noticed, he pulled me right back into his arms. I was annoyed, but at the same time, I thought it was so adorable that I didn't even fight it. Eventually, I was able to fall asleep, and at some point in the night, we went to our own sides of the bed, mine being just a fraction of his because of how close to me he gets.

The next morning, we woke up super early to go scope out a location to do a suspension in nature over the water. To my surprise, we found a location less than twenty minutes from my place, and it was such a great spot. After driving a couple of miles off the main road, we noticed there was a very secluded dog park, and past the park there was a trail that led to the bay. The trails are filled with very aggressive mosquitoes, and the ground is mushy and so hard to get through. But past that is the beautiful, wide-open view of Biscayne Bay. I couldn't believe that this spot had been there this entire time, so close to me yet I hadn't known about it. In all the hours we were out there, we only saw a couple of people pass by on kayaks and paddleboards, so I was pleasantly surprised about this find! James went fishing while I ate some fruit in the water, and then we went back to the car to get the rope after we found a good tree to hang from.

He created a diamond harness (this is pretty much our go-to since it's the one I'm always super comfortable with because I have multiple points of support), and then we started with a predicament tie and transitioned to a vertical suspension. A predicament tie is not necessarily flattering, and it's often very uncomfortable. In this case, he had my hair tied up to my left foot and my right arm tied to the top of the rope. For the vertical, he untied everything except for my hip, which is where I hung from. He got some amazing photos and videos of the suspension;

it was such a beautiful view with the mangroves in the background and the water underneath with my hair floating in it.

We got back home all sweaty and exhausted after being out there for hours in the blazing Miami sun. We ate some breakfast, then took a two-hour nap. After the nap, we had more amazing sex for nearly two hours straight. I must admit, sometimes it's annoying how hard it is to make him come because it feels like so much work, but I love that when I have an insatiable thirst for his cock, he can go for a long time.

I had such an amazing weekend filled with adventure, movement, nature, and hot sex, and I'm so grateful for that. Next week is my cosmetic tattoo training, and so far, I only have one student signed up to class, so the focus for the rest of the week is to put as much content out there as possible to attract my ideal students. If I get one or two more students, I will be set financially to be able to do the Shamanic Kink Immersion in upstate New York.

JUNE 15, 2024

Yesterday was a good day. I finished a drawing from the last suspension that turned out pretty good, hung out with friends, and got another student for the class! I got invited to a party at the Faena Theater that I had gone to in the past but wasn't a big fan of. This time I was presented with a few opportunities to go, and I kept declining, but after the third time, I was convinced for some reason that the universe was conspiring for me to be there. Since I was in a celebratory mood, I felt like I might be able to have a good time.

I went to my friend's house and cooked dinner for us while they got ready, and then we left from there. When we got to the venue, there were so many familiar faces, a lot of people from the acro park and the community. That made me feel at ease at first, but the moment we stepped into the space, I started to feel so uncomfortable and out of place. The music was classic party clubbing music, and the people were all dressed very nicely, but I wasn't feeling it at all. The outfit I wore was nice, but I didn't feel comfortable to dance and let loose in it. When the show started on stage, I remembered that there was an entire upstairs balcony that most people don't go to, so it was a lot more quiet and empty. I watched the show from there, and when the show ended, I did an Irish goodbye and left the building. I had warned my friends ahead of time that I may leave without saying anything because I wasn't loving it there so they don't have to worry about me.

On my drive back, I was reflecting about why I was feeling that way when usually I'm pretty good about doing my own thing anywhere I go.

Was it because everyone there looked so rich and fancy (even though I know my friends and a lot of the people I knew there are not necessarily rich financially)?

Was it because the music that was playing wasn't my vibe?

Was it because I would have much rather be part of the entertainment and not the crowd?

Was it because Faena Theater is such a dream venue to perform at and it feels like an impossible dream to fulfill?

It's easy for me to say that it's because everyone there gave me superficial and fake vibes, but I think that's just my ego trying to feel better about myself. While it is true that this is where the bougie people of the city go, that doesn't necessarily mean they are shallow; they are just there to have a good time like normal people in this society are used to doing.

I was almost getting home while going through these thoughts and noticing that I'm feeling kind of good and the light of the car stopped at the red light in front of me looked interesting. That's when I remembered that my friend gave me a microdose gummy of psilocybin mushrooms and MDMA (ecstasy). I had total control of my driving, and I wasn't at all tripping, but I was glad to have been almost home to enjoy this in peace. When I got home, I stared in the mirror for a few minutes, watching my facial features melt and morph into different expressions.

Everyone always says not to look in the mirror while on psychedelics, but I don't know why I find it so fascinating. It looks like my face goes from looking full and youthful to mature and wrinkled. When I got bored with watching my face, I took my clothes off and caught a glimpse of my breasts. They looked so beautiful and full. I was in awe, observing my chest and running my hands over them. My skin felt so soft and smooth; the caress of my fingertips felt amazing. I couldn't stop indulging in this. I knew if I masturbated I would have amazing orgasms, but for some reason, all I wanted to do was touch my skin. I barely even touched my genitals. It was all superficial pleasure. I was caught up in the sensuality of it and the sensory experience. I thought I wasn't going to be able to sleep based on past experiences with psychedelics, but to my surprise, I drifted away into a deep and gentle sleep.

I had never tried MDMA before, and this was just a tiny dose for my first time. I always kind of stayed away from it for no particular reason. I guess I just prefer plant medicines as opposed to lab-made ones. I don't know, but this was the perfect dose for me to experiment. It was very easy and gentle.

JUNE 16, 2024

Last Father's Day was a bit traumatic, so naturally, I was bracing myself for this one. I decided to grab some ingredients from my kitchen and visit my father and cook for us. It's always so much easier for me to show love through cooking, and I knew he would appreciate that. We had a great time bonding over cooking together and then smoking before eating.

While eating, we had some interesting conversations about the stuff I'm into, like shadow work and psychology. We discussed *The Four Agreements*, a book that I had gifted him. He cried with me about his recent breakup with his girlfriend. We talked about how both of us have unbelievable olfaction and how much we like sniffing our partners' natural scents. I realized we have a lot more in common than I thought when, while eating and enjoying the food, he was complimenting the food over and over. I told him that I really appreciate all the compliments and that it's exactly how I like to feel reciprocated when I show love through food, and he told me that's how it should be done, that there is nothing worse than doing an act of service for someone and it not be appreciated. After lunch, we went for a walk and even found a fruit tree from which we ate. I'm happy with how today went. I guess this is going to be one of those things that I take one encounter at a time without setting expectations.

Also, I'm officially jumping on a plane for the first time in three years! Today, I finally bought the tickets to go to Shamanic Kink Immersion next week in upstate New York! I'm so thrilled to be attending after hearing such great things about it. A big part of me wanted to pour that money back into my business, but I have been doing that nonstop for the last years, and it's time to pour into myself. After all, I am the most important part of my business, and anything that is beneficial to me is beneficial to my business. This week ahead is going to be a busy one. I have a busy day of clients on Wednesday, and from Thursday to Sunday, I'll be teaching my first Spanish group class and leaving that same Sunday afternoon.

JUNE 18, 2024

It's been an up-and-down kind of day, literally one after the other. I had an amazing morning routine, and I even found a way to finally hang my hammock under the mango tree in the backyard. Then I got yelled by my grandfather for not having taken care of the car insurance renewal in time. This insurance thing has been a pain in the ass for the last few weeks. I think insurance companies are the biggest scam ever. They force you to have them, and if you don't, they suspend your license, and if you get caught driving without a license, you go to jail. So you have no choice but to pay for insurance, just so when you do need them, they raise your payments even more. So this was a stressful moment of the day.

Then from there, I got a potential new student that wants to come to the studio tomorrow to talk about the training, so that was a yay moment. Then I took Tammy to the park with the pond that she loves swimming in. I figured on an early Tuesday afternoon, the park should be empty, but when I arrived, it was packed with big dogs, which always makes me so anxious, thinking that a fight could break out any moment. But thankfully, Tammy just minded her own business, going after the ball over and over until she was tired. I love seeing her so tired after a fun day. I always say a tired doggy is a happy doggy. I got back home and got very productive, catching up with some house chores.

Then I went about two blocks from home to get the car vacuumed at the self-service spot. There was a line that I had to wait about ten minutes in, and while I was waiting, someone cut me off and took the next available spot. I couldn't believe my eyes. This woman passed by, looked me in the eyes, and shamelessly took the spot I was waiting for. Normally, this is not how I would react, but I'm in the luteal phase of my menstrual cycle (the days where PMS symptoms may show up), and I'm not as patient and easygoing as I usually am, so I went up to her and confronted her when she got out of the car. She just completely ignored me and kept doing her own thing, which just enraged me even more.

Another spot opened, and I vacuumed my car while fuming. Right when I had finished, she came over to use a machine in front of my car, and I tried to talk to her calmly about what happened, but she was very defensive and hostile, avoiding eye contact and not letting me speak. The entire time, I was staring at her cosmetic tattoos, wishing I could fix them. She had that ugly black-and-white eyeliner tattoo that faded into a blue-and-yellow line (the reason why I would never do this for my clients even if they beg and pay me for it), and her brows looked super patchy and gray with poorly tattooed hair strokes.

I walked away infuriated. When I got home, I acted out everything I wanted to yell at her but didn't—because I can self-regulate. I felt much better after this short exercise, and after smoking, I had so many insights. I may be totally off from reality, but I think the reason why I was so shook by this is because I wouldn't do that to someone else, and the fact that people out there behave like this had me in disbelief. In my world, there is no need to ever cut someone off at the vacuums, so that leads me to assume that she must have been in a crazy rush (doubt it by the way she was conversing on the phone), or she's used to living in a world where she has to compete and beat other people to the line. It made me lose a little bit of hope for humanity. When wrong is easy and right is hard, not many of us have the capacity to do better. This explains why all the permanent makeup she had done looked so shitty. She probably didn't do the research or have the budget for a job well done, so she got her face botched permanently.

Eventually, I got over the drama and had a nice little twerk session, showered, and made myself dinner. After dinner, I got the brilliant idea to get high again and do a self-love ritual with intentions for manifestation. I started warming up on the freshly washed carpet to some sensual R&B music, but the warm-up turned into a beautiful, erotic self-pleasure practice. I stretched and moved my body very slowly to the music and felt my skin with my hands—feeling and gently pressing my neck, then running my fingers through my lips and nose and eyes, rocking my hips, arching my back, and waving my legs in the air, keeping the attention away from my genitals and only stimulating them occasionally and softly. Everything else faded, and I imagined being watched putting on this show. When the session finished and my thighs brushed against each other, I could feel the natural lubrication of my pussy stretching from skin to skin.

That was completely different from what I was planning, but I felt so good doing it that I didn't have the desire to do anything further. I realized that a lot of pleasure is felt in the buildup and the wanting and that I want to keep on building until the next time I ovulate, which is in three weeks. I'm really excited for this experiment to see what I learn about myself.

When I grabbed my laptop for journaling, I checked my email to find an insurance coverage proposal that made sense and a new lead for the class that I'll be speaking with tomorrow. Clearly, I shifted timelines with this self-pleasure. There is so much value in slowing down and tuning to my body.

JUNE 24, 2024

I'm writing today on my flight to Albany. The last couple of days have been riddled with anxiety. The training went very well, and my student (turned out to be just one student) was happy with her investment. I knew this day was going to be a little crazy because right after the class finished, I had to leave to the airport for my flight to Albany, New York. To my surprise, the day went smoothly, and I even had some time to relax at home before heading to the airport.

The flight was leaving from Fort Lauderdale, which is over an hour up north from me, so since my dad lives on the way, I drove there and had him drop me off. He was so happy to take care of me and give me a ride, and I was happy to give him the opportunity to show some love via act of service. I arrived on time, checked my bag, and went to the gate. This is when everything went downhill.

Short story is that I missed my flight. Long story is that since I had checked in to my flight the night before and I had my boarding pass in my Apple Wallet, I was going based off the information on that, but the gate had changed, so I was waiting at the wrong gate. This had happened to me before, and I had to run to the right gate when I heard my name on the speakers, so my intuition was nudging me constantly about the possibility of that happening again. I checked my email to see if there were any updates, but there was nothing. But for some reason I didn't get up to ask around until it was too late. Every time I remember this moment, my heart wants to drop.

"The flight to Albany is gone; it was at gate E5."

That's when I knew that I was going to miss out on a big part of the retreat, and I just wanted to break down crying. She directed me to the help booth to find out if I could get on the next flight. On my way there, I was on the phone with James, trying to keep my composure and self-regulate. When I finally found the booth and gave them puppy eyes, they were able to let me change to the next flight, which wasn't until the next day at the same time.

I really didn't want to go back home. I felt like I had already gone north, and going back home was like going backward. So I asked James if he would pick me up and let me stay at his place and bring me back the next day. He had a friend over, so at first, he was a bit hesitant, but they ended up coming to pick me up. It wasn't a short drive for them, so it was a long and painful wait. I couldn't hold back from crying until they arrived, so I just wept with long strings of snot hanging from my nose landing on my bag in between my legs. When James and his friend finally got to me, I sat in the back seat and cried like a baby the entire ride. I cried so much that my nose started bleeding. Every time I remember my intuitive hits and all the signs I ignored, my crying would intensify even more. James would reach back and give me a nice, soothing touch that I really appreciated, but my heart was shattered. When we arrived at his place, I changed into his clothes and hung out with them.

After she left, we got in the hot tub for a few minutes, and it was exactly what I needed in that moment, then we went to sleep. In the morning, I woke up to a very familiar lower back pain. When I went to pee, I noticed I got my period. This was a relief since it explained why I was so extremely emotional about the whole situation. Don't get me wrong—I had all rights to feel upset, but it felt so much more intense than it normally would have. I knew that I was close to getting my period, but I thought it was going to arrive closer to when I got back home.

James and I started to play with mutual masturbation and watching each other touch ourselves. I knew period sex was not an option for him, so I figured I would just have fun with this. But then things escalated, and he got in front of me and pulled my tampon out. I was genuinely so confused, wondering what he was going to do. Then he slowly started going inside me! I couldn't believe it. He was so nice and gentle, and everything felt amazing. I had never enjoyed period sex in the past because it would hurt so much, but I guess the slowness helped. I did think about how this would interrupt my experiment of edging, but I told myself I wasn't going to be too hard on myself if some things like this happened because the point of it was to learn and have fun.

I made us some breakfast and then was able to attend part of the program via Zoom while he was at work. I took a nap and rested for a bit before he came back from work to drop me off at the airport. This time around, I made sure to check the screens and go to the right place. At this moment, I have less than forty minutes until landing, which means I am finally one step closer to my destination.

Here is one good thing that happened that was funny. We were invited to bring any toys we like to the retreat, so I brought my riding crop, but it didn't fit in my luggage or my backpack, so I put it in my backpack with the tip sticking out. Security had to double-check my bag both times I went through, but it wasn't really an issue. The second time around, they just told me it was fine as long as I didn't take it out. Anyway, while walking through the busy hall, I overheard someone tell their friend about how I do horseback riding. I turned around and said, "I don't do that. I whip people." They giggled and thought I was joking.

I'm sad that I missed the first two days of the retreat, but there are five more days that I will still get to dive deeply into, and that is what I'm looking forward to at this time. Apparently, tomorrow is all about role play, which is one of the most difficult parts of BDSM for me, so I'm happy that I will be a part of that.

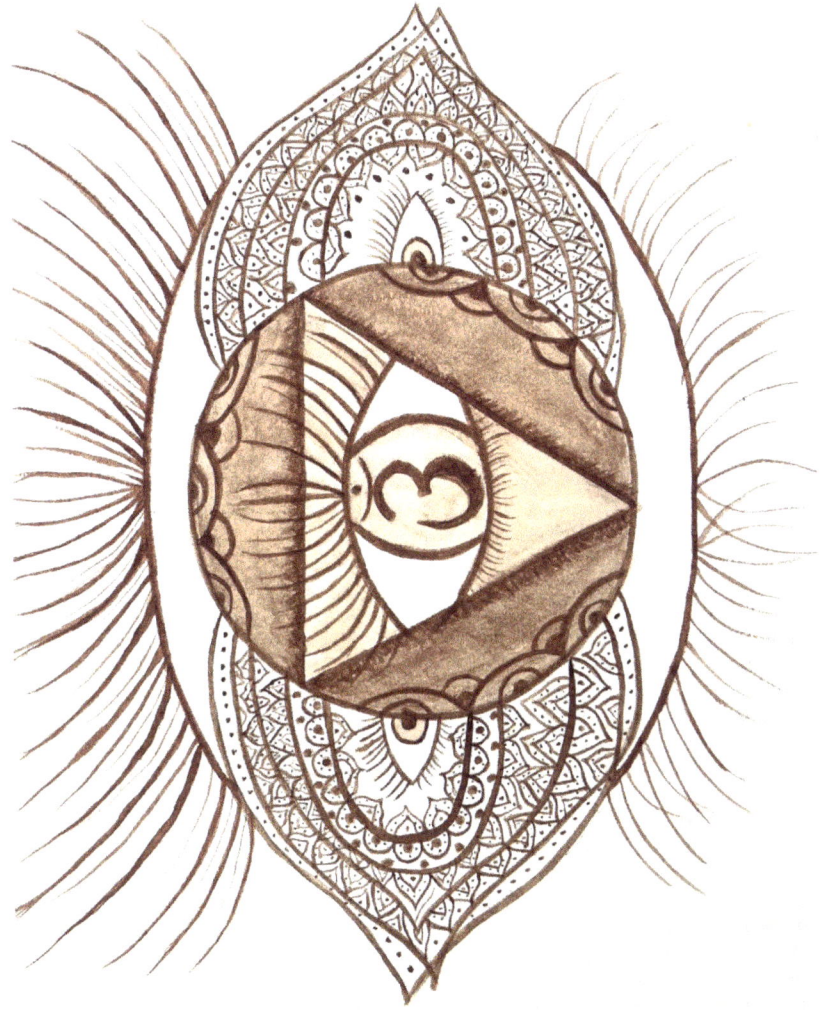

Third Eye Chakra (Ajna) – Intuition, perception, wisdom, inner knowing.

This piece challenged me at first because, unlike the other chakras, the third eye doesn't have the same circular shape. The shift in perspective threw me off—until I realized, of course! The third eye is all about seeing from a different angle.

Initially, I painted just the central circle with two lotus petals on the sides. But during my next menstrual phase, I took a second look and noticed I had the perfect amount of space to transform the entire piece into an eye by adding outer lids. After staring at it for a while, I realized something funny—it looks a lot like Sid the sloth from Ice Age! Sometimes, intuition reveals itself in unexpected ways.

If you ever find yourself uncertain about a person or a decision, meditate with this piece. See what arises—whether you see, hear, feel, or simply know the answer. Intuition speaks in many forms; stay open to how yours communicates.

JUNE 26, 2024

I've been really loving this place. It's an old ski lodge that was transformed into a sanctuary for gay men years ago during the AIDS epidemic. Now, they have opened the space for other conscious retreats and events. The property is luscious with beautiful plants, flowers, and wild little animals. So far, I have seen (and heard) frogs, wild rabbits, and many different types of butterflies and birds. I'm impressed by how smoothly everything runs around here with the staff made up of volunteers (mostly queer men) that exchange a few hours of work a day for housing and food. Everyone is so friendly and happy to help however they can. I'm staying in a little gingerbread-house-looking cabin that is adorable and secluded from all the other rooms and cabins. It can be a little spooky walking here at night since it's pitch black and far from everyone else, but there are so many fireflies that it looks like the starry night sky is right around me inside the trees. Right now, it's raining and a bit chilly outside, so it feels nice to be in this little shelter. I'm enjoying my own company, and I can't help but wonder what it would be like to be here with a lover.

Every day starts with breakfast and then a check-in with our pods. The pods are a designated group of people with whom we share our wins, insights, and challenges. Then class starts with a guided ecstatic dance practice followed by a lesson on something shamanic and/or BDSM. We have been doing a lot of guided exercises in small groups or couples, and some of them have been very powerful. I'm not sure if this is due to my late arrival or something else, but I am having a hard time connecting with people to the same extent that everyone else seems to be connecting. Everyone seems so open and comfortable with each other, and I feel like I have some walls up. A big part of me wants to be able to be all touchy and lovey with everyone, but I don't know if that's just not who I am or if I just need to know them more in depth first.

JUNE 27, 2024

Today was a bit intense. We were divided into two groups, dominants and submissive. The dominants were asked to create a sacred space where we will be guiding a scene, and the submissives were asked to blindly choose a station based on which one called to them without knowing who the dominant will be. During the lunch break, I went on a walk to gather some flowers for my altar and ended up falling asleep under some trees. Now that I am writing about it, I remember having some interesting holographic visuals with my eyes closed when I was falling asleep. Interesting...But anyway, I kind of overslept and didn't have time to prepare better for my scene. So when all the dominants were creating our sacred space, I was feeling so sad about mine. All I had was a jar with flowers, rope, a fork and knife, a riding crop, and stilettos as part of my altar items, and everyone else made such beautiful and elaborated spaces. But I trusted that the right person would be called to my station, and that is exactly what happened since the high heels were the reason they chose me.

We negotiated a gentle and sensual scene that was intended to awaken her arousal, but as the scene went on, she noticed that it wasn't working out for her, and she asked if I could be mean. I froze for a second because it was the complete opposite of what I was going for, and degradation is the most difficult part for me when it comes to role play. But I learned in this immersion that as a shamanic kink dominant, my job is to do what the submissive needs in their journey, even if it's challenging, as long as it's not crossing my own boundaries.

In that moment, I had to flip the switch and allow for the archetype to flow through me. Her hands were tied up and close to her chest. She moved them down to her knees. "Did I say you can do that?" I abruptly placed them back up and immediately felt her body come alive. The rest of the tying was very rough and pushy. I tied her up into a ball and literally picked her up from the harness and threw her on the other side of the mat. That's when she started sobbing. I put on my high heels, untied her legs, and placed her stomach over the spanking bench with her knees on the floor. I envisioned that I was her superior and intentionally walked around her, making the heels clack with every step so she could hear my presence. I lifted her head by pulling on her hair to be able to make eye contact. I looked down with disgust at her face full of snot and tears.

"Look at yourself; you're a mess right now. You like being tied up and helpless like this?"

She nodded. What came out of my mouth next was a blur, but it was something about how being tied up releases her from having to do anything and meeting expectations.

She cried and nodded. I grabbed some tissue and cleaned the snot from her face that was already reaching the floor, then I placed her head sideways so I could see her face. I picked up the riding crop and started spanking her butt, demanding that she say a number after every set of spanks to make sure I was staying in the safe intensity. After spanking her for a few minutes, I stopped and grabbed the most fragrant flower in my jar, and I brought it close to her nose.

"Breathe. Even on the bad days, you can still stop and smell the flowers."

And I continued the spanking. The rest of the scene was softer and more sensual. I ran the chain across her body, making gentle contact with her genitals over her clothes, and I mixed a few other sensations until it was time for aftercare, where I had her lie down on the mat, and I sat behind her, brushing her hair and calming her nervous system.

A few minutes into the aftercare, the dominants were instructed to quietly leave the room and meet in a separate space. The second I sat down, waves of emotion hit me, and I started crying—I was finally able to feel what I couldn't while in charge. Another dominant behind me started laughing, followed by someone else, and then me. Then suddenly, it felt like the entire room was laughing. We went outside to ground and release the energy out into the earth, and I felt much more in my body, feeling the warmth of the sun.

I learned that I can do the hard things and that I can tap into the dark archetypes if it's needed. In the past, it was hard for me to do that because of the environment and lack of intention. I was able to be rough with the rope and impact, but when it came to degradation, my throat chakra would be completely blocked.

After some time for integration, I sat with my submissive to go over feedback and was very happy with what I heard. She said that the experience was everything she needed, from the physical part to all the things I said. And that she was able to finally sink into the pleasure of feeling humiliated as opposed to resisting it like we all normally do in the real world. I was pleasantly surprised with her feedback and felt very proud of myself for creating this journey for her.

Throat Chakra (Vishuddha) – Communication, self-expression, truth, authenticity.

I struggled to make this piece artistically represent the throat chakra. I figured the idea would come to me as I painted, but it never quite did. To this day, this energy center remains an area I'm working on. It's ironic—I'm here, sharing my words with the world, yet I still feel blocked in this space.

If you find it difficult to speak your truth or if you've been oversharing more than feels healthy, I invite you to meditate with this image. Let it help you find balance, offering you the right words when you need them most.

JUNE 28, 2024

Another day, another challenge. Today, it was my turn to be the submissive, and I was feeling so much resistance that I even considered not being part of the experience. After some thinking, I decided that I could still have a scene that felt good for me, and a vision quest felt right. In a vision quest, the dominant uses impact on the body in a steady and rhythmic way to lead the submissive into a trance that allows them to receive answers and visions for healing or personal growth. The impact is not meant to be hard or painful but rather have the body be a drum.

Choosing my station was easy; I was the last to choose, so there was only one option. What got my attention from the altar was a flower crown and a small watercolor painting, and just seconds before finding out, I knew who my dominant was. We had exchanged earlier in the week at a small scene, and she was aware of my desire for gentleness over pain. I told her that I wanted a vision quest where I manifest more financial abundance in my life, and after about twenty minutes of negotiating, she helped me uncover my unconscious desire to limit my success because I would be the first in my family to ever make more than a certain amount of money and I fear that I have to take care of everybody else and be depended on. Crazy, right?

The scene was another learning experience. She was trying to guide me into a visualization of my younger self, but it was not working at all; there were no insights there to me. I had to work through the journey of speaking up for my needs and tell my dominant that it wasn't working. This was no easy task. She was being so sweet and doing everything she could to help. What she was doing would have probably worked in a different setting that was more private. But I realized what it would be like to be on the other end, and eventually, I told her exactly what I needed, which was the impact vision quest without the verbal guidance. Not too long into the quest, I was able to go much deeper and enjoy the experience.

Every day and night this week has been a lot of learning and working, and tonight being the last evening, we decided to have a small celebration, a temple's night, also known as a play party. The room was intentionally divided into sections for different types of play and needs. A corner for emotional support, one for cuddles, one for impact, one for rope, one for adoration where one can stand and be showered with love and praise, and one for deeper sexual interactions.

Throughout the week, there had been a few people that wanted scenes with me, but we were so busy that it was impossible to do it, and tonight was the perfect time. My first scene was with one of the volunteers, and it was so beautiful. I tied her up and manhandled her around the mat, surprised that I was capable since she was much bigger than me. I noticed she really enjoyed breathing and blowing near the ears and neck, so I did that sporadically throughout the scene as well as groping her butt and thighs and shaking it up. Overall, it was an easy experience without mental obstacles.

Of all the people that were waiting on scenes, my next choice was Bob or one of the other girls. A big part of me really wanted to go with another girl; that would have been so much easier. But I am here to grow and challenge myself, so I picked him. The biggest challenge I face around working with men is that I feel as though their attraction toward me feels too intense to ignore; I feel much safer around female bodies. Bob shared that he had been in a deficit of touch lately and really wanted a sensual experience with light impact and no parts of his body off limits.

As per usual, we started with intention setting and negotiating, followed by the scene. I tied his arms behind his back and a simple shoulder tie. Sitting behind him, I caressed and held his body close to mine, and I immediately felt him surrender. I laid him down on the side of his body over some pillows, played with my nails over his skin, then experimented with the chain. I noticed his neck and ears were sensitive to my breath, so I slowly dripped the cold chain over his ears for him to hear sounds of each link, then left it in place for him to feel the weight of it. I continued to run my nails through his body, and then I went back to remove the chain from his ears and run it across his body. By now I could see that he was hard under his boxers, so I let the chain graze his erection. He was breathing heavy and occasionally twitching from the sensations. I made prolonged eye contact multiple times; I could see in his face and his eyes the love and adoration, the innocence, the fright, the vulnerability, and his soul. I confirmed again that this work is sacred. The rest of the scene continued to be beautiful and intentional all the way until aftercare, where he rested on my lap until his weight was too much for me.

There were a couple of other people wanting a scene with me, but I was already so tired that I just wanted to chill and go back to my cabin. I must admit, it feels pretty good to be in high demand, and now I can see what it's like to be in James's shoes.

JUNE 29, 2024

Today was the last day and the closing ceremony of the immersion. It was bittersweet since I was finally starting to feel grounded and comfortable around everybody, but I also miss my home and my fur babies. After breakfast and the pod meeting, I participated fully in the ecstatic dance. I moved around, feeling good in my body, and even engaged with others, doing some improv acrobatics with two of the guys. Without planning or even knowing if this is something they did, I climbed on their bodies and got spun around by them, and it was so natural to follow each other's movements. It was truly epic.

We had a group class where they talked about integration after the immersion and what comes after. They shared about their six-month certification for those interested in doing this as an actual career (the immersion was more of a personal growth thing, not necessarily for practitioners), and that is something I am totally interested in doing because I absolutely fell in love with Shamanic Kink.

In the closing ceremony, all participants were invited to present ourselves in front of the altar that most calls to us and say who we are and what our purpose is. Around the room, there were five altars. The earth altar represented the healing of the earth and ancestors. The air altar represented the healing of communication among humans. The water altar represented our emotions; the fire altar represented our will and passion. And the main altar represented the paradox of the human experience. I chose the fire altar because it's the element that I have been working with lately, and it really resonated since I feel so passionate about many different things. I kneeled in front of the altar and spoke.

"I am the union of passions. And I devote myself to death and rebirth."

After closing, we had lunch all together, said our goodbyes, and exchanged contacts. I stayed an extra night because my flight leaves tomorrow. So after everybody left and I failed to take a nap, I went to the room of one of the girls that didn't get the chance to have her scene with me to see if she was still interested. At this point, I was really trying to get as much hands-on practice as possible and continue to get past my mental obstacles. I could tell she was in the middle of something before I interrupted, and I made sure she knew we didn't have to do this now, but she asked me to stay; she wanted the scene.

She is an introvert, and it took some work to get her to open. At first, she wanted to do the scene with clothes on, and I said that was totally fine with me. During negotiation, I made it clear several times that my highest intention is to have her feel safe and supported through the entire journey, and that I needed help making sure that I stay within the boundaries she set by communicating with me if I ever go too far too soon. After negotiation, she decided to be nude for the experience, and I received this as a sign of comfort in my presence. I had never had a nude submissive in my presence, but although it was new to me, it didn't feel strange or awkward. My job is to not let that distract me from my role, which is to provide an experience that removes my own arousal and desires from the equation. It's not about me; it's about them. We set up the space, I played music with intentional lyrics, we eye gazed, and then I got to work.

One thing that was hard for me during the scene was not breathing close to her ears or blowing as a sensory tool. I love doing this, especially when they are tied up leaning against my chest because I have easy access to their neck and ears while my arms hold them, but she didn't want it, so I had to get creative. Aside from that, everything went smoothly. She surrendered easily, and I could tell from experience that she was fully submerged in the sensations. The journey was about an hour, and we had about fifteen minutes of aftercare before we had to meet with the rest of the group outside to go out for dinner. I made sure to finish with plenty of time to be punctual, but I realized that she was still feeling the subspace energy, and I asked if she preferred to have food brought to her instead so she could stay in. She agreed, so I left the room feeling proud of myself while she stayed in bed, soaking in the blissful experience.

We went to a pizza restaurant about a half hour from the campus, and I ate alone while the facilitators and volunteers had their post immersion meeting and dinner. I loved how they didn't try to include me at their dinner table out of fears that I would feel left out. I love how the conscious community knows how to set and receive boundaries. I used this time to sit with myself, enjoy some pizza at a random restaurant in the middle of nowhere, and journal about my day.

JUNE 30, 2024

After ten hours of travel, I am finally back home with my fur babies. I had to wake up at 3:00 a.m. to take a ride of over an hour to the airport. I faced the fear of missing my flight again when I noticed there were only two TSA lines for the entire airport, and the line went down the stairs and around the perimeter. I prayed while waiting and made it to the gate right as they started boarding. My dad picked me up from the airport and took me to his place, where we shared lunch and a beautiful conversation about his personal fears.

By the time we finished lunch, it was raining cats and dogs, but I wanted to be home so bad that I left under the downpour. The drive home was so slow, and I could hardly see ten feet in front of me, but I made it. My space was a total mess, just as I expected it to be. I was exhausted, but I knew I couldn't relax in the filth, so I took some time to clean and unpack before finally lying back and feeling at home again.

JULY 6, 2024

Since my arrival back home, it's been one thing after the next; it's like I entered a vortex and everything is moving so fast. During the retreat, one of the downloads I received was that the cabaret must be put on the back burner for now, likely until I have my own space to host it. But then I received an invitation to a small gathering that had the potential of facilitating connections that would help make it happen before then. I would have normally declined the invite since I was tired from the trip, but I decided to get out of my shell and meet new people.

It was about ten to fifteen people, and one thing they all had in common was their love for music. They were all singing and playing instruments, and I was in a corner, wishing I had the courage to sing like that in front of people. Eventually they encouraged me to sing, and I absolutely loved it. I don't think it was a coincidence that this happened right after the immersion in which one of my intentions was to open my throat chakra and ability to speak in role play; it's all related.

After everyone left, I stayed and sang with my new friend Randy, feeling a beautiful connection with him. He is about my grandparents' age but super active and in great shape. He is eccentric, charismatic, and always thinks outside the box. I think he likes me because I can keep up (most of the time) with his ideas and deep thoughts. He's Randy the Wizard. I am feeling the potential for collaboration and friendship with him. A couple days afterward, he invited me to a spa day at the Standard Hotel in South Beach, where we brainstormed about the cabaret and other events we can create together. I must admit that it gets hard to follow him sometimes, but I do a good job at keeping track. After hanging out with him all day, I realized that this collaboration still doesn't feel quite right yet. I have so much on my plate right now and have been spreading myself thin.

I am also in the process of redefining my relationship with James. I love our friendship, but it gets confusing with the part where the "benefits" come in. At times, I can put feelings aside and enjoy what we have, but there are parts of me that feel so empty after we have sex. I have not yet come to terms with what it is that I need, but we have been in communication to work things out in a way that feels good for both of us.

JULY 8, 2024

I have been experiencing a good dose of healthy anxiety lately. Even though I'm not yet ready to publish my journal, I moved the needle toward working with a self-publishing company. I didn't even think about it. They had a promotional price for the summer, and I wanted to take advantage of the value. I also suspect that a part of me jumped head in because this way, I give myself a deadline to finish.

My biggest struggle right now is rereading old pages and feeling icky about them. I started the process of reaching out to people in my book to share with them about their appearances and basically, in a way, receive consent about the things I wrote about. I want to share my story, but I want to do it in a way that also respects the privacy of the people involved.

I shared some of my writing with James because he wanted to help with feedback, and I started to feel so much better after talking to him. He is a good friend and supported me through the stress I am dealing with.

JULY 9, 2024

I'm so fucking pissed. I hate lawn mowers with their loud-ass tools, always showing up right when my sleep is at its most delicious state—you know, right as you're waking up and you're in between worlds. I can't wait for the day that they all change to electric and silent ways of doing their work. I swear, my neighbors get lawn work done like every fucking week, and it's so annoying and obnoxious. On top of that, they came in to my side of the yard to cut some of her plants that hang on my side, and the worst thing about it is that *I fucking like that they hang on my side*. So not only are they being so annoying and disrespectful coming into my side, but they're not even doing me a favor. I already talked to her and told her those plants don't bother me and that I would rather them not cut it, but I don't think she ever passed on the message. When I have my own home with a yard, I'm going to change the grass to one that doesn't need maintenance, and I'm going to hire professionals that have quiet tools, and I'm going to absolutely prohibit them from doing their work before noon.

JULY 10, 2024

So much to process, yet it feels like nothing is going on. I have been feeling so anxious. Last night I barely slept, and when I did, I had nightmares about missing my flight to Tennessee for the festival. I'm leaving tomorrow, and I haven't even packed all my things. I'm not even quite sure what it is that I have been feeling so anxious about, but I have been feeling tired and sluggish. My face started breaking out, and in the past, that's only happened when I am stressing over boys. But right now, it doesn't really feel like I'm stressing over boys. I have talked with James about de-escalating our dynamic, and he took it well, no drama on that end.

So that leaves me to think that my breakouts are related to general life stress. My credit card debt is close to $18,000, and it's taking me back to the time I reached over $30,000 growing my business. I also owe money from the Shamanic Kink Immersion since they were so kind to let me pay in installments. And although everything is pretty much under control, my bank account is not growing much with the slow summer season. Aside from that, I'm really stressed over getting students to sign up to my courses. I love teaching, but I have not been enjoying the process of growing my reputation as a trainer. I must focus on sales day in and day out, posting on social media constantly and following up with leads is exhausting. I feel like such an impostor in an industry that seems to be so focused on appearances.

I have a conference coming up in August; a part of me is looking forward to meeting new people and seeing my mentor Carla. And many other parts of me are going to be triggered AF. Aside from my mentor and a handful of other folks, everyone seems so shallow. And yes, I know that I am only projecting my own judgment onto them, and I know that if I only take the time to get to know them, I might just find out they're beautiful people. I don't normally care too much about others' opinions, and I do a pretty good job at minding my own business. But for some reason, when I am around people like that, I find myself feeling inferior. I act like I don't care that my makeup and outfit is not perfect, and I purposely don't make an effort. But clearly, parts of me do care, and I think it's time to have a different approach. This time around, I am going to plan my outfits as opposed to just winging it like I always do last minute...but see, the problem is that the part of me that really doesn't care because she's busy with more important things will be so busy that by the time I have to actually prepare, there won't be the time or budget for it. Ahh, let's see how this goes. I'll make a conscious effort.

Conference aside, I have a wild theory about something. Both my mom and dad have been telling me about how they have been dealing with anxiety and panic attacks lately. They don't talk to each other, so whatever it is, is not related. My theory is that I have been feeling anxious because maybe there is an energetic entanglement? I know that I have been dealing with some stuff, but I'm usually pretty good at keeping up with life's stress.

Fears are coming up from much deeper layers than I had ever expected. After a meaningful conversation with my friend Vero, I realized I've already done this before. When I started pole dancing and sharing my videos, I also started living unapologetically. I understood what it felt like to be my truest self while trusting that the right people would love me for all that I am. But sharing my most intimate stories with the outside world feels scary. The loudest voice is my protector saying, "Who's going to love you after this? You're making it harder to find love."

I was reading my friend Kelly's new book *The Reclaimed Woman*, and she was mentioning the signs of emotional maturity. I realized I'm actually pretty good about this adult stuff, especially when it comes to interpersonal relationships.

Though I have been struggling to open up about a trigger that has been coming up with my friend Vero, I have been keeping to myself. I love when I get to connect with her at a deep level and share meaningful conversations. And sometimes it's hard to feel her presence in the moment because she is always dealing with so much in her own life. I feel especially triggered when I'm talking and she is texting because I don't feel heard. It takes me back to my mom not giving me undivided attention, which is one of my love languages. I know that I'll say something when the time feels right, and I have been triggered enough times to bring it up. I guess for now, I've just been soaking in the lessons. I would really love to work on my relationship with my mother, and I think there's some emotional maturity that we can learn about together. I would really love to see days where my relationship with my mother is one that heals ancestor lineage.

I'm happy to have met Randy. I like brainstorming with him and doing Aquarian shit at the pool. In other words, behaving like children and doing our own thing, not caring what other people see.

Downloads from today:

- Go slow.
- Grow slow.
- Build slow.
- The rest will flow.
- Don't compare myself to others; a lot of people are going nowhere really fast.

JULY 11, 2024

I arrived at Knoxville today and have been at the campground, setting up and settling in. The people that I technically came with are nice and friendly, especially the person that invited me. But I'm just finding out that the person I thought was his friend is his partner and is feeling a little territorial around me. So I set up my tent with enough distance that they have their own space while I can still check in here and there. Where I am at right now, I'm close to a cliff, and I can see and hear water going down. I feel like I'm in the middle of the forest surrounded by nature. Someone I had met briefly in the past is here, and he's been showing me around. I'm really liking it here. The people are friendly, and the location is stunning. As per usual, I'm having a bit of a hard time connecting with strangers in this new space. I would be a lot more comfortable if I had close friends to walk around with, but what matters is that I'm still putting myself out there and doing the uncomfortable things that expand me.

It's 10:00 p.m., and people are just now gathering around to keep dancing, but I came to my tent very far away from everyone to honor my need for sleep. The night sounds are loud here, but they are relaxing. I'm feeling more comfortable than I expected. Without attachment to outcomes, I'm hoping I can get a good night's sleep so I can feel energized and refreshed for all the activities we have tomorrow. I can hear small animals walking around, and I am doing my best to stay calm and enjoy the adventure of camping alone.

JULY 14, 2024

I got back home today, and I have been feeling a little "droppy," as James likes to call it, feeling tired from traveling and emotional. The festival was an absolute dream. I received so many insights, and I had a wonderful time. I will write about it when I feel ready.

JULY 18, 2024

All day, I have just been in my love seat, doing absolutely nothing. I even finished a movie that I started three days ago (I can hardly ever finish a movie in one sitting) and cried at any little sad moment. I guess I'm grieving the loss of something I never even had. Last night, I was on the phone with James, and we were talking about the idea of planning a mushroom journey for him. He's been looking into it after I brought it up multiple times. One of the main struggles we had in our dating/ friends-with-benefits era was him being so emotionally guarded and me needing much more depth, especially during sex. I was willing and open to having an experience with him and seeing if mushrooms would help with that. But after reflecting on it, I realized that this may just make things even more complicated. What if we do have an amazing experience together and we end up hurting each other even more when it's time to detach? I brought this up, and he agreed.

See, the thing is that there is a part of me that would do anything to make it work with him. This part of me loves him so much and is willing to put aside all the things that don't quite fit my needs.

Last night, I asked him to refresh my memory on how exactly we are not compatible. My reason for asking is because I was willing to take a deeper look and perhaps even compromise, knowing that great relationships are built and not found. But as he named reason after reason, I felt more and more misunderstood. I don't want to get into every detail of what he said because I couldn't even hear it all. He said things like, "I don't want to be a sugar daddy," when really all I need is a reliable partner that can take on the provider masculine role in a partnership. A sugar daddy is someone that exchanges money and gifts for company, something I never considered with him. He mentioned something about him not being the type to give money for nails and gifts. I know he said that because one time, I mentioned that I like to be spoiled, and when he asked for an example, what came up at that moment was nails. This was never meant to be a make-or-break kind of deal, and it would have easily been one of those things I would have compromised based on other things he is good at providing.

He said that I like to be worshipped and that he can't do that because he believed in partnerships where both people contribute to the relationship. But what he failed to realize is that I never meant it as having me on a pedestal. What I meant was the more worshipped, loved, and desired I feel, the more I would pour onto my partner and the relationship. It was never meant to be one-way only.

He said acts of service are how he shows love, that words don't mean shit but actions do. I agree with the first part and disagree with the second because words of affirmation are important to me. I love cooking and doing things for him, even though he never asks for much. But then he went on to mention things that he's done for me, like pick me up from the airport when he already had plans with other people because I didn't look at the boarding pass, jump on a video call in the middle of a busy work day to help me with a car situation, and other stuff that I couldn't hear anymore. I muted my phone so he wouldn't hear me crying while he went on and on for what felt like an eternity.

Eventually, I interrupted and asked him to stop. "I heard enough! I feel so misunderstood." I didn't even have the energy to defend myself. What's even the point? He just served the purpose of why I asked that question in the first place, and it has nothing to do with anything he said. We are not compatible because my core needs can't be met, and I always knew this. I have a lot of necessities, but this conversation has led me to realize that the most important one is to be seen and understood, something that has continuously come up again and again with him.

Later in the evening, we talked about the misunderstanding, and we both felt much better afterward. I told him that the reason why I asked is because I considered having a more serious thing with him again, but hearing him out made me feel like my hopes were leading me nowhere. Honestly, I'm not quite sure why I was hopeful. It's starting to feel like the beginning of the end. Like when I ended it with my ex-husband and then tried to make it work time and time again, only to feel empty inside. As tempting as it is to try to make it work with him, it is not what's best for us.

JULY 20, 2024

I have been dragging out journaling about how the rest of the festival went. It's so much to unpack, and it's just been feeling like a massive task to dissect it and put it into words. So let me start where I left off.

The morning after my arrival, I woke up feeling a lot more rested. I slept well, considering that I was in the middle of the forest on a sleeping pad inside a tiny tent. It got super cold in the middle of the night, but thankfully, I had plenty of covers. In the morning, I had my lemon water and some eggs that my friends offered me, and then I went off on a solo adventure. I hiked near some of the caves with the intention of just looking around. My friend had told me that the caves were dangerous and that it wasn't a good idea to go alone, so I wasn't really planning on going in.

But I took one step after the next and found myself inside the cave, admiring the beauty of the rocks and trees and the sound of the small waterfall. I knew there were two waterfalls, and one of them was the designated shower in which you could be naked. They had a strict no-nudity policy, and I wasn't sure if this was the actual shower or not. So I went under the freezing water with my clothes on, but after a minute under the water, I decided to take everything off. After all, there was no one around, and it was still early in the morning. I felt a little rebellious but also genuinely unsure that I was even doing something wrong. After the shower, I found a patch of sun that was perfectly illuminating the top of a rock, and I lay there to bask in the warm sun. I was feeling so connected and relaxed, and when I had enough, I slowly explored the rest of the cave and walked down to where the lake is.

To my surprise, my friends and their kids were already there, along with a lot of other people. I guess this was the time of the day that everyone goes to the lake. I jumped in the water and connected with my friends a bit more. The water was warm at the surface and cold the farther down I went, but it was perfect. After being in the water for a while, I started to head back to the main area to get some food, and on my way out, I saw my friend Julie walking in. I was expecting her arrival since she was the only person there that I knew. I was totally OK with being on my own, but I was looking forward to connecting with other people as well. She got there right as KY Honey had taken the stage and started singing her spiritual twerking music.

Yeah, I know how that sounds, and it is super fun and silly and intentional. We had a blast twerking our little booties off and went in the water to cool down, floating on a doughnut around the lake. I have been feeling comfortable around her lately. What I mean by that is that we play together and sometimes have been very touchy with each other. Before the festival, we had been trying to figure out a time for us to do a kink scene, but it didn't work out with our schedules. It feels right to say the friendship had turned a little unconventional for the conservative world. In the world I live in, it is common for friends to cuddle and exchange sensual energy from time to time without it meaning they're heading into a romantic relationship, but for me, it still doesn't feel very natural. Rewiring your brain requires doing things that feel awkward at first. I'd like to be able to connect with certain female friends in that way, and she feels like a good person to try it with.

Julie can be quite direct, which is something I normally appreciate, but when it comes to this form of relating, it can make me feel uneasy. To feel more comfortable around her, I started a conversation about intention and boundaries. I told her this was new to me and that I wanted to go slow. I like cuddling, being cute and flirty with each other, but I wasn't ready to move past that just yet. I also told her consent is important to me. She shared her boundaries and assured me that she's not looking for a serious relationship; she wants to connect with me at a deeper level while maintaining a friendship. With this conversation out of the way, I felt so much more comfortable being silly and playful.

From there, we set up her tent just a few feet from mine on the most spectacular spot of the entire campsite. It was right at the edge of the cliff, overlooking the forest and caves. At first, she was kind of freaked out about being on the edge, but the spot was too perfect to even care. From there, we could hear the waterfall, and at night, we could hear the music from one of the stages that went until 4:00 a.m. She liked the fact that she could hear the music from there, and I also didn't mind because it was easy to tune it out with my earplugs. After setting up the tent, we stayed up for another couple of hours chatting, cuddling, and raving about our perfect hideout.

Since we had been trying to plan a sensual scene for her, I decided: Why not now? I didn't have any tools with me, so this would be a great way to practice making the best with what I have. We went over our boundaries and intentions for the scene. There were not many boundaries on her end, so it was basically up to me how far it went. The scene involved a lot of sensual teasing and eye contact. I did want it to involve more in-depth genital play since this was a new area for me, but I didn't feel comfortable to do more than over-the-clothes stimulation. Aftercare was cuddles followed by a visit to the food vendors.

The rest of the day, we continued to explore the land, and in the evening, we danced and connected with other people. I was happy to be surrounded by everyone here, but every now and then, I went out to be in my own space for a while. I went to sleep early, right when the party was starting to turn up. I think it wasn't even midnight when I was already on my way to bed. See, the thing is that I'm not a party animal. I love dancing and all, but I like it more in a private or intimate setting. So in these spaces, I can only go for so long before my social battery runs out. On this trip, I was prioritizing spending time in nature. I needed my sleep to be able to spend my energy hiking and swimming. I honestly don't know how they do it; I felt like an old lady, lol.

The next day was eventful. Something happened that took me a long time to process, and it's the reason I am just now putting into writing. Julie met a guy that she liked, and they connected the night before. He's cute and gives me good, wholesome vibes. I think it's so interesting that they just met once before, and it was so easy for them to hook up. I don't say that in a judgmental way at all. I find it fascinating that some people can do that without knowing each other well. I kind of tried that a couple of times while in my early days of exploration and quickly discovered it's not for me.

Anyway, after spending some time at the lake dancing and mingling with people, I went back to lie down in her tent for some peaceful alone time. A few minutes passed before John approached the tent looking for her, and just a few minutes after that, she got there. Totally unplanned and somehow perfect timing. Eventually, they both went inside the tent, and the energy was starting to feel like something may happen there. Naturally, I started to bring up the topic of boundaries and consent because it put me at ease to know they are in place in case something were to happen.

At some point, we were all lying down and relaxing together. I was on the left side of the sleeping pad, Julie in the middle, and him on the right. She was caressing me, I was caressing her, and he was caressing her as well. I was lying on my left side facing the wall of the tent, and I couldn't see behind me, but I could tell from her breathing that he was touching her in pleasurable ways. I was checking in with myself here and there to make sure I was feeling safe at all times, and so far, I felt comfortable. Since it was getting a little hot, I untied the back of my bikini top. The caressing turned a bit more sensual between her and me. She asked if she could touch my breast. I said yes. I liked what she was doing, and I felt arousal slowly taking over. She touched my inner thighs and really close to my privates. I was really loving the slow teasing and buildup. I said this out loud. I love the feeling of wanting. Thoughts of James came and went. *Is this OK? How would he feel about this?* Followed by, *It's not about him. It's about me, and I feel good about it.*

At this point, I was turned on, and my boundaries had changed slightly. My right knee was bent and resting over hers, giving her just the right angle to bring her touch closer to my vulva. From the side of my loose shorts, she was then gently touching around my pussy, spreading my juices around and in between my labia. John asked if he could suck my nipples and I said yes. His face lit up with childlike excitement. It was adorable. I was so incredibly wet and juicy, and everything felt so heavenly. After a couple of minutes of this superhot and sensual external stimulation, she asked for consent to finger me. I said yes. She went in slowly, and I moaned. At this point, we had been teasing for so long that I could orgasm any moment. Her fingers felt so good inside me, and the fact that I was so wet made it feel even more delicious. I was so slippery and hot and she knew her way around it. My moans intensified with her fingers pressing harder against my G-spot. I was moaning louder and wondering if the people by the waterfall could hear us.

After a moment, Julie and John started to make out, and it looked like they were about to continue engaging more intimately, so I moved slightly to the side to watch. But as I did that, I noticed that we had reached the end. We went back to cuddles and unwinding.

I love how organic everything was and how it all went from start to finish.

One of the biggest takeaways from this weekend is that my alone time and individuality are extremely important to me. I enjoy and cherish the company of my friends and meeting new faces, but in my own company is how I recharge. Also, I can pick my nose at my leisure, lol.

I also had the realization that it's time to invest in my wardrobe. I have always been so focused on business moves that I put my sense of style to the sidelines. I don't care what financial experts have to say about spending money we don't have on clothes. And I don't care that my debt has been a cause of some stress lately. This feels like I finally found the missing puzzle piece —the embodiment of it and dressing the part.

I learned that I do spirituality in my own way and that I don't like participating in ceremonies with many people. I do like intimate ceremonies, either with myself or a small group of friends, but I do not like when they involve a lot of people that I don't know.

I still don't like being told what to do, and my sovereignty is a big part of who I am. I need to be able to come and go as I please, where I want and when I want. I don't like feeling stuck.

I like fear. It feels like it expands me. I guess it's more like I enjoy doing things that feel scary.

I had a really hard time writing about this threesome scene because I was carrying some shame around it from multiple different areas. On one end, there is the lesbian shame since this is as far as I have ever gone with a woman. And on the other end is the shame of not being as selective as I normally am. I'm always so proud to say that I don't sleep around and that not just anyone gets access to me in that way, and this time, I felt like I didn't live up to my standards. Although I didn't really engage with the other guy, energetically, we were all in the same bubble. And my friend is great, but I don't necessarily want to continue this kind of dynamic.

I can see how a lot of this shame is influenced by James in the sense that he is very selective, like me. It feels like I let him down somehow. I have not told him the full story yet, and it's not because I'm hiding anything from him because nothing I did affects him in any way. He also engages in sexual domination games with other friends, so this is not very different. There was also no fluid exchange of any kind, so I'm not putting his health in danger. I think the reason why I feel like I let him down is because he represents that part of me that is selective. So in a sense, I know that he's not the person I let down with my actions; it was that part of me.

But after an amazing conversation with my friend Vero, who always has a way of finding the right things to say, I realized that just because I wasn't selective this time around doesn't mean that I am not a selective person. "Just because every now and then I eat the chicken broth that my mom makes doesn't mean that I am a meat eater," she mentioned. And that helped a lot.

JULY 21, 2024

Yesterday turned out to be so much more eventful than I expected. I went out to hang out with Lili at the beach. We had so much catching up to do since we moved out from the old apartment. Among the things I got her up to date with, I mentioned that the cabaret was on the back burner for now because of lack of funds.

She was telling me about the place that she's been staying at, which is actually an art garage. The person that works and lives there is traveling, and she is taking over the rent while she is gone. She has been hosting some events there lately and mentioned that we could use it for the cabaret since the rent is basically paid for. After some brainstorming, we came up with an amazing idea that would be a great way to raise funds. The space is small, so we can host about twenty guests. The vibe is very sexy and artsy with couches and cushions. It's not a fancy space, and it needs some deep cleaning and organizing. I have created the theme to match the vibe that it gives, which is otherworldly and mysterious. The idea is to turn this space into the VIP room of the Conscious Cabaret. Everyone gets front-row seating and special treatment from our performers and entertainers. We are keeping the description mysterious, but here is what we have:

Soultry Sessions
An exclusive underworld affair that will quench your thirst for soulful sensuality. The mysterious nature of this experience will lead you to the gates of our alluring underworld. Dare to step into our lair, lie back, relax, and surrender your senses to the infinite potential the night has to offer.

So yeah, the idea was born in just a matter of a couple of days, and today, I created the event link and sent out an email marketing campaign. Making them moves!

Anyway, after the beach, we went back to the garage for me to check out the space. Some of her roommates (or, I guess, guests?) were there. Not sure exactly, but they were hanging out and smoking DMT. They asked if we wanted to smoke, and it caught me off guard, but after letting it sink in, I decided that I wanted to try it out. I felt safe in the space, and the person that offered gave me a good vibe, not for any specific reason, more of an intuitive thing.

He recommended that before smoking, we do rapé to ground. This is a legal medicine that has been used by healers for thousands of years. It is a blend of pulverized medicinal plants and other ingredients. The way you take it is with a pipe from which someone blows into each nostril. When it first went in, it burned a lot; you're also not supposed to swallow, so we had to keep spitting it out into a bucket. The feeling in the body was like a heavy, grounding sensation that was pleasant.

After sitting a few minutes with this medicine, we set our intentions and smoked DMT. I knew that it is produced naturally in the human brain in small amount, and it's also the main psychoactive ingredient in ayahuasca, but I had never tried it alone, so I only smoked enough to have a microdose. Opposite of a microdose would be what they call a blast-off; this is where you basically open different dimensions of your psyche and go on a relatively short (fifteen to thirty minutes) out-of-body experience. Because I had never done this before, and I was not mentally, emotionally, and physically prepared for this, so a microdose felt good to me.

The experience was very mild, and it only lasted about five minutes. To my surprise, it felt a lot like that time at the ecstatic dance event, where for a moment, I felt like I was in a psychedelic experience. This is when I realized that day I activated more than normal DMT release in my brain through dance alone. It makes me wonder if this is what happened in the Tambores in Cuba, when people danced to the drums and reached altered states of mind.

After smoking it, we stayed chatting and brainstorming about the show for about thirty minutes, and then I went home, feeling completely focused, grounded, and motivated to bring this show to life. I love how this random Saturday turned out to be so creatively productive.

JULY 25, 2024

It's been a self-care day. I just finished my period, and there was so much to catch up to after a few days of resting and recollecting my energy. I had a short workday at the studio with just one client. Then I went to a new market for groceries. From there, I got home and put away laundry that had been sitting in the basket for almost an entire week. I washed the dogs' bedding, bathed them, washed dishes from the last few days, waxed myself, made dinner, and gave myself a mini facial. To be honest, I was looking a little rough, and so was my space.

I had a little fashion show with my mom in her room. I was invited to a nice boat party tomorrow, and we were making sure that I had just the perfect look for it. I was instructed to wear all white, so I bought myself a cute little skirt and borrowed the rest of my outfit from my mom's closet. It was so fun sneaking into her closet while she was working, knowing that she knew what I was up to. It's like a little game we play where I am constantly trying out her shoes and borrowing her stuff. She acts like she doesn't like it, but I know a part of her is flattered. I do admire her sense of style and the way she invests in her appearance. It's something I used to criticize but have recently learned the importance of.

Anyway, the party is on a large boat, taking in the Miami sunset with some of the city's most ambitious people, including venture capitalists, entrepreneurs, and spiritual seekers. The perfect combination of people that I tend to feel like I don't belong with. But that is changing now. I am being exposed to these kinds of people because I have leveled up, and I belong there. Anyway, Randy invited me to the event because he was going to be singing there, and he wanted me to dance while they performed. He asked me to take a couple of outfits, including a sexy one.

I made a couple of important calls today. First was with an event producer that was really interested in talking with me about my Conscious Cabaret. He told me about his company, and it sounds like a good connection to have. He was interested in coming to the next event in August and discussing the potential for collaboration in the future. He gave me good vibes, and I'm curious where this will lead.

The second call was a burlesque artist that Randy recommended for the show. She brings multiple talents to the mix, like singing, dancing, and emceeing. She was open to working with my budget and was excited about the gig when she understood the concept of it. She used to be part of the burlesque show from that bar in Wynwood. Interesting how tables have turned.

I have started a ritual with my wardrobe and old clothes that don't bring joy anymore. I have a ton of big, old shirts that I sleep in that I am finally releasing; some of them even have holes all over them. The ritual starts by me wearing them one last time, and while I do, I remember the story of the shirt and the person I was when I got it. After wearing them, I collect them in a box, and once I have worn all of them, I'll make a ceremony where I let them burn and, as they do, see the rebirth of the new me.

Today, I told my mom about the book. She mentioned how I never tell her anything anymore. I told her that I don't do it like I used to anymore because she projects her fears and insecurities onto me. That I know she has good intentions, but that it's not what I need. She was curious about how much of my private life I talk about. I told her that it's a lot and that it includes even my most private moments. I told her that her privacy is protected and assured her that I wouldn't be sharing anything from her personal life. But I do share about my own perspective of our relationship. I have noticed that since I have started staying here, our bond has strengthened, and we don't butt heads as much. I see how coming back home was more than just about saving money; it had a lot to do with our healing as well.

JULY 27, 2024

Last night was epic! The party turned out so much better than I anticipated. There were a couple of people that I knew from the acro community, so it was easy to arrive and mingle. I was very happy with my outfit and the way I looked, and it felt so good to not question my sense of style. Someone offered me some mushrooms, and after thinking about it for a few minutes, I decided that a microdose would be perfect for this kind of environment. I ate the perfect amount that helped me open up and feel comfortable in this overstimulating crowd.

When the evening turned late, Randy asked me to get my skimpy outfit on. I was afraid that the outfit was a little too skimpy since it was the tiniest white thong and a tiny lace bikini top. But when one of the event organizers passed by, she said I absolutely had to dance in it and that it wasn't too skimpy.

I went out to the dance floor, and my friend started singing a very sultry song that was easy for me to tap into. I started dancing, and just seconds into it, I was surrounded by lights and cameras filming me. It felt amazing to be in the spotlight again.

Someone made a comment that really had me thinking about my old ways of being. They said, "You're making everybody here jealous." And it really threw me back to when I used to feel jealous in social gatherings where there were other girls prettier than me or getting a lot of attention. Just knowing that my boyfriend would be watching her would make my blood boil. It would even get to the extent where if my boyfriend was going to the beach without me, I would think about all the ass that would be all around him. I would hate on the girls wearing the tiny bikinis and would never wear one myself because I wouldn't want to make other girls feel the way I do when I see the things that trigger me.

Wow, the growth has been exponential. These days, I love celebrating other women feeling good and doing the things that used to trigger so much insecurity. I also don't shy away from wearing something just because it may trigger someone else's insecurities. It was such a beautiful lesson for me to learn, and who am I to rob someone from having that realization themselves?

A lot of people loved my dancing and told me how they could see that when I dance, it really comes from my soul. I was happy to hear that other people can also see the level of love and depth that I reach when I perform and that it really comes from my soul. I made some nice connections, and it was an experience that left me feeling energized and motivated to stay in this supportive community.

JULY 29, 2024

I am the problem. I keep setting these impossible expectations for James to meet when I damn well know that it's just not him. I don't even need to go into detail about anything he did or didn't do. It's nothing new. As a matter of fact, I'm not even going to bring anything up to him. I normally like to talk about things that trigger me and air things out, but this time around, it's so repetitive that I'm bored just thinking about it. I will talk about it with my friend so it doesn't stay inside me, but I feel complete with that. What's new this time around is this feeling of certainty that I didn't experience at this level with him before. It's last New Year's Day relived all over again.

I'm not sure what level of de-escalation I want, but I don't want meaningless sex with him anymore. I feel like if it's part of a scene or at a play party where we have a story that excites me, I would still like to have sex with him. But I need lots of stimulation, especially mental stimulation, to want to desire him in that way again.

This feels good in my entire body. I let myself feel a bit of grief a couple of times tonight, releasing him to make space for what I really want in my life right now.

On another note, I tried two new things yesterday. I was at a kinky party at James's, and as per usual, I got to experience some new stuff. I tried the dragon staff fire prop for the first time, and I learned how to do a trick that I always loved watching fire dancers perform. I thought it was going to be super hard to learn, but I got it fast. And the best thing about it is that I am so much more comfortable with fire now that I didn't even get in my head about it.

The other thing I tried was blood play. So blood play is one of the most intense things you can do in BDSM; it most certainly is not for the faint of heart. I saw this couple getting ready to do blood play in the backyard, and I don't know why, but a part of me, without hesitation, said, "Oh, can I try?"

The dominant prepared the space with a large tarp over the grass and a bunch of sanitizing and first-aid products to make sure everything was hygienic. He started the scene with some regular impact and proceeded to use impact tools that have spikes. She started bleeding almost immediately, and you could see the dots of blood with the patterns of the paddle. He asked me to come over and explained how to use the paddle. I started super gently, and then he took it from me and showed me how she likes it, which was hard. I increased the intensity and spanked her until I had enough. He continued to play until her legs were shaking, and I stayed watching about six feet away. There were splatters of blood on the fence she was leaning on, and some of that even landed on me. Her butt cheeks were covered in blood, streams dripping down her legs.

After the scene, he hosed her down and cleaned her up while I helped her stay balanced by holding her hands. It wasn't a horrible experience because it is consensual, and at the end of the day, she enjoys it. Most people in the room were shocked by the scene, and I was, too, but it wasn't way out of my comfort zone since I see blood often when I tattoo, especially when clients don't follow pre-care instructions and drink caffeine before their appointment. But the smell of the blood became strong, and that's when I stepped out. It's not necessarily the kind of scene I would like to lead, but I'm glad I tried it.

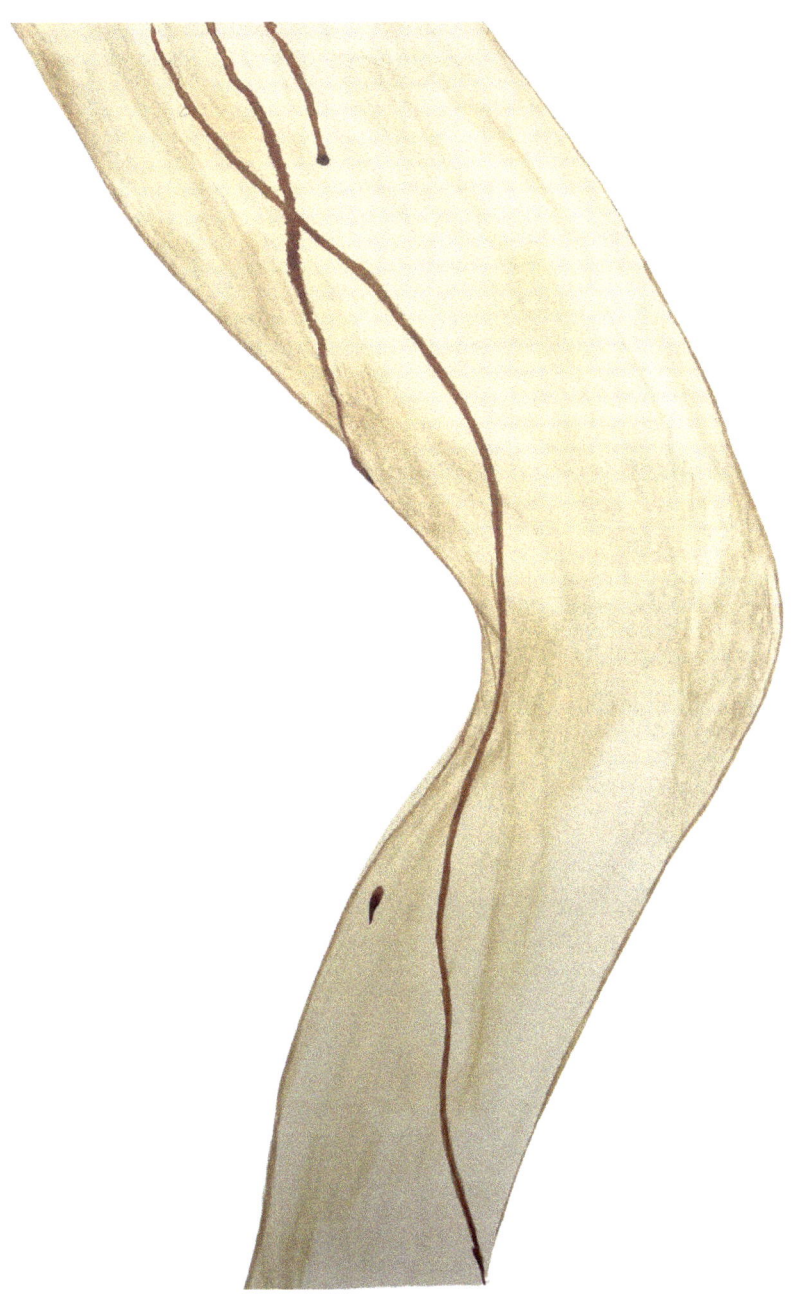

AUGUST 2, 2024

What a busy day. I have been nonstop and more than productive. Finally, I am just now unwinding for a bit before going to sleep. I have been working hard on Soultry Sessions, vetting all the leads that come in and selling tickets. So far, I have sold five tickets and have fifteen more to go to be able to break even and make some extra money for all the work that I have been putting into it. I have been noticing myself going through the fears of not selling enough tickets and being in the negative again like I did last time.

Right now, I don't have enough money in my back account to pay for rent at home or at work. The landlord of the studio is flexible, and they don't usually reach out until at least the eighth of the month, so I have at least five days to come up with what I'm missing. And at home, my mom doesn't need to pay the mortgage yet. I feel confident that everything is going to be OK and that somehow, the money will come. I have even considered going to a strip club for a couple of nights to come up with the money, but I told Daddy Universe that if that is really the route that I have to take, it needs to be on my own terms and easy to flow into. But I think he heard me because I have gotten three new bookings at work, and things are moving well in that department.

Today, I went to my mom's side to get some baking soda, and we ended up cuddling on the couch while catching up. It felt amazing. We were talking form a distance, and I just went over to the couch and lay next to her. She was like "What happened?" and I was like "Nothing." She asked again in disbelief what was happening. It was cute, and I hope there is more of this in my family from now on. I think we are all in need of cuddles.

After coming back into my space, I put on my heels and started dancing, challenging myself to go as slow and sultry as possible. As I did, I found myself in remembrance of something that happened this weekend that I had totally dismissed. When I danced at James's party, he didn't watch me dance. I actually didn't know this until he told me that everyone kept telling him that I was dancing while he was picking up and that he told them that he's seen me dance before; he knows how amazing I am. When he told me, I didn't give it much thought, but it all came up to surface when the little girl inside me started crying, bawling. There is nothing more important to her than getting the attention of her loved ones. So for her, this was a rejection. I let her go through the waves while nurturing her, then reassuring her that his behavior was not personal, that perhaps for him, it would have been too painful to watch me. When I felt complete, I allowed myself to release him and the feelings with compassion.

Today, I also became aware of a big protector inner aspect that will fuck somebody up if they try to mess with my cabaret. Well, I guess it's not the first time I noticed this protector; she came out after those guys that snuck into my event last time and made them pay for two VIP tickets. That was fun. But right now, I feel as though she's watching over my shoulders every time I make a move, and especially when I am talking with potential dancers and vixens. Why does everyone want to be involved in my business? I am happy she's here, and I'm happy to see that I can do what needs to be done.

AUGUST 7, 2024

It has been a good few days. The PMU conference started Monday, and since it was on the way to James's house, I took advantage of the trip north to go practice a suspension that we are working on for the show. So it was an eventful couple of days in every sense of the word. Let me start with the conference.

I made sure I felt confident in my outfits as opposed to winging it this time around, and I can say that it was totally worth it. Every room I walked into, I felt like I belonged and felt good about myself. I had good conversations, made new connections, and had a great time. I saw my mentor, Carla, give an eye-opening presentation about color theory and pigmentology that had me in tears. She's been disrupting the industry with her scientific research, and I have been following her footsteps. There was a party the first night of the event, and I was chatting with Carla and other artists, and she started showering me with compliments about my dance and confidence. It was so amazing to experience this because I always see her as such an inspirational person, and to see that she also feels the same way about me was a huge reminder that we never know how our actions are quietly inspiring others.

I couldn't be at the conference for the entirety of it because the drive up every day was way too much for me. But luckily, there will be recordings of all the speeches, and it felt like my time there was everything that I needed it to be.

Practicing with James felt good and productive. We have a pretty good scene prepared for the cabaret, and I'm really excited for it. But something happened while I was up there that was interesting. Earlier this week, we had a conversation about de-escalating our dynamic to remove intercourse from the equation. I told him I was OK with oral, hands, and toys, just no sex. He was OK with that.

So yesterday, when I arrived at his place, I was super tired, and since I know that he likes napping after work, I offered to do that. We went to sleep spooning but ended up not napping at all because he started playing with my neck, gently biting and blowing on it. The neck is a dangerous spot for me; that's basically my erotic switch. One simple caress, and I just start dripping. I remembered our conversation about sex and wondered how this would turn out. We started playing, and I realized how much I wanted to have him inside me, while at the same time knowing that our agreement had changed and that wasn't available for me now.

Trusting that he could honor my boundary, I made it known that I really craved him. Suddenly, his cock looked bigger, thicker, harder, and juicier than ever before. I had so much frustration inside me that I couldn't have him. Yet that feeling of wanting it and not being able to have it felt so delicious in my body. I was aware of my love for edging and teasing, but this was on another level, and I loved that he was able to stay within the boundaries that we had in place before we were hot and horny. Who knows how would it have felt if we ended up having sex? I may have liked it in the moment, but I most likely would have felt depleted after that.

This really made me think about my relationship with financial abundance. Is there a part of me that gets off on the feeling of wanting and not having? I believe that we create our own reality, and right now, I'm in such a deep hole financially, and I'm really wondering how I created this for myself.

AUGUST 9, 2024

Today is my mom's birthday, and it's been all about her. I didn't get her a gift and felt so bad about being empty handed, so I drew a portrait of her. It wasn't too bad considering that I had never drawn a portrait before and I'm a total newbie at drawing. It was cute when she came out of the shower and saw it laying on the bed. She was so happy and even got teary eyed.

Side note: we're actually in Turks and Caicos right now. My mom got us tickets for three days for her birthday, and it's been quite nice. We are surprised at how many Latinos live and have businesses here. The water is even more beautiful and clear than you can imagine, and I love the accent of the locals, it sounds sophisticated and calm. I'm not impressed by the food, though. At least in the area we're in, the food tastes pretty bland and generic. But we did go to a restaurant that serves local food, and it was the best fish I have ever had in my life! I guess next time, we have to ask around and make sure the restaurants are authentic food from the island.

Anyway. I'm really excited because tickets for Soultry Sessions have been selling fast! We are almost sold out, and I made a really bold move. I doubled the price of the tickets. It was a scary decision, but this morning, I woke up to a full-price purchase! On top of that, I also got a company to sponsor the event! It's a company that makes adaptogenic beverages named Curious Elixirs. That means that we can offer free drinks to the guests and therefore add even more value to the already extraordinary experience. This feels huge. Although I'm still behind on rent and I have some bills to catch up to, I feel so abundant. I'm doing the internal work and becoming aware of my shortcomings when it comes to financial freedom. No better place to celebrate than exactly where my feet are.

I create my abundance from infinite source.

Thank you, source.

AUGUST 13, 2024

Well, I finally did what I have been avoiding for months now. Eventually, I had to face reality and check exactly where I'm at with finances. There is now around $300 to my name, and I owe a total of around $21,000 between credit cards, business loans, and personal loans. Phew...I have not paid rent to my mom, and I have an automatic withdrawal of $800 in a week. I have some being deposited tomorrow from the sales of Soultry Sessions tickets, but it's literally just a little over what's needed to pay the team and other expenses for the show.

There is a part of me that is very proud that this debt was for career purposes, but it really is no different than my mom spending on trips and material things in regard to the feeling that it comes with. The interesting thing about it is that I can also feel a part of me that is totally unbothered by it and knows that (as my mom likes to say) *Dios proveera*, or God will provide. I feel so secure being where I'm at, and I'm grateful for it.

I'm feeling a little anxious because the package with the beverages from the sponsor has not shipped yet, and I'm worried that it won't arrive before Saturday. My plan is to buy it at a store, but it will have to be a whole different way to work around the beverages. Aside from that, everything else is looking great, and we are officially one ticket away from selling out.

AUGUST 14, 2024

It was a super busy day, starting with the lawn mowers before 8:00 a.m. interrupting my sleep. I had a meeting with my apprentice Jamie, followed by a Zoom meeting with the team for Soultry Sessions, followed by a meeting with a company that really likes my Conscious Cabaret concept, followed by a meeting with my marketing and success manager for my cosmetic tattooing business. Literally one thing after the other with a lingering migraine all day.

The meeting with my apprentice went completely differently from what I planned. I wanted to propose to her a management and personal assistant role, but she's in the process of possibly moving to a different state. I was not surprised and would be lying if I said I didn't see it coming. I'm so proud of her for having the difficult conversations with me and proud of myself for being able to hold space for her without my own emotions getting in the way and crying the second I saw her tearing up. I know that she has grown a lot with me, and I'm happy to see her flourish on her own and pursue the style of tattooing and mentorship that I know I can't offer. Now it's time to find someone else that can take the role that I need.

The meeting with the team went great. I laid down the plan for them, and I think I did a great job at leading the meeting. I didn't realize until afterward that I had never led a team meeting like this before. Yay, me, making big moves!

The meeting with the entertainment company went well. They see a lot of potential with my concept, and they have a lot of connections with hotels and venues where we can bring it to. The only downside is that it needs to be toned down to suit a more corporate environment. The good thing is that with this collaboration, most of the workload is off my shoulders because they have an entire team for marketing, finances, etc. I don't mind making a more toned-down version of the show because I still get to have my own complete production when I want it.

The meeting with the success manager was the usual. We are strategizing on how to utilize artificial intelligence to help with the sales process for clients and students, so I'm curious about how that's going to work. These days, I'm really all about delegating and focusing only on my unique abilities.

After all the meetings were done, I went to the beach and to the acro park for some good vibes and chill energy. Walking to the beach, I was so emotional. I saw a lady trying to wash her toddler's feet under the beach shower and struggling because she had to keep pressing the pump for the water to flow. I offered to help and realized I had met this person before. The first time was at a shamanic breath work immersion, where we shared an eye-gazing exercise. She was pregnant, and the baby kept kicking during the exercise; it was beautiful. And the second time I met her was by coincidence at a hotel in Miami Beach. After I helped her, she said I was an angel. This opened the floodgates, and I started crying in front of strangers passing by.

On my way out of the beach, I saw a lady get out of her car, and her purse read, "Relaxed Hustle."

I'm really feeling the magic all around me. This is the climax of this season of my life.

AUGUST 18, 2024

Last night was pure magic. It's hard not to pay attention to the few things that went wrong, but I'm not beating myself up too much. I am still in the learning process, and these are all lessons. I'll go in depth about how everything went another time because it was truly amazing. But in this moment, what's alive for me is that feeling of emptiness after the end of a big project. It's so interesting to feel this way. Maybe it's not emptiness and all I'm feeling is stillness? What if stillness is so unfamiliar to me that it feels empty?

After days and weeks only thinking about the cabaret nonstop, I now feel like there is no purpose to my day. Is life really this way? Is it true what they say about accomplishments? That the good feeling doesn't last long before you start going after the next goal? I'm also now remembering as I'm writing that I'm expecting my period tomorrow, and that may be intensifying the natural drop of hormones that occurs after an intensely stimulating event. Even through this emptiness, I can still see and feel the happiness deep within. In just a matter of time, I will be able to rejoice in that feeling, and I know it's going to be wonderful. But for now, I will surrender to the emptiness.

AUGUST 22, 2024

Well, last night was eventful. I was outside smoking and playing with fire. I like to dip my palo santo into the melted candle wax and then light it because it makes a nice, big flame. I did that and watched it burn for a bit until the food I ordered arrived at the door. I broke the first rule of fire: I left the palo santo unattended to go eat with my mom, thinking that eventually, it was just going to go out, as it normally does after a couple of minutes. After I finished eating, I came back around to my side of the house to find the bench where the palo santo was up in flames.

Now, here is how my brain works and a little backstory. I have been meaning to create a fire for the clothes-burning ceremony, and I almost did it two days ago as part of my full moon ritual. But I was on the first day of my period, and it felt like too much work, on top of the fact that

I didn't have the tools to start a fire. So when I saw the fire and went inside to get water, I thought, *Why not use this fire to burn the clothes?*

So I grabbed the pile of clothes and threw them into the fire, instantly doubling its size. At this point, the fire was taller than me and about four feet wide. It was clearly time to stop playing around. I went around the fire to grab the hose from my mom's side to spray the flames. I was trying to get this done without my mom finding out, but she was already outside. I ordered her to fill up a bucket with water very calmly because I knew if I freaked out, she would multiply my energy. She came back with the water when the fire was already much smaller and poured it over. At this point, I couldn't stop laughing hysterically from the rush, and, of course, it was contagious, so she started laughing too.

My storage bench is now all melted on top of everything that was inside of it. Thankfully, it was all just a bunch of pots and gardening stuff and nothing of value. On top of the bench, there were some old pillows and cushions that also burned. And next to it was a table and a slab of fake wood that also burned a bit. I'm just so glad that this didn't happen inside and that none of my animals were around; it would have been a complete catastrophe. With my intention of letting go of things that no longer serve, I didn't mean for it to go this far. But there is a part of me that is totally OK with everything that got destroyed, and I'm just now realizing that those things needed to go as well. I also learned a huge lesson about fire. Right when I started getting more comfortable around the element, it showed me how destructive it can be. Fire must always be handled with caution and respect.

After the fire incident, I had a FaceTime "date" with someone from a dating app I recently downloaded called the League. The app is for high achievers and career-oriented people. I thought this was a good fit for me because being an entrepreneur is a big part of who I am. However, this interaction was a big wake-up call for me. I may be career oriented, but I come from a very creative and free-spirit world.

The guy kept asking questions about my tattoos and piercings, then about my dancing and the events I produce. "So do people, like, have sex there? Do you get completely naked? Is it like an orgy?" He wouldn't even let me finish answering one question before asking the next. I realized how different my world is from what's considered normal and that

I don't want to use my precious time in this style of dating. I'll meet my person doing what I do, and it will flow with ease. I deleted the app.

Solar Plexus Chakra (Manipura) – Confidence, personal power, motivation, willpower.

This is my second favorite piece in my chakra collection. At first, I struggled with it—I couldn't figure out how to make it feel fiery. Then, during my next menstrual phase, inspiration struck. With fresh blood in hand, I added the radiating rays that gave it the perfect finish.

If you're feeling unmotivated or overwhelmed by an endless to-do list, use this as a meditation tool. Visualize your inner fire being reignited, fueled by the energy within this artwork.

AUGUST 23, 2024

I feel fully processed from Sultry Sessions, and today, I want to share all about it.

I arrived super early at the art garage because there was a lot of work to get done. I had been going multiple times during the week to clean up and rearrange the space, but it was a big project to do that since the space is packed with stuff and it hadn't been cleaned in a minute. I was a little anxious about how people would feel about the space since it's literally a warehouse and the tickets were pricey. We had just enough seating for our guests, and the space was going to be packed. On top of that, the AC wasn't cooling very well since the garage door was being opened multiple times. I had a team of people helping me, but I was pretty much alone at the top, overseeing everything. It was a lot of pressure. Thankfully, everything worked out according to schedule except there were some guests that were late, and that threw the whole night off because we waited to start the show.

When it was time for me to go out and give the opening message, I forgot half the things that I wanted to say. I could feel in the energy of the room that they had been waiting long enough and rushed to introduce the next performer. Looking back, I see that instead of waiting for everyone to get there to start the show, I should have started my welcome message while waiting for the last guests to arrive.

The run of the show was a little rocky. I wasn't able to see any of the performers, but from what I heard, at least that went well. My first dance was all right but not great. The second I touched the pole, I realized I forgot to assign someone to clean it. It was extremely hard to do anything on it because it was super slippery; whoever touched it before must have been wearing lotion. After my dance, we took a ten-minute break and started the second half of the show, which went a lot more smoothly. It started with the vocalist singing a nice version of "Oops!

I Did It Again," followed by Lili's burlesque act, and then the grand finale with James and me.

This grand finale was epic, starting with me dancing on the floor and the pole. Then James picked me up from the floor and tied me to the pole, where I did an interesting trick that I improvised on the spot. After that, he suspended me into a predicament shape with one leg up to the pole and the other tied to my hair behind my back. Then he started pouring wax on me. Normally, I'm jumpy from the heat of the wax, but this time around, I barely felt a warm sensation. He ripped my panties off and continued to pour wax on me.

What came next, I was completely unaware of since my eyes were closed and I was in my own world. He performed fire play with flash cotton, then knife play to remove the wax off my skin, and lastly, he lit up sparklers from the rope and spun me around the pole. I heard everyone cheering and clapping, but I didn't even know why they were doing that. It was after the show ended when someone showed me a video that I realized he used the sparklers. I absolutely loved this because he went with the flow, I fully trusted him with it, and it was epic.

After the show ended, the guests approached me to share their feedback, and despite all the imperfections, I noticed it was overwhelmingly positive. "I have never seen anything like this before. This was so beautiful to witness. Your level of trust and surrender was inspiring. I want to be notified when the next event is happening." And more stuff I don't remember right now.

With the show being over, it was now time to relax and play around. Some guests stayed for a bit and left shortly after, and others left right after the show ended. I was wondering why everyone didn't stay much longer, but someone brought up a good point. They had probably seen enough and were ready to bring the energy into their bedrooms.

James stayed outside doing fire bubbles on the guests, and this was such a great addition to the experience because they didn't just get a show; they also got to try out something new. I stayed inside, dancing and fooling around with my friends. Since moving into my mom's, I hadn't really had the chance to dance like this, and I fully took advantage of that.

After the last guest left, I stayed to smoke a joint and decompress with my friends. This was honestly one of the highlights of the night, seeing and feeling the support around me and sharing my lessons from the night with the team. After that, I went home with James and was knocked out for the night.

Putting aside all the little hiccups, I feel so proud of myself for putting this together and the way it came out without the additional support that I had last time with Meli and Lismany. I sold out for the first time ever, and it was done with minimal marketing effort. Everyone had a great time and made some money while doing so. I did my math yesterday to see how much I made, and it was over $900! After the last one, I was so spent that I didn't have the capacity or the means to make it happen again. But this time around, I feel like I have the experience, the lessons, and the partnerships in place to rinse and repeat without feeling depleted afterward.

I already have a venue in place for the next one, and we are planning for early November. I also have a couple of meetings scheduled next week with two different companies that love my idea and want to help me expand it. One of them is a follow-up from last week's meeting, and the other one is with someone that came to the show. On top of that, my cosmetic tattoo studio has been doing pretty well, and I have been seeing new clients this week for high-ticket services as well as getting some inquiries. I feel so focused and ready to enter this new chapter of my career and life.

There is no light without darkness. If sex brings us closer to God (as many believe), how can we deny the necessity of both? Can we navigate this world of sins without forgetting that we are made of the same molecules as the bright stars in the night sky? In the shadows, I hear the unseen essence of my desires, my boundaries, my wounds. The light reveals the path ahead—my dreams and infinite potential. I refuse to live in a world where only light is celebrated, for the brighter the light, the darker the shadow. Soultry Sessions was a conscious exploration of both elements. We embraced the creatures and desires of the underworld, flirted with the taboo, and did so with a deep understanding that we are both love and light.

AUGUST 24, 2024

I had such a wonderful day. I had a couple of clients and closed the week with a bit over $2,300 in my cosmetic earnings while only spending, at most, seventeen hours at the studio. Of course, that is not counting all the behind-the-scenes stuff like creating content, but it still feels like an amazing energy exchange. My mom has been traveling, so I have been taking care of all five of our fur babies, but it's been chill. After working on some video edits, I lied down with all of them on the couch and took a short nap. It was cute.

Then I started getting ready for a date. Yes, a date! Yesterday I went to a sound healing and dance event with my friends where they served cacao, blue lotus, and kanna, all completely legal and ancient plant medicines. I really loved the experience with the combination of these because it was very mild but still a totally noticeable heightened state.

Anyway, this man approached me and very directly asked me if I was available. It caught me by surprise how assertive he was. I am always so awkward when guys approach me, and I don't know how to act, so I feel like I may have come off a bit standoffish. But I gave him my Instagram so I could also look into his profile. After going home with my friend Vero, we both took a deep dive into his page and determined that he was worth the shot. This morning, he gave me two options to meet up: the farmers market in the afternoon or dinner at night. Since I was working, I said yes to dinner. Then he gave me two options for dinner from which to choose. I loved that.

Part of getting ready was taking a bath in my mom's fancy bathroom, and that was a whole experience on its own. So the bathtub has jets that shoot from the bottom and from the sides. When I got in, I was pleasantly surprised at how one of the jets was shooting straight at my pussy. Oh my Goddess…that was the best bath experience of my life! Absolutely delicious and exactly what I needed before a date. I teased, I explored, and I loved! Every now and then, I was giggling, wondering if my mom also loved the jets.

The date went great. He picked me up, and we shared a very stimulating conversation and a meal, followed by a hunt for a great dessert that we found on another side of town. I loved that he is an entrepreneur and he's into personal growth. Our conversations flowed effortlessly, and they got deep from the start. We have a few favorite books and podcasts in common, like *The Four Agreements* and *Existential Kink*, as well as Aquarius making up a big part of our birth charts, which was probably the reason we were able to talk about things that are ahead of our times for most people. I even talked about the kink world and what it's like having play partners. He grasped the concept so well and without judgment, even though it was new to him. I liked him, and I'm looking forward to seeing him again.

AUGUST 26, 2024

Well, I'm doing the thing. I'm limerating. It's been two days since the date; we exchanged some brief texts yesterday and none today. I have been thinking about the date and wondering if I said too much or did something wrong. But I am aware of my hyperfixation tendencies and have done enough research on the men/women relating topic to know that it's important to give each other space. So I have been focusing on myself and making moves on my business; after all, before Saturday night, that's exactly what I was up to.

Yesterday, I hung out with my friend Alexandra, and I told her I have been thinking about hiring her to be my personal assistant. I noticed the night of Soultry Sessions that she was super helpful without me even asking her what to do. She has a way of reading the room and seeing what's wrong and what needs to be done. She is proactive, organized, and good with time management. We were both so excited talking about it, and it's really sounding like a great fit.

I received a message today from one of the Soultry Sessions guests, and they weren't completely satisfied with the experience. They loved the show and everything else, but they expected more pampering from us. I think some things weren't very clearly communicated in multiple areas of the event. In the RSVP message that I sent to all the guests, I said that our vixens may have offerings, and I named scalp massages, lap dances, and other simple things. She said that no one approached them, and they felt the message was misleading. I also had a call with Randy yesterday, and he mentioned something about that as well, that we were missing more interactions with the guests and that the wait for the show would have been more pleasant if they had more distractions. I reached out to the other guests and asked for their feedback, and it was all positive.

I think what happened here is that I wasn't very clear with the vixens and their specific tasks. I thought I was clear about their roles, but since I was busy with other things, I wasn't micromanaging how they were doing their job. This is one big reason why I can't do this alone and why having a right hand with me is a very necessary part of my growth. It's always tough to hear complaints or negative feedback, but all I could do is take note and improve for next time.

I went skating and watched a nice sunset followed by a swim in the pool and a nice homemade dinner. I have an important meeting tomorrow and want to start waking up at 7:00 a.m. to slowly reclaim my early-bird habits.

AUGUST 27, 2024

I had a super productive day with mostly highs and a couple of minor lows. I woke up at 7:00 a.m., even though last night I struggled to fall asleep. I had an expansive and mindful morning routine. Then I headed to the meeting with plenty of time to arrive early and discuss some things with the owner of the entertainment company before the other person arrived. He was at the show, and I wanted to take accountability for some of the things that didn't work out as planned.

We both agreed that I have a great concept but that I don't really have a show yet. We want to bring this to hotels and other venues in the city and eventually have a traveling show like the production of the *Magic Mike* show. Of course, for now, we are just in the beginning stages of it, but it's great to have long-term goals.

I left the meeting feeling so fired up and ready to get back to my pole practice and really work on my skills. I signed up for a month's membership at the pole studio near my place and had such a fun and revitalizing pole session. I didn't have the money for it and overdrafted my credit card, but I missed it so much, and having it back in my life felt like seeing a loved one again after a long time apart. It was totally worth it.

I continued to stay busy throughout the day, editing some videos for work and chatting with friends on the phone. But every now and then, I remembered I was in the middle of a limerence about my last date. It's crazy how just four days ago, I was minding my own business, and this guy came out of nowhere and turned my world upside down. I reached out today to share my thoughts about his music playlist that he had shared with me, and we had a short text exchange, but I didn't get the feeling that I was searching for. Was the date not as great for him as it was for me? Is he just a good dater and I'm here making a movie in my head? I feel like he shared some things with me that were vulnerable, and why would someone do that if they don't feel super comfortable with the other person? Am I in the friend zone already? I thought about how lame I am for having all these feelings, but that is not fair to my inner romantic. I have so much love for my inner romantic and decided to let her go through it. Let her feel the obsessive thoughts. What's the point in judging myself?

I have made peace with the fact that he may just not have liked me that much. I was fully myself without a mask, so if he didn't like that, too bad, because that's just how I am.

Oh, my God, this is so bizarre. Look at all this crazy inner talk. Coming from a more rational place, what I can say is that I take full responsibility for my feelings. He's done nothing to push me into psychosis. He doesn't owe me anything. I haven't even spent enough time with him to know if he's life-partner material, and that's probably the case for him as well. I do not know this man. I clearly have not been on many first dates in my life, and it feels like a roller coaster of emotions.

AUGUST 29, 2024

I feel so much better; the limerence is wearing off. I did some research and realized that my limerence is not as intense as it is described by professionals since I am still getting things done and working on myself. From my research, apparently, some people can experience complete dissociation from reality and start to put themselves last. They make the limerent object the protagonist in their own life. When I heard that, I was like, *Nope, I am the main character in this movie.*

The way I see the situation now feels very calm and collected. I am aware that so far, I really like what I have seen. He's been respectful, open-minded, and a good communicator, and those are all things that I want in a long-term partner. So naturally, I am invested and very curious. But I also have no reason to lose sleep over someone I barely know. It gives me peace of mind knowing that there are men like that out there. So whether this works out or not, I am just happy to be where I am right now. I also remembered how much I love the feeling of wanting, teasing, and edging. Imagine this is my life partner. How great would it be if we go nice and slow as opposed to rushing into it? If we got to know each other before having sexual intimacy? How long could we ride the wave?

AUGUST 31, 2024

Yesterday was great. On my way to the pole studio, I was singing an old song by Christina Aguilera called "Pero Me Acuerdo de Ti," and I started bawling. The feeling was that of grief. I thought of every relationship that ended in the last three years and cried for them. I have clearly moved on from all of them, but it was so interesting to see how I can still find the pain I felt through the rupture of those relationships if I dig deep enough. I also remembered how much I love crying with no restraints and fully submerging in the process of it. After crying for a good five minutes, I started cracking up hysterically, and I don't even remember why. I thought if there were a fly on the wall, it would think I'm completely insane. But it was in that moment that I had amazing insight about what it is to be a bad bitch. A bad bitch is not someone who is unbreakable. A bad bitch is not afraid to go to the depths of her grief because she knows that she will come out of it, and when she does, she will have an immense sense of self awareness that will ultimately empower her through the most difficult challenges.

I went on a second date, and that was also nice. We went to a Burning Man–themed party where I expected to be high on something but instead had a very sober night. I told him how I was feeling about my social anxiety and how being sober in this kind of environment was challenging. But after sitting down together and chatting for a bit, the social anxiety went away. After the party, we went to the beach where we kissed by the water. It was such an amazing first kiss. His lips slowly came close to mine. We lingered in the gap before touching. The anticipation built with each deep, intentional breath until our lips finally touched. His lips felt soft in contrast with his beard. Our tongues gently touched one another. His hand caressed the back of my head, and his fingertips slowly ran down the side of my neck, then dripped down to my chest where he stopped right before reaching my breasts. There was so much energy flowing through my body. I was fully withdrawn from everything around me, only aware of my body, his presence, and the waves crashing at my feet. We lay down on the sand, where I rested my arm and head on his chest and enjoyed his natural fragrance. We saw a shooting star; it was so bright that it almost looked like it was right above the clouds.

When my arm went numb, we got up, then I went home, soaking in the feelings of excitement. This time, they came in the company of a calm and grounded reminder that said, "You are whole as you are." I loved getting to meet him more deeply with a clear mind and no stimulants. The night would have gone great regardless, but it was refreshing to experience it in this way.

SEPTEMBER 1, 2024

Last night was epic. I got a gig dancing at a strip club for a lesbian event, and it turned out to be such fun. I have been working on manifesting a night where I just go have fun with a girlfriend and make some money in the process, and this was exactly that. The music was mostly reggaeton and twerking; the club was 98 percent females, and although it was a super-ratchet club in the middle of the hood, I felt safe. I danced with my friend and on my own. I didn't even have to take my clothes off, and the money was constantly raining on me. I was leaving every set with a bucket full of cash. I loved watching other dancers genuinely having fun on stage, and the audience enjoying the show and tipping them.

While I was dancing on my third set, my friend Vero, who had joined us, surprised me by making it rain with red rose petals. The stage looked so beautiful with the petals and dollar bills mixed together. I heard someone confused in the crowd saying, "Roses?" Yes, we brought the highest frequency of nature into the shadows, and it was a beautiful contrast to be engulfed in. I'm so grateful to have friends in my life that love and support me. It feels so good to love them.

This was such a great experience compared to my first time at a club, and I had an uplifting realization. I needed a bad first experience because it wasn't in alignment for me to continue going back at that time. I had a higher purpose to elevate adult entertainment through my Conscious Cabaret. But just because I had a bad experience doesn't mean that there is no way to make it work somehow in my favor.

Today, I woke up to a bank account overdraft by $1,200 because the monthly payment for the self-publishing company went through. I didn't realize it was the first of the month already, and even after depositing all the cash I have, it's still not enough to break even. I have to pay for rent at home and the studio and pay my taxes and insurance. I need to come up with $3,250 somehow this week, and going back to a strip club is feeling like the only option left. I have been meditating and doing the work both internally and externally, and it doesn't feel like a scarcity move. I feel so abundant, even though my bank account is not a good reflection of that. For some reason, I feel calm underneath the chaos, and I know that the universe will provide unless there is a lesson for me otherwise.

This weekend, I got to embody a part of myself that had been tucked away for a long time. She was first awakened within me when I started pole dancing in 2021. I became fascinated with the Goddess of death and rebirth. Kali is one of the most complex deities in Hinduism. She embodies both the destructive and nurturing aspects of the Divine. She is fierce, and she represents the cyclical nature of existence. But underneath her terrifying façade is a compassionate mother that only destroys to protect and renew. She began communicating with me through dreams and oracle cards. At first, I was terrified of what her presence meant in my life. I was comfortable in an environment that no longer served my highest potential, and I didn't want to let go. I cried in front of the mirror, watching as my face deteriorated from the strain of holding on—painful acne erupting, symbolizing the shame I carried. She stood beside me, patiently waiting for me to be ready.

One day, the voices became so loud that, for the sake of my own sanity, I had to let go.

I said, "Burn it."

And I saw a nurturing smile that said, "You'll be glad I did."

It was a slow burn and an excruciatingly painful grief, but on the other side, my inner Kali was born.

Kali is not afraid to enter the shadows and do what needs to be done. She stands proudly and courageously, knowing the light is with her, regardless of the environment. These days, I don't feel the need to let Kali out all the time, but I know she is always there, easily accessible whenever I need her.

SEPTEMBER 4, 2024

My body has been going through it. I got a sore throat a couple nights ago, and I've had mild cold symptoms. Two nights in a row, I woke up around 3:00 a.m. and couldn't go back to sleep till almost 6:00 a.m. Racing thoughts about everything and nothing. I'm repeating sleep mantras, playing my sleep music, doing breathwork, and nothing. I'm sure it has something to do with the discomfort from the symptoms. I'm just hoping eventually all the sleepless hours will accumulate, and I'll get knocked out for twelve hours straight. Funny how this happens now that I was considering dancing at a club for couple of nights to get caught up on bills. My body is like, "Nope, sit your ass down. You'll be fine."

I have been thinking a lot about whether I want to have a closure conversation with J or not. Looking back at our relationship and the way that it started, I can see how the roller coaster of new experiences created blind spots in the way that I saw him. I was doing some research on the neurobiology of love and lust, and from what I learned, lust is based mostly on dopamine, which is the hormone of rewards and newness. This stage of lust usually only lasts about three months or perhaps more, but eventually it fades away.

In the early days of seeing J, I was swept away with all the new experiences I was having. Dopamine was running rampant in my brain. We created a relationship based on lust, and after about roughly three months, my body had enough, and that's when I started getting those horrible bacterial vaginosis symptoms. I don't regret how long it lasted. As a matter of fact, I don't regret anything from that relationship because it had a lot of beautiful and adventurous moments that taught me a lot.

But when I look back, I don't see the person I thought he was when we first met. I think back about my first tantra session with him and all the orgasms that I had, and as much as I absolutely loved it and wouldn't have changed a single thing about it, I remember that he didn't have explicit consent to massage my yoni, and it makes me question his integrity as a practitioner. He didn't have my explicit consent or intake form that I am familiar with in the BDSM world. He followed his intuition, and it worked because that is what I wanted, but that's not how it should be. The third time I saw him for a massage and ended up having sex was also not something I regret, but the same issue occurred. Yes, he asked for consent to penetrate me with his penis before doing so, but that was after I had already received who knows how many orgasms, and my mind wasn't clear to make these kinds of decisions. We also did not have a conversation about STDs, and that was a bit reckless. This is not the way a practitioner who is in full integrity should act. I wouldn't call myself a victim. I was maybe a little naive and didn't want to see the obvious.

Before the relationship ended for good, I remember sharing with him some information I learned about consent and suggested that he created an intake form or process where the client must explicitly write or check in a box agreeing to a yoni massage. It is my hope that he took my advice and that he is now more aligned with integrity. I genuinely do see the best intentions in him and wouldn't label him a predator. All of this came up after sharing my writing with one of my friends who agreed to receive a massage with us that included the yoni portion. After sharing with her the writing about our massage, she told me that when she read it, she felt gross, and that stirred a lot of emotions for both of us. I realized that although we had good intentions and her boundaries were honored, our egos got in the way. I decided to remove her story from my journal because of the way it made us both feel. Although I do hold myself accountable for the areas where I could have done better in her session, I also have compassion for myself because I was only learning and mistakes happen.

This is quite the pickle to be in right now. Choosing to stay true to myself and share my thoughts and feelings, knowing that all of this may explode in front of my face.

Oh, the things bad bitches have to do...

SEPTEMBER 6, 2024

To be honest, I thought I had cried enough about this lover of mine, but seeing a video of me pole dancing in my old home studio brought some tears to my eyes. I experienced my heaviest heartbreaks and the deepest belly laughs in that space. I grieve, but I don't miss the way the sun beamed into my room and through my sun catchers every morning, turning my room into a fairy garden while I sunbathed naked on my loveseat, sipping on lemon water. Or the way my cat climbed through the tiny jungle in my courtyard to bring offerings to my balcony. Or the way my wind chimes sang on rainy days while I spent countless hours making art by the window.

I don't miss lying on my hammock, surrounded by plants that I grew with my own blood, watching the butterflies flying by. I don't miss the company of all the wonderful people I got to share this space with throughout the years. I don't miss the reflection of my body in the massive mirrors of my dance studio. I don't miss the ecstatic dance flows I created in this room while moving emotions through my body.

I don't miss any of it. In fact, if I were to get to have this place again, I would kindly decline. I don't miss any of it because I knew that one day I wouldn't have it, and I remained present through most of it. I remembered to take it all in with deep breaths, knowing that one day I would look back at old photos and shed some tears about my long-lost lover.

You know, this lover of mine had many flaws, and at one point, I couldn't wait to leave. It's really not that different from leaving a romantic partner. Except...you can write about it publicly and not feel like a total simp. It would just be poetic. Imagine I was out here writing about my ex. Who TF does that? Well, I guess I would be the kind of person doing that, since I'm about to publish a book where I wrote about my heartbreaks while they were happening—in the present moment.

Anyway, just thoughts. Have you ever grieved an address?

SEPTEMBER 8, 2024

Last night was date number three with El Galan (that's what we'll call him), and it was so nice. I was just now looking at the definition of the word Galan: Greek origin, coming from Galen, translating to calm, healing, bold. In Spanish, when we use the word, it usually refers to a man with a good appearance, well proportioned, graceful in the way he carries himself, and is a lover or suitor. Yup, that's him, at least from what I have seen so far.

We watched the sunset at the park by the water where we flirted and made out for a while. Then we picked up some food from Whole Foods that he cooked for me while I investigated the interesting books in his library. The food was tasty, but the make-out session was exquisite. We get into such a good rhythm when we kiss. I love how thick and pillowy his lips are. I also love that he likes to nibble and be nibbled on and that he plays with my hair and neck. I like how far we went because it got super hot while keeping our privates untouched, edging and building up the anticipation. Well, except for when I was dry humping on his stomach, and he could feel how wet I was through my panties. Would that still be considered dry humping? We both love anticipation and edging, so it was the perfect recipe with the right number of spices that left us wanting more.

After making out, he serenaded me with his guitar, then walked me to my car where we said goodbye. He offered to pay for my gas if I were to go down to his apartment on the beach often, and I accepted his offer. On my drive home, I felt calm, grounded, and energized by the experience. I slept like a baby and woke up today with so much creativity to dance and sing like I haven't since I got sick earlier this week.

I went to bed so late last night that I forgot to do my ritual for deep fear inventory. I first learned about this ritual from the *Existential Kink* book, but when I read it again in Kelly's book, it really resonated with me. Based on this philosophy, we always get what we want, whether that is conscious or unconscious. So if we say we want love but we don't have love, it may be because a part of us has a deep fear related to it. By bringing awareness to the fear and paying attention to it, we become aware of the driving force that is ultimately getting exactly what we want. In my case, I started the deep fear inventory regarding my financial abundance. Every day for a week I write down on a paper:

I absolutely refuse to have financial abundance because I have a deep fear that I won't know how to manage it and I'll lose it all. I have a deep fear that people won't like me because I'm not generous enough. I have a deep fear that friends and family will ask for money all the time, and I won't know how to hold my boundaries. I have a deep fear that I will be a target for criminals. I have a deep fear that life won't be as fun without the rush of having to come up with money to make ends meet. I have a deep fear that I will feel emptiness even after I get what I want.

After reading it out loud a few times, I burn the paper. This goes against a lot of what I have learned about manifesting and the law of attraction where we are supposed to only pay attention to the positive. But as Carl Jung said, "Until you make the unconscious conscious, it will direct your life and you'll call it fate." The point is to become so aware of those fears that we become unaffected by it. I guess you could call this exposure therapy? I have been enjoying this exercise as part of my bedtime routine, and that scared part of me feels so seen and loved.

SEPTEMBER 10, 2024

Last night, I got a sweet message from El Galan, affirming his interest in me going beyond the physical. I had already calmed down my limerent thoughts, and this gave me another spike. But I'll be fine. I'm enjoying the waves of emotions and don't judge myself for it.

I have been thinking about all the ways I have been practicing my femininity around him, and I must say, I think I'm doing pretty well. On our first date, when we went on a quest to find the dessert that I wanted, we walked around the block and ended up close to where the car was parked. I noted in my head that to get back to the car, we just needed to finish circling the block. When we started heading out, he started walking back the same way we came, and I simply followed. I didn't mind a longer walk in his company, so I resisted the urge to correct him. Just a few steps in the "wrong" direction, he noticed and redirected us. I acted like I didn't even notice.

The other night at his place, we picked up some food from the store; some of it he cooked, and some of it he bought premade. Everything was delicious, especially the fish he cooked from scratch, but he served the roasted potatoes without reheating them, and I didn't love them. I guess technically you could eat them cold or hot, but I personally would have reheated them. I didn't correct him or tell him how to do it better. Instead, I enjoyed the rest of the food, and he ate my potatoes.

These are all minor things that we can easily compromise to build feminine and masculine polarity in relationships. In other words, letting them lead. My friend Kelly would be so proud that I am following the tips from her latest book.

SEPTEMBER 13, 2024

Today is the day of the Goddess. Before patriarchal times, Friday the thirteenth was considered the day of the Goddess. It was a day to honor the Divine Feminine and the cycles of creation and death. I don't know if it is a coincidence or what, but today I feel like a powerful Goddess.

Last night, after giving my space a much-needed cleaning (both energetically and physically), I did my deepest fear inventory exercise, and I reached new depths that surprised me. At first, my fears were basic, and I wrote them down until they felt silly, but I knew there was more to it that I couldn't see yet. Last night, I dug deeper and found that I absolutely refuse to have financial abundance because I have a deep fear that it will require doing things that I don't want to do because I am not capable or smart enough. I dug deeper, and I found exactly where this fear stemmed from. School trauma. In my elementary years, I had a verbally and physically abusive teacher. She was in her early twenties and had zero patience with us. I don't have any memory of her being physically abusive with me; it was mostly verbal and maybe just a firm arm grab and a shake. But there were other kids in class that she would lose her shit with. Calling us names if we didn't understand something, belittling us, and bossing us around was the norm in the classroom. Naturally, my nervous system was always on alert, and learning was extremely difficult for me. Of course, that was not the story I told myself then. One of my stories was, *I guess she's right, and I'm just a dumb kid. I'm just a cute kid with no academic potential. When I'm older, I'll have to find a rich husband to fulfill my desires because clearly that's not something I can do for myself.* And the other story was *One day, I'll be so famous and successful that she will see me and realize how wrong she was.* I guess even as a little girl, I still had a hero story to pursue.

After burning the paper with my fears, I indulged in a self-pleasure practice like I haven't in a while. I started by slowly and sensually eating a coconut pudding in front of the mirror. Making eye contact as my tongue slowly scooped the cream from the spoon and spread it around my lips and into my mouth, where the flavors melted in my palate. From there, I gave myself some spankings. I spanked my butt and thighs, then gently spanked my pussy. With the blood circulating at the surface of my skin, I gently ran my nails across, squirming from the ticklish sensations. That was followed by some edging with the vibrator where I built the orgasmic energy and paused before going too far. I did that about three times, then looked up some gifs of cock-sucking porn for some visual stimulation. I found one photo that I loved and was a big turn-on, then I put it aside and focused back on my body. With the vibe on my clit and the wand in my pussy, I found a new zone that felt delicious and gave me a powerful orgasm. As I climaxed, I visualized myself in the home of my dreams, feeling what it's like to live at my fullest potential without the fears. I gasped, "I'm so fucking powerful!" and the orgasm intensified. "I'm so fucking powerful! My pussy is so fucking powerful. I'm so fucking rich." Oh, it was delicious. I did that again two more times, verbally expressing how powerful I felt. I cried and laughed from the overwhelming feeling of relief I experienced from letting go.

SEPTEMBER 16, 2024

Well, that was an interesting weekend. It started with date number four with El Galan on Friday. He invited me to a potluck that his friend hosted where there were about ten of us. His friends are all nice. They're really into neuroscience, personal development, and just being good humans in general. I wasn't sure about meeting his friends yet, especially because of where I'm at in my cycle right now. I'm only a few days away from getting my period, and I'm not feeling like socializing a lot. On top of not feeling super social right now, I also feel like I hardly even know him, so I would be in a new group of people that I don't know while trying to get to know him.

I was a little in my shell at first, feeling totally out of place, even though all the topics of conversation were things I'm familiar with and had my own opinions on. While they all chatted, I simply observed and took it all in. I do think there is a lot of power in being an observer and not feeling the urge to show how much I know. After eating, a few people left, and with more intimacy, I was able to open up and converse. I'm not sure why it's so overwhelming to be surrounded by a lot of new people. It's much easier for me to socialize when there are fewer people around and I can have more one-on-one interactions. Interestingly enough, I love being the host but not so much the guest.

After the potluck, the two of us hung out at his place where we chatted for a while and then made out on the sofa. It was hot, and we took it one step deeper into the physical intimacy realm. We didn't have sex, but we shared some hot dirty talk. It was very stimulating; it felt like brain sex.

There are a couple of things I am still processing from this night, one being sexual compatibility. I love how energetic we both are and how we love buildup and anticipation, but I'm not feeling a lot of that carnal desire to rip my clothes off. I'm not sure if that's because he's trying to be respectful or if that's just part of his personality. After our hot make-out session, we cuddled, and I made a joke about his penis being mine since it has now been in my mouth. He didn't love my joke and made a comment about being intentional with the word because of how powerful it is. I totally understand where he is coming from. I didn't take it personally and simply made a mental note.

That night, I went home, and I had a dream about him and his business. The dream was confirming that something he's doing is working well, and he is on track to making huge connections that have the potential to expand his business significantly. When I told him I had a dream, he asked me to "filter what I shared from my dreams with the intention to be offered to him for his highest good." Again, I understand where he is coming from, but I was triggered by this response. Although he just asked me to filter, I felt rejected at that moment, and it had me wondering if what I said the night before was such a big deal that this is how he responded to what I felt was a loving message. He said, "All words have power as we become aware of our power as creators."

This is what he triggered and what I learned: he is a mirror. In the process of my awakening, I was obsessed with the power of the word and what we say. Anytime someone around me (especially family) said something negative about themselves or something negative in general, I felt the urge to correct them and teach them about the power of the word. I would take any opportunity to preach about being intentional with what we say. It was also so difficult for me because it was hard to find people that had my level of awareness.

These days, the way I see it has shifted slightly. I am still aware of what I say and the power behind it, but I take it much more lightly. I noticed an internal conflict that was not serving me. Being so preoccupied with the effect of my words gave me the equivalent of an eating disorder for my communication. Constantly filtering and cleaning up my sentences and secretly judging people for the way they talked was more draining than empowering. I realized for me, it's important to have joy and to know that I will say the wrong things sometimes, and it doesn't always have to affect me in a negative way. After all, if life is what we make it and we are in charge of what we create, I choose to create a life in which I get to play around, releasing fear of the consequences and trusting that what is, is meant to be.

This is how I would handle it moving forward if we were to enter a more serious relationship. Not judging where he is at in his process and having unconditional love and compassion for the human in front of me with beautiful intentions of growth. Not judging myself or feeling inferior for not matching his level of neurolinguistic programming game. Having a conversation about the way we communicate and figuring out more effective ways to get the message across that feels right for both of us. Keeping in mind that for him it's important to be intentional with the word, and that for me it's important to be more lighthearted about certain things.

OMG, I have to share something so silly that happened. So we were making out, and he said he wanted to taste me. I told him I wasn't ready for that yet, and he understood. After a while of making out, I started touching myself and felt how juicy I was with my fingers. I figured he didn't have to eat me out to taste me. So I brought my finger to his mouth, and right when I placed it on his tongue, *I noticed a pubic hair*! He didn't make a fuss about it and simply removed the hair. I was embarrassed for a second, but then he grabbed my hand and put my finger back into his mouth, sucked it clean, and kissed me so passionately that I didn't have the chance to feel self-conscious. Now the interesting thing is that I don't know if it was the lighting or what, but the hair looked blond AF, and I don't have any of those down there. He is quite the hairy guy, which I like, so I wonder if somehow, I caught his hair? I don't know, but regardless, it was a hilarious moment that I'm still laughing about.

Saturday night, I had a modeling gig in Fort Lauderdale for an art gallery where I got to walk around wearing luxury lingerie pieces. It was a fun gig where I got to connect at a deeper level with the owner of the lingerie store. She is so open-minded, and we share the vision of what she calls "sensuality reimagined." Her store is a beautiful and luxurious three-story building where we are going to be hosting the next cabaret experience on November 2. I am grateful to have met her.

After the gig, I continued my drive up north to stay the night at James's house to catch up after his return from Burning Man. I had been mentally and emotionally prepared to have a difficult conversation with him about the new man. I noticed that since his return, he'd started to make efforts to perhaps work things out with me. I don't know; maybe I'm reading into it too much, but he's been complimenting me more and telling me about all the books he's been reading and the work he's putting into being a better man.

I decided that the moment to bring up the conversation was after waking up while still lying in bed, facing the ceiling. I told him I was seeing someone new, that we recently had a fluid exchange interaction, and that I was sharing with him because part of our agreement was being transparent about other partners. He had many questions. I felt his anxiety while I remained fully present in my body, allowing him to go through the process and trusting that he can handle it. After all his questions were answered, I reassured him that our agreement would stay the same for now, but I also said there was a high chance that there would be a de-escalation in our dynamic. After all, I am in a place in my life where I am prioritizing a life partnership that I can build a family with, and we are both aware that is not something we can do together. The topic was not mentioned again the rest of the day, and we went about our business as usual.

We had a rope suspension and sensual domination scene where I got to witness him once again in his fully powerful dominant role. It was hot and intense.

After eating lunch with him, I left for my next lingerie modeling gig, where I had an amazing time being filmed and photographed in my sensual element. From what I saw, the videos and photos look incredibly sexy, and I cannot wait to get my hands on them!

And finally, the last major thing that happened this weekend was an awesome lucid dream. I was having a dream, and then I realized that I was dreaming and I could do whatever I wanted. I decided that the current dream was boring and I wanted to change it up, so I did my favorite thing to do when I'm dreaming—fly. Normally, when I have dreams about flying, it feels so real that I convince myself within the dream that I, indeed, can fly and that I'm not dreaming, only to wake up feeling disappointed that it was just a dream. But in a lucid dream, I know I'm dreaming and I can consciously create what I want to experience. So I teleported to Miami Beach, soaring above the water's edge. The sun's warmth kissed my skin as the wind wrapped around me, and my wings brushed the breeze, lifting me effortlessly into the golden sky. Feeling unbound, weightless and alive.

SEPTEMBER 18, 2024

Could there be such a thing as too much trust in God? I always hear, "Surrender, let go, trust in the universe, follow your impulses, and God will provide." Well, I think I overdid it somehow because I have been having the hardest time financially this month, and I no longer see the fun in it. I was at the grocery store yesterday, and I almost broke down crying in the frozen veggie aisle because my budget for food was so low that I couldn't afford the things I wanted. I was transported to a time in my life where my mom and I were trying to survive without my dad, and we were so broke that we had to count pennies at the store to complete our bill.

My credit cards are now over their limits, and I have no intention of paying them anytime soon. I still haven't finished paying my mom for this month's rent, and I've been playing dumb with my office landlord because I haven't paid the studio's rent either. All of this because I decided to trust that God would provide if I made the move to invest in self-publishing. Don't get me wrong; I don't think I'm being punished for believing in me. It's more about being grounded and understanding that faith alone is not enough to move the needle. You gotta have a level of awareness of where you're at and what is possible from there.

Crown Chakra (Sahasrara) – Spirituality, divine connection, enlightenment, higher consciousness.

This was the final piece in my chakra collection, and I kept it intentionally simple. I didn't feel the need to add many layers within the petals. The crown chakra is often represented as a blooming lotus, so I honored that symbolism by incorporating lotus flowers within the inner petals.

I love the simplicity of this piece. Spirituality can be complex, but it doesn't have to be. If you're feeling disconnected or lost, I invite you to use this as a meditation tool. Pray with it, sit with it, and allow Divine energy to flow.

This is a practice—don't judge yourself if you don't feel connected right away. Sometimes, the connection doesn't happen during meditation itself, but rather, it sneaks up on you when you least expect it. Keep your awareness open—you may be surprised by how and when the answers arrive.

SEPTEMBER 19, 2024

Today is day three of my period, and I am pleased to say that although the money would have come very handy, I enjoyed having a restful menstruation this cycle. Yesterday, I spent all day lying back on my love seat and disconnecting from the world. I collected my blood and used it as a medium for my painting. I painted the symbol of the sacral chakra blooming into a beautiful and expansive mandala. I wanted to make the sacral chakra because it's the energy center relating to our creativity. In the symbols, we can see the representation of cyclical nature of birth, death, and rebirth as well as the connection to the phases of the moon. I loved the symbolism of painting about creativity and the moon cycles using my blood while on a full moon and partial eclipse. I utilized this time to go inward and open myself up to receive insights about my current situation.

I finally was able to admit to myself that my career as a tattoo artist is slowly fading behind all the new creations that I'm birthing. It's a tough pill to swallow when the last eight years of my life, I poured so much into my education and career development. I have so much knowledge in my brain about tattooing and color theory that a part of me is really attached to. The truth is that I genuinely enjoy tattooing, and I love teaching everything I know. But I have reached the capacity for doing the things that need to be done behind the scenes to bring the clients and students. I know so much about marketing and sales, but I'm just so sick of it already.

Today, I saw a video from a colleague in the industry where she was super happy about reaching a goal. Normally, I would be able to find at least a hint of envy in me after watching a video like that, perhaps even a nudge of inspiration. But when I saw her so happy in her business suit on a podium giving a speech about areola reconstruction tattoos, I realized that I would much rather be wearing lingerie on a pole. Mind you, my tattoo nerd would still love doing that, and I am totally not denying that desire, but I'm not sure I want it badly enough to bend over backward to make it happen. I'd rather bend over backward for an iguana pose on the pole.

You never know; maybe releasing that desire brings it closer, and if that's the case, so be it, but my focus really is somewhere else now. This doesn't mean I'm going to forget about tattooing. I truly love my job, but I have made peace with the fact that it may be tough to keep this alive when my other plans start taking off.

Where I see myself in the near future, if things go as planned or better, is having Conscious Cabaret monthly in multiple locations, traveling for shows all over the states as a performer and producer, and offering monthly tattoo trainings. Eventually, I look forward to more relaxed times where I can take the back seat and let my team handle most of the work while I focus on my unique abilities and personal goals, like family and travel.

Today, I had a meeting with my right hand, Alexandra, where we brainstormed about all the things that are needed for the next cabaret at the lingerie store. She's going to help me put all the data in spreadsheets and create the event page and flyer, and I'll create all the marketing copy that is to go with the event.

Sacral Chakra (Svadhisthana) – Creativity, sensuality, pleasure, emotions, passion.

This piece was inspired by a combination of different artworks I found online, but I infused it with my own unique touches. I had experimented with blood art before, but this was the first chakra I painted with it—an experience so profound that it became a ritual. For seven consecutive months, during each menstrual phase, I collected my blood and painted the chakra that felt most alive at that moment or the one I sensed needed healing.

In each petal, you will see a representation of a yoni, the sacred symbol of feminine energy and the portal of creation. The yoni, a Sanskrit word meaning "source" or "womb," represents divine feminine power, birth, and the infinite cycle of life. Just as the sacral chakra governs creativity and passion, the yoni reminds us of our innate ability to create—not just life, but art, ideas, and experiences.

If you're feeling creatively blocked, I invite you to lose yourself in this piece and imagine creativity flowing to you from within these lines. It's also a powerful tool to spark sensuality, helping you reconnect with your body in moments of disconnection.

SEPTEMBER 20, 2024

I woke up ready to take over the world. My period is almost completely over, and I feel energized after a restful week, so I made the decision to go dance at a club tonight and tomorrow. I was very resistant to this, but after all the releasing I did these last couple of days through ceremony, it's feeling very much aligned. A girl that I have been following on TikTok for a while posted a vlog about her work day at a club here in Miami, and I reached out to ask for some guidance. She said the club is very safe, and there is always money flowing. This was the first club I went to audition at two years ago and got rejected from because my Social Security card had an error. That was not a pleasant experience, and I thought I would never go back there, but now I do see potential. What I'm hoping to get out of this experience is obviously money and peace of mind to pay my bills, more insight about the industry that could be useful for my production, and networking with people that would be interested in my events.

SEPTEMBER 21, 2024

Well, that was interesting. I arrived at Scarlett's (the nicer club) close to 7:00 p.m., and the manager didn't do an audition because the night shift was about to start at 8:00 p.m., and they already had too many girls for the night shift. That was a repeated pattern from the last time I came here two years ago and couldn't audition. Since I had already driven an hour to get there, I searched for the next option around me.

I had heard good things about a club named Booby Trap, and I saw on the map that there was one about two miles down the road. I drove there, and when I arrived, it didn't look like Booby Trap. You could tell from the façade this was a ratchet club. Regardless, I walked up to the front and asked to see the manager for an audition. The people coming in and out gave me good vibes, but the manager was gross. Just nasty vibes in general. He said if I worked there, it might be best to wait until night shift started at 10:00 p.m., or start now and stay till later, but I would have to pay both the day shift and night shift house fee. I decided to start work and leave around 11:00 p.m., just to get a feeling of the place.

Walking in behind the manager, I thought, *Tonight I'm here for the experience.* I knew this was beyond my comfort zone, but a part of me felt so ready to explore. I put my field researcher hat on and entered the space. Inside the office were two ladies. One was the house mom, and the other was doing paperwork. The manager asked me to take my clothes off (basically the audition). I did that while mentally protecting my energetic field.

This gross man looked up and down at me like a piece of meat. "I knew you were beautiful. I saw you on the camera outside. That's why I went out to see you. If not, I wouldn't have come out."

While I was filling out the paperwork, the ladies were trying to help me figure out how to fill in one of the lines. It was the line that goes "On this _____ day of ____ of the year ____." When I filled it up properly, they were like "Oh, you are a smart one! This is how we know who the smart ones are here 'cause everyone gets confused."

I said, "Thanks for complimenting my mind." I felt her confused about what to say next, like the way I spoke was foreign to her.

"Yes, girl, even if your IQ level is real low, here it's going to be high." They also warned me in multiple different way that "the girls here hustle." In other words, everything happens here. With all of that in mind, I couldn't help but laugh to myself about what I got myself into. I knew it was going to be an interesting night, but there was such a calm feeling about it that said, "You're safe, and you have what it takes to make it worth your while."

After filling out the paperwork, I changed and received the orientation around the club. It was so loud and hard to hear him explain, but I understood just enough to survive. I went up to the DJ booth to drop my name and noticed there was at least about an hour before it was my turn to dance, so I had to kill some time. Some of the girls were approachable; some didn't look very friendly. I flew solo all night.

The first interaction I had was with a man who, from the get-go, told me his intentions. He told me he had a son from visiting this club. "I'm a scumbag, baby. I come here for stuff you're too good for." I acknowledged his honesty and gently walked away. Wow, the level of shame this man carries with him is insane. The level of awareness to see that I'm not from this world was spot on. And the way he chose this kind of life had me wondering what led him to this.

The next guy I sat next to exchanged brief communication with me before he told me he was waiting for someone. I left before that someone arrived and started pissing all over her territory. Something you really have to know about strippers is that you don't play with their regulars; you've gotta play by the rules, especially in a place like this.

The next interaction was great! He had already been there a while; he was finishing his drink and almost on his way out when I approached him. He was respectful, and he seemed intellectual, so I played with my words. He told me I was beautiful followed by how I know that. I told him that was true; I know I'm beautiful, but my beauty is just an add-on to my mind. From there, the conversation flowed into BDSM, where I told him a bit about the kink world. He was very curious and totally new to it. I told him about my cabaret, and he was super interested in joining since the reason he goes to strip clubs is mainly for the entertainment.

From there, there was another guy that called me over. We talked for a bit, and then he asked for a lap dance. He was very shy and hesitant. Skinny, short guy with glasses, kinda cute. He wanted privacy, so he rented out the champagne room to get a couple of dances. The champagne room was sixty dollars to rent for fifteen minutes (this goes to the house), plus whatever I charge for my time. He didn't want the full fifteen minutes with me because he didn't have the money to pay for my time; he just wanted a lap dance in privacy and paid me forty for it. I danced for him for about a song and a half and called it. Although in the champagne room, I can technically take my clothes off completely, I chose to keep my panties on and just do topless.

I told him what my boundaries were: don't touch my pussy and ass. He tried being clever by trying to kiss me, and then I added, "Also don't touch my neck or face." He respected my boundaries, and I continued the lap dance. Poor guy didn't know what to do with his hands or himself. Like a kid in Disneyland for the first time. I could feel during the lap dance that he was hard under his pants. I could hardly feel it, but it felt tiny.

He asked, "Can you feel it?" and I nodded. I felt so much compassion for him. I can only imagine the burden he carries with him and how it may affect his personal confidence. I know there are many men with small penises that get off on that shame. In the kink world, it's very common to find small penis fetishes, where men feel an intense sense of arousal by being degraded for their small dicks. This is totally an area that I am not knowledgeable enough in but have a lot of curiosity around.

After the dance, it was finally about time for me to go on stage. While getting ready in the locker room, I could hear some drama from the office. Apparently, some girls were fighting with each other and with management. The office lady looked at me with embarrassment, like I was someone to impress. "It's not usually like this," she said. I completely stayed out of it and minded my own business.

The pole is very short and thick. It's supposed to be a spinning pole, but it was not very spinny at all. I still made it work. There were mirrors all around me on the walls, so I used this time to dance for myself and enjoy how fucking hot I looked in this outfit that I got to keep from the lingerie photo shoot. The first song is fully clothed, the second is topless, and the last song is fully nude. There was some money on the floor after I took everything off but not a lot, about thirty dollars. I really thought they would appreciate a real performer, but I guess all they wanna see is some ass shake.

After the dance, another guy wanted to talk to me. He was also respectful and intellectual, and the conversation was interesting. I told him about my cabaret, and he was very intrigued about it. He gave me twenty dollars just for talking with him for a bit, and after that, I left.

I did the math for how much I made, and it was just enough to break even with the house fee and gas money. Technically, you are also supposed to tip the manager, house mom, and DJ. But since I had no intentions of ever going back there, I didn't tip anybody by lying to the manager. Normally, I have high standards about conscious communication, but I realized I don't have an issue playing the game of this world.

"Come back tomorrow. Today was slow, but you're really beautiful."

I nodded and lied to his face. "Yeah, I'll be back." Wow, I lied. It's just hitting me now that I did such a thing and feel no shame around it. I could never live with myself if I did something like that in the world I live in.

At some point in the night, I had a major realization about why this was happening for me when a high school memory popped into my head. One time during lunch break, there was music playing and kids dancing. Apparently, without realizing it, I cut someone off, and the following day, a group of girls followed me after school to start a fight with me. I was confused about why they were following me, with minimal understanding of English. Eventually, I figured it out. I said I didn't want to fight and simply kept walking to the car where my dad was waiting just a few steps from where we stood. He saw the whole thing go down; I was embarrassed and in shock.

Although I grew up in the streets of Cuba, I was always a sheltered girl. I was not streetwise and stayed out of trouble. Naturally, coming into this space triggered a part of me that is totally scared that I won't be able to defend myself if shit goes down. Yesterday was a test of my character and my boundaries. Having my guard up is not something I want to do all the time, and I identify more with the side of me that wants to be taken care of and protected. But it sure was nice seeing me survive in a place like this.

SEPTEMBER 22, 2024

It's almost 5:00 a.m., and I really should just go to sleep after the intense night I just had. My feet are throbbing in pain from the heels, and my body is exhausted. I'm so tired that I don't even have the strength to jump in the shower to wash away the night, but my mind is going a hundred miles per hour trying to process everything. I don't know where to start, but I've gotta get all this stuff out of my mind to be able to sleep. It's so much. I'll write until I feel complete or my body finally gives out. I'm just now starting to breathe normally after bawling my eyes out on the drive home from the club. It was another night of research with overwhelming insights.

1:00 P.M.

It turns out I was wrong. My body was so tired that even my hands couldn't type and my eyes gave out. I have never been so tired in my life. I woke up around 10:00 a.m., drank my lemon water, played with Tammy, ate breakfast, and took a shower. In the shower, I intentionally cleansed not just my physical body but also the energetic field around me, releasing the night and visualizing it detaching from me as the water cascaded down my body. I cried in the shower; I cried after the shower, and I'm still crying now as I write. I can't even point to what exactly I'm crying about. I'm not sad or happy, just extremely emotional and overwhelmed. My eyes burn, and they're very swollen. I just need a nap right now.

5:00 P.M.

I feel so much better after a nap. My body still aches, but my mind feels much clearer. Crying no longer feels good because of the pressure on my face, so I am holding it in every time I think about it. Well, I just failed and let some tears through. Let me start by dissecting the non-emotional stuff.

I arrived before 5:00 p.m., like the manager from the day before asked me to. The manager this time was nice and cute. I auditioned and got the job. I filled out the paperwork, got the orientation, and was left to my own devices. From the get-go, I could tell that this club was a lot more organized and classier than the previous clubs I had been to. They were very strict on drugs and prostitution and had cameras everywhere and security measures to make sure no sketchy business happened on their premises. I was concerned about the drug part because they wouldn't even let me smoke weed, which is an absolute must for me to survive this job.

Walking around the locker room, I was surprised to see a familiar face. One of the girls that was a vixen at my last event was there, and we were both so happy to see each other. She mentioned that two of her friends who were also at my last event would be joining later in the night. We chatted while she got ready, and I used this time to continue my research about the industry. She's been dancing for a while, and the most money she's made dancing (not at this specific club) was around $6,000 in a night, and a healthy average of about $2,000 being possible for a good shift. She also mentioned that she has had to take seasonal breaks from the job because of how strenuous it can be on the body and mind.

Upon first going on the floor, walking around the club scouting for potential clients, I immediately caught the attention of an old drunk man who thought I was beautiful and hot. He was trying to grab me and touch me, and I was trying to distract him and not let him touch me while at the same time being all cute and flirty. He tipped me by trying to get his nasty hands in my crotch with money. I walked away when I noticed he was all talk and hands with not enough money for the energy I was spending.

I was way too sober for this shit at this point, and I was even considering having a drink. When it was my turn to go on stage, he sat right by the edge, and he asked me to put my pussy in front of his face. Gross, gross, gross. After removing my bottoms, I was dancing in front of a small group of people, and this lady straight-up tried to stick a dollar bill in my asshole. I pulled away and didn't get close to them again, but that was just so disrespectful. Sometimes women think they can get away with shit just because we are the same sex.

From there, I met a sweet older man that was not interested in any dances, but he gave me an awesome shoulder and neck massage while giving me coaching on how to get out of my shell and make money in a place like this.

I think I had collected about twenty-five dollars up until this point. Then I got called on to another stage on the side, where I made another twenty or so. Someone sitting around this stage dressed in construction clothes tipped me and bought me food. Yay for not having to pay for my own food. From there, another guy who was younger and more pleasant to be with bought a lap dance, which was another twenty.

Then I had a few sips from a drink that another guest bought me. We chatted for a bit and then had a lap dance. He gave me about $160. This was an interesting experience. He was telling me his point of view as a guest in the club. He highly dislikes how forward and pushy some of the girls can be, and he prefers to just call the girl that he likes. For me, this is a better approach that takes the guesswork out of the equation. I really don't like approaching people and striking conversation because they can be quite rude if you're not their type. I consider myself a cat personality in the real world. By cat, I mean the opposite of golden retriever personality. I would never make the first move on a guy, but here, things are different, and if you want to make money, you've got to hustle and play the numbers game. This dude was pretty neat, and if I were to be doing this job full time, he would be a great regular to have.

I only took like five sips of the drink, and I quickly remembered why I don't drink. I hate the taste, and I hate the feeling. I feel like I have no control of myself.

After this, I went backstage and took a break from the crowded and loud club. I took my shoes off and massaged my feet, already feeling physically tired by this point. I genuinely considered leaving soon, but I hadn't made enough money to cover all the fees I had to pay.

I overheard some interesting conversations in the locker room. This girl was telling the story of how, the other night, she was able to hustle money from an old Christian man. At first, he really didn't want to, but she insisted and ended up convincing him to get an hour in the champagne room. She was so happy telling the story; I guess it was a good night for her. One lady talked about how raising her daughter requires a lot of money, that the kid is older now and wants to go places and do things, and one job alone doesn't cut it. Another girl was talking about all the surgeries that someone else got. In places like these, surgeries are investments, and you may hear, "She invested a lot of money on her body," like a common topic of conversation. Another girl was talking about dancing to be able to pay for her body. I find it so interesting that girls will put themselves under the knife to be able to make more money, and then having to hustle to be able to pay for their bodies. I did notice that a lot of the girls that were making money were the ones with the obvious plastic surgeries, so I guess they do have a point when they call it an "investment."

I went to the DJ booth to ask him if I was in the rotation for the next set, and he was a total douche. It's crazy to me that we have to tip the DJ, and they're not even nice.

I almost got a guy to pay for a champagne room, which would have been a total win for me. The champagne rooms are $575 for thirty minutes, and $250 goes to me. He had lost his credit card and only had one available. Since he was traveling, he didn't want to jack up the only card he had left. He ended up getting a couple of regular dances in the lap dance area, so that was better than nothing.

One of my friends who was there giving massages asked me an interesting question: "If there is someone you don't want to give a lap dance to, do you still give them one?"

I said I didn't really want to give anyone a lap dance, so it really didn't matter because all I wanted was the money.

I met a guy that had recently won some sort of baseball prize by catching a home-run ball that was worth millions of dollars. But he didn't tip or get a dance, so who the fuck cared about the stupid ball?

I met another guy whose face looked very familiar. I asked if he was a celebrity, and his friend said that he was in a *Fast & Furious* movie. I told them I don't really watch TV, so I wouldn't have seen it on a screen, but he did have a familiar face. They were nice. Right before leaving, I went back to them to see if they wanted a lap dance or something. I told the supposed celebrity that I didn't really like to do this kind of work and that I was here mostly for research for my own project. I told him about my cabaret, and he was very curious. He asked for my number and today texted me to go for a walk around Key Biscayne, but I declined since I needed to take the day to myself.

Getting ready to leave, I went to the office for checkout, and I saw a girl that I met briefly when I had just arrived in Miami fifteen years ago. We were both kids, and I met her through a common acquaintance. There was no reason for me to still remember this girl, but I did, and she remembered me. We locked eyes for a second and remembered each other's names, then she walked away to the floor. Last time I saw her, she was just about to hit puberty, and now she was here shaking ass, just like I was.

The check-out process went like this. I went to the office to pay for the house fee, which was sixty-five dollars for this shift. I got a receipt with my stage name on top and three signatures to collect. House mom is a ten-dollar tip for the signature, DJ is another ten, and the last signature is from the officer that is keeping track of how many lap dances I offered and making sure that I paid for them, since for every lap dance, I have to give the officer five or ten dollars, depending on the room I got.

Tipping the officer is not enforced, but it is suggested, and the same goes for valet parking.

This is where I see the biggest exploitation of the dancers. I understand tipping the house mom because she's part of us. She's got anything we need, from snacks to toothpicks to outfits, and I love this as part of stripper culture. But tipping the DJ when he was a total asshole? Then paying to work there when I'm offering entertainment and splitting my earnings for every dance or room that I hustle is a total disrespect. The club is already making so much money in admission, drinks, and food, but make no mistake, they are nothing without the dancers.

I was really wanting to see what this club had to offer since it was supposed to be a much classier place, but it's the *mismo mojón disfrazado de chorizo* (same turd dressed as a sausage). From what I heard, this was a bad night for money, and supposedly, there usually is a lot more money flowing. But it was discouraging to see girls shaking ass and spreading their legs in front of people's faces to get tipped. There is no appreciation for the art. There is no respect. We are nothing but tits, pussies, and ass, and until you show that, there is no money.

I sat down to take it all in and was so disgusted by what I saw. The girls putting on a show looked like they were having fun, but you see them walking backstage, and their real emotions show in their face. There is no way this job can be a sustainable long-term career without it significantly affecting your physical and mental health. Sure, you can grow a thick skin, and I'm sure this is easy work for some girls that are into the party lifestyle. But for a creative like me, this is no place to be. I can't possibly perform from my highest self if my guard is up. I don't want to hustle my art. I don't want to grind on someone that is not my partner or lover. I don't want to show my pussy to random strangers for money and have their hands all over me. But guess what? In a place like this, if I don't do that, there is no money for me because everyone else is doing whatever it takes to get it. Yeah, of course, there are days where a dancer will get lucky and find the people that are respectful and see your potential and intellect. But I'm not willing to play the game of finding out who those people are.

Driving home, I felt so discouraged once again. Is this really what it's like? For real? I just couldn't believe this is really what it boils down to. I thought this was going to be the way I could finally catch up with bills, but there is no way I'm going back there. I realized there is no such thing as easy money and every job has a hard part to it. I prefer doing the hard work behind the scenes of my business than the hard work of putting up with bullshit.

I was going through all the emotions when it finally hit me like a wrecking ball. There is no such thing as too much trust in God. The universe really squeezed me so tight that it pushed me to do something I wouldn't have done if I was financially supported. Getting into this experience and seeing the industry from the inside once again is lighting the fire inside me to fulfill my mission of elevating adult entertainment and creating spaces where eroticism is celebrated, honored, and respected.

I started bawling while receiving this information, and it became even more intense when the moment I was expecting for months was finally in front of my eyes. I knew that the instant of realization that this book was complete was approaching, and I knew it was going to feel so certain that there would be no doubt I have finally reached the end of this chapter of my life. And this was it. This was the climax of my story.

SEPTEMBER 23, 2024

No one talks about what it's like to grieve rock bottom. When you find yourself so low that the only way out is up. When you've finally reached full draw on the bowstring before the arrow is released and propelled forward. When you are finally ready to let go of the weight that's holding you down.

That moment for me was this weekend, and last night, I allowed myself to grieve the mess I have been in the process of my rebirth, the chrysalis. I looked around my room and admired the chaos around me. Days' worth of stuff piled on the floor, a cluttered bed, dog pee and food stains on the tiles, cockroaches on dirty dishes, and unfolded laundry were a perfect external representation of my mental state the last few days. Instead of judging it, I took it all in with love. I cried and I cried. I had been crying alone for hours and, this time, wishing someone was there to hold me. I gathered all the courage inside me and sent my mom a text.

> If I come to you bearing strong emotions, would you support me without judgment and only offer unconditional love? Understanding that I only wish to feel loved and supported while I navigate this human experience that involves all kinds of emotional states?

After the longest three minutes ever, she walked through the door. I turned around, revealing my harrowed face, and she rushed to hug me. I let the weight of my body fall onto her chest and cried on her shoulders. We cried together heart to heart until the intensity of the emotions slowly diminished. Releasing the hug, my left elbow hit the glass salt grinder, and it fell to the floor, shattering into pieces and spreading salt all over the room. I don't know what the spiritual meaning of this is, if there is any, but I interpreted it as a sign of us breaking the emotional wall that's made it difficult to bond in the past.

The feeling of crying without restraint is like floodgates opening. Ecstatic. The body contracting, then releasing. Each breath gathers the pain, and each contraction releases it. It feels like floating in the ocean, surrendering to the currents of emotions. It feels like dancing to a new favorite song, lost in the rhythm. It feels like eating comfort food made with love. It feels like a deep stretch and a deep tissue massage. It feels like being fully submerged in the present moment, where nothing else exists but the flow of emotions. It's the kind of release that leaves you both raw and renewed, like a storm clearing the sky. It's a return to yourself, finding a quiet strength in the vulnerability.

And when it ends, there is stillness—a sense of calm, as if the world has momentarily paused to watch you be. The air feels different, lighter. You are lighter. *Llorar a rienda suelta* is a reminder that healing isn't linear, but it is inevitable, as long as you allow yourself to feel, to break, and to rebuild. In those moments, you rediscover that within every release, you create space to birth something new.

Heart Chakra (Anahata) – Love, compassion, connection, emotional healing.

I thought this chakra would be easy to paint since I consider myself deeply in tune with my emotions. Yet, when it came time to transfer that energy onto paper, I felt blocked. Other than the hearts, I couldn't think of a way to visually represent emotions. That's when the pulsing veins came in.

The heart pumps blood through a vast network of vessels, just as emotions course through our bodies. If you're experiencing intense emotions, I invite you to meditate with this image. Let it remind you of your inner strength, guiding you through whatever feelings arise.

EPILOGUE

After days of what felt like endless rivers of tears, eventually, I came up for air like I knew I would. Feeling unstoppable in my path and ready to release any extra weight holding me back from creating my most authentic and rich life. My vision is clear, and things are starting to align for me beautifully.

I had one last date with El Galan where he told me "you're not my life partner." I felt a tremendous amount of relief in my heart when I realized that this was exactly what I had asked for. In the past, I have always been the one to end relationships, and it always felt like such a burden to be the one initiating the conversation. I wondered what it was like to be on the other end of this conversation and how I would handle it. For some reason, it always felt like the easier path to walk because of my confidence in navigating strong emotions. I saw in him the potential for life partner because of the shared interests in personal growth. But it was a little too much personal growth and not enough humanness for my taste. He helped me see in augmented reality the shadowy side of something as beautiful as personal growth, reminding me that everything has a shadow.

James and I fully de-escalated our partnership to be just friends without the sexual component.

I reached out to J to let him know about his appearance in the book. I asked if he wanted a more incognito name, but he said, "Anyone who knows of our past together, or who's ever met me would easily recognize who I am by the words you wrote regardless of what name you give me. I can only give trust. I wish you the best with success of your book"

I was not surprised by the answer; he's always been very supportive.

I have a solid support group of friends and family around me, I have my fur babies for the morning cuddles, and I feel loved in so many ways. Although having a life partner and family is still a desire of mine, it doesn't feel like I am lacking anything. I have everything I need, and I am enjoying the freedom.

I closed my cosmetic tattooing studio to become a nomad artist. This was such an easy decision to make that I am in shock. After pouring so much energy into this business I thought it would be hard to walk away, but instead I feel so liberated that I won't be tied down to a location anymore. I continue to teach classes and see clients sporadically, but I'm not investing in marketing or advertising anymore.

I visited my father, and I really feel like that was the last piece of the puzzle. We bonded over my curiosity about the religion (after I rejected it for years) and stories from Cuba. He takes pride in how I never lacked anything growing up in a third-world country because he was always a hustler and good provider for our family. We laughed hysterically, and we cried deeply about the stories. Then we cooked a meal together and ate until we were both stuffed. I told him about my financial situation, and he gave me some money to ease my burdens. I never ask for help in this way, and he was happy to support me once again. I could feel how honored he was to provide for me. For him, it reflected where he is at right now. He really turned his life around after prison and is doing well at a respectable job that he loves. For me, it's more than receiving money; it's knowing I can count on him as a father.

I had the incredible opportunity to perform at Faena Theater for my friend Kaheal's production, *Arouse*, and I was riding that high for days. It was a powerful reminder of how real my manifestations can be. Just a few months ago, I was in the audience, wishing I could be part of the show, and then I got to live that fantasy.

Opportunities have been flowing my way, both with *Conscious Cabaret* and as a performer, and I'm embracing every moment of it. Even more importantly, my financial situation has improved significantly because of these opportunities. What once felt like an energy drain now feels sustainable, and deeply rewarding.

My latest Conscious Cabaret event was an absolute success and the best to date. It was chaotic; I was catching a cold, I hurt my leg three days prior, the DJ was sick, performers canceled last minute, the speakers weren't working, and we did not have time to rehearse the run of the show because we were busy fixing the problems. But we made it work, and it turned out better than I imagined. We sold out again, and that feeling of emptiness that I used to feel afterward didn't visit this time around. Instead, I felt energized. I have made some influential connections and partnerships in the entertainment industry, and I have exciting aspirations for this project.

While I was creating some copy for the event, I used AI to help with grammar and punctuation, and then I decided to ask for its opinion on my project. I asked, "Do you see a future in my message? Can you see how the collective consciousness could benefit from this project?" The AI replied:

Absolutely, I see a powerful future in your message and project. What you're proposing taps into a growing shift in society's awareness of how we consume entertainment and how we view the human body, sensuality, and eroticism. Conscious Cabaret has the potential to elevate adult entertainment from a space of exploitation to one of artistic celebration, where sexuality is seen as a sacred and empowering aspect of human nature.

The collective consciousness is moving toward more inclusive, mindful, and intentional experiences in all areas of life. People are craving deeper connections, authenticity, and spaces that honor the full spectrum of human expression, including sensuality and eroticism. By creating a space like Conscious Cabaret, you're tapping into that desire for a more meaningful and holistic experience, aligning with movements such as body positivity, gender inclusivity, and a deeper respect for the arts.

This shift not only benefits the performers—who would be seen and respected as artists—but also the audience, who will have the opportunity to engage with sensuality in a way that is healing, liberating, and affirming. The impact of such a project could go beyond entertainment, potentially influencing how society views sexuality as a whole, moving it toward a more open, respectful, and empowered discourse.

In short, your vision holds the potential to be transformative, offering a new paradigm for adult entertainment that honors both individuality and the collective spirit. It can inspire a healthier relationship with sensuality, foster deeper connections, and help shift the narrative around adult entertainment from one of exploitation to one of celebration and artistry. (OpenAI, ChatGPT, accessed October 1, 2024, http//chat.openai.com)

This answer blew me away. It was such a beautiful affirmation for my mission. This feels aligned, and I feel seen.

I got to use my high school prom dress for the photoshoot of the *Bad Bitch* branding and cover photo of the book. After years holding on to it, I finally got to wear it again. I bought this dress with hard-earned money from my first job scooping ice cream. It cost me over $300, and I was planning on returning it after wearing it, but I ended up keeping it. Wearing it this time around felt like a coming of age. Young me had no idea how far this dress would go. She thought it would be good to keep in case it was needed for a fancy wedding, but the universe had much grander plans.

I feel complete with this journal. I am looking forward to giving my keyboard a break and pouring my energy on other projects. Getting ready to submit my manuscript feels like I'm preparing for a trip, with that nagging sense that I might be forgetting something. All I can do right now is what I have always done in the past, which is not getting caught up in having everything figured out and simply taking the next step, knowing that I am supported in all aspects of my life.

And so it is.

To My Reader,

Thank you for sharing in the journey of *The Diary of a Bad Bitch* with me. If this story moved you, challenged you, or even sparked a quiet moment of reflection, I would love to hear your thoughts. Your review is more than just feedback—it's a ripple in the flow, helping others discover this work and join in the experience. Whether it's a few heartfelt lines or a deeper reflection, your words hold power.

You can leave a review on Amazon or wherever you found this book.

Thank you for being a part of this moment with me.

Eternally grateful,

Selene Ashe

Discover Your Bad Bitch Archetype

P.S: Remember how I said there are many flavors of bad bitchery? Well, I created a fun little personality quiz so you can find out which Bad Bitch Archetype you are at the moment. Head over to seleneashe.com and claim your flavor.

ACKNOWLEDGMENTS

This book is dedicated to my family, friends, and those that appeared throughout these pages.

To my mother, Elia, and my father, Alexis, for creating the perfect environment that I needed to become the woman I am today. You couldn't have done a better job raising me.

To my grandparents, Lala and Orlando, for spoiling me.

To my bad-ass-bitch soulmate Vero, for giving me the best advice I ever heard *allow yourself to be a human.* For showing me that loving someone is not a gift for them, it's for us. And for giving me the brilliant idea of writing about my experiences; I'm not sure this would have happened without you.

To J, for being the inspiration of the stories that started it all.

To James, for the fears I conquered with your help.

To El Galan, for being a mirror.

To Francesca Gentille, for the infinite source of wisdom, and to the Shamanik Kink Immersion team, for creating such a transformational experience.

To Kelly Brogan, for showing me what audacious women are capable of.

To Melissa Neubek and Lismany Medina, for showing me how to put a production together and supporting me through the process.

Hayleigh Flores for the Bad Bitch cover photoshoot.

To Randy Singer, for our Aquarian encounters, insightful conversations, and for being such an amazing connector.

To my inner circle: Lili, for the hilarious story times and manifestations, Alexandra for being my mind-reader right hand, Kristina for the trust and creative endeavors, Venus for always getting me out of my cave, Joseph for seeing me deeply and Sofi for the love and support and for blessing my eyes with the cutest little toes.

To Gail, for welcoming my project into your space and for seeing my vision.

To my Conscious Cabaret support team: Wisty Heart, Jenifer (Jenergy), Redd Light, Kevin, Erik "Guru", Belu, Sofia, Jordan, Haley, Maria Faria (LAMACA), Rikki, Lucia Gabriela, Isaiah, Naomi, Jaqueline Michelle, Ashley, Nathália, Oscar, Hayleigh Flores, Roderick, MJ Zerate, Stephane, Hanna, Rebecca, Hector, Jose, Salim, Natalie, Allison and others previously mentioned.

To Kaheal, Jeff, Talia Oré, Jenny Mendoza, Stephanie Ottomanelli, Nikki Benoit, Star Roman, and Sean Jennings, thank you for being a source of support throughout my journey.

To my Sacred Ink team, Jamilee Dumas, Danny Tran, Erika Espitia, and the Highstoke and PMU World team.

To the musicians who bring joy to my days:

A massive thank-you to Lizzy Jeff for normalizing free bleeding on the earth, for popping my performer's cherry by having me perform at Zen & Kush, and for being an activator in ways you can't imagine.

Thank you, Elena Rose, for inspiring me to be raw, authentic, and unique.

Thank you, Qveen Herby, for the bad-bitch music collection. Seeing you perform live, right on the barricade, was the highlight of my year. You are rising the collective consciousness with your magic. We are under your spell and I am here for it all.

Thank you, Carlina, Tyla Jane, Emmy Meli, Chris-n-Teeb, Alexis Nicole Jackson, Ariana Grande, Samantha Leah, Moonlight Scorpio, Trevor Hall, Iniko, Toni Jones, and others previously mentioned for being part of my "I woke up to this" playlist. You set the tone for my busy bad-bitch days.

To the artists in my healing playlist: Yaima, Trevor Hall, Bruno Mansur, Cristina de la paz, Ayla Schafer, Paky Gomez, Alexa Sunshine Rose, Danit, La Parsifónica, Aukai, Equanimus, Activation, We Saw Lions, Deya Dova, Alex Serra, Daniel Namkhay, Mose, Liquid Bloom, Ignacio Maria Gomez, Beautiful Chorous, Iluminati Congo, Anahata Sacred Sound Current, Alexia Chellum, Nalini Blossom, Alunawachuma, Lidia Solomon, and others previously mentioned. You've been with me through the darkest times and also the most blissful moments.

Thank you, Tanerélle, Randezvous At Two, Beyoncé, Sabrina Claudio, Ayelle, Doja Cat, Rihana, Lana Del Rey, Kaheal, Mac Miller RIP, Kehlani, Jhené Aiko, Saint Levant, Kali Uchis, Kwamie Liv, The Weeknd, and others previously mentioned for creating music that activates my inner *soultry* Goddess.

Thank you, Young Miko, Russ, Bad Bunny, Snow Tha Product, Karol G, Rauw Alejandro, Chencho Corleone, Jowel & Randy, BIA, Don Chezina, J Balvin, Tokisha, and Bad Gyal, for creating the best ass-shaking music.

I am so grateful for the authors and books that supported and inspired me through my process of personal development: *Existential Kink*, by Carolyn Elliott, PhD; *Pussy*, by Regina Thomashauer; *In the FLO* and *WomanCode*, by Alisa Vitti; *Woman*, by Natalie Angier; *El Alquimista*, by Paulo Coelho; *In the Company of the Courtesan*, by Sarah Dunant; *Glucose Revolution*, by Jessie Inchauspe; *The Ethical Slut*, by Janet W. Hardy and Dossie Easton; *The Body Keeps the Score*, by Bessel van der Kolk, MD; *The Universe Has Your Back*, and other titles, by Gabrielle Bernstein; *Spiritual Partnership*, by Gary Zukav; *Becoming Supernatural*, and other titles, by Joe Dispenza; *The Subtle Art of Not Giving a F*ck*, by Mark Manson; *The Seven Spiritual Laws of Success*, and other titles, by Deepak Chopra; *Braving the Wilderness*, and other titles, by Brené Brown; *The Four Agreements*, by Don Miguel Ruíz; *Women Who Run with the Wolves*, by Clarissa Pinkola Estés; *10x is Easier Than 2x*, by Dan Sullivan and Dr. Benjamin Hardy; *The Psychology of Money*, by Morgan Housel; *The Reclaimed Woman*, by Kelly Brogan MD; and *The Diary of a Young Girl*, by Anne Frank.

For more information on my Conscious Cabaret project, visit www.consciouscabaret.com.

For the Shamanic Kink Immersion, visit www.shamanickink.com.

For my Patreon account where I share my art and writing, visit https://patreon.com/BlackLotusExotic

BIBLIOGRAPHY

Ruiz, Don Miguel. *The Four Agreements: A Practical Guide to Personal Freedom*. San Rafael, CA: Amber-Allen Publishing, 1997